W9-AOA-630

SOUTHERN FRIED FOOTBALL

The History, Passion, and Glory of the Great Southern Game

SOUTHERN FRIED FOOTBALL

The History, Passion, and Glory of the Great Southern Game

Tony Barnhart

TRIUMPH
BOOKS
CHICAGO

Library of Congress Cataloging-in-Publication Data

Barnhart, Tony.
Southern fried football : the history, passion, and glory of the great Southern game / by Tony Barnhart.
p. cm.
Includes bibliographical references.
ISBN 1-57243-367-1
1. Football—Southern States—History. 2. Football—Southern States—Miscellanea. 3. Football—Records—Southern States. I. Title.

GV950 .B37 2000
796.332'0975—dc21 00-056787

This book is available in quantity at special discounts for your group or organization. For further information, contact:

Triumph Books
601 South LaSalle Street
Suite 500
Chicago, Illinois 60605
(312) 939-3330
Fax (312) 663-3557

Printed in the United States.

ISBN 1-57243-367-1

Front cover photos (clockwise from top left):

Archie Manning, photo courtesy of the *Atlanta Journal-Constitution.*
A celebrating University of Florida football fan, photo courtesy of the Associated Press.
Georgia mascot UGA, photo courtesy of Dan Evans/University of Georgia.
Legendary Alabama coach Bear Bryant, photo courtesy of Alabama SID.
Auburn fans at Jordan Hare Stadium, photo courtesy of the *Atlanta Journal-Constitution*/Lanna Swindler.
Georgia Tech celebrating a win over Georgia in 1949, photo courtesy of the *Atlanta Journal-Constitution*.

Back cover photo:

The famed Bear Bryant celebrating with his team, photo courtesy of the *Atlanta Journal-Constitution.*

Book design by Patricia Frey

To my mother, who taught me the love of reading and writing;

To my father, who taught me the love of athletic competition;

To Maria and Sara Catherine, who have given me all the wealth I have, and all that I will ever need.

TABLE OF CONTENTS

FOREWORD

College football as played in the Southern region of the United States defies absolute definition. The mechanics and techniques are much the same as other regions. Hats and pads and socks are the same. It's somewhere in that mysterious area of FERVOR that we probably should seek the difference.

But what is the point of doing that? Isn't it more fun to just enjoy it? Jump at every chance to be part of it!

If you are like me, with white growing under your cap, Tony Barnhart's *Southern Fried Football* will be a memory jogger.

If you're waiting for your first mortgage, you will learn something about the history and evolution of the game of football in the South.

Long before the Falcons and Dolphins and Jaguars and Saints and Cougars and Ravens and Redskins and Oilers and Buccaneers came along, the old game was doing nicely down in Dixie.

Yale played Georgia. Vanderbilt was a powerhouse under McGugin. Centre and Sewanee took no guff from anybody. There was a Paladin over at Furman long before Richard Boone ever set a horse.

Folks were eating fried chicken, potato salad, and white cake under the shade tree long before Henry Ford's folks gave us the station wagon and created a new buzzword, *tailgating*. My Grannie never did trust that word!

Coaches were characters and at least Feudal Barons, if not Kings. There has been one general who actually coached more wins when he was a mere major. He gave the profession a list of ten basic principles of coaching, but I always liked the eleventh unwritten one the best. On game day he reminded his troops that touchdowns follow good blocking just as surely as night follows day.

There was a Notre Dame quarterback who was head coach at Alabama for sixteen seasons for cryin' out loud!

There was the Auburn guy who coached forever at Georgia and the Georgia guy who was a big winner at Auburn. In college football WINNING has always been the bridge over troubled waters . . . leading occasionally to forgiveness and acceptance.

For six decades I've lived and loved college football. Good games, bad games, good people, and bad people. I think I have heard every preachment and parable from the coaches. I think the best one defining the game of football came from Wallace Wade. "Nobody ever wins a football game . . . somebody loses it."

Enjoy!

—Keith Jackson

Editors note: Keith Jackson, one of the most decorated announcers in television history, has been the voice of college football for ABC since 1966.

ACKNOWLEDGMENTS

My love affair with college football began innocently enough. In the fall of 1965, Ms. Lois Cheves invited a group of seventh graders to make the thirty-mile trip from our home in Union Point, Georgia, to Athens to watch the University of Georgia play football. She said it would be fun. I thought it would be a good opportunity to spend some time with Becky, Ms. Cheves's daughter and my classmate since the first grade. Even a twelve-year-old must have his priorities.

At that time, college football wasn't really on my radar screen. Like most boys of that era, I was a Yankees fan. I knew that Bobby Dodd was winding down his great coaching career at Georgia Tech, ninety minutes away in Atlanta. At the University of Georgia, a second-year coach named Vince Dooley was starting to make some noise. But that was the sum total of my knowledge of the game.

The week before my trip to Athens, I saw something remarkable. The University of Georgia opened its 1965 season with a televised game against Alabama. Oddsmakers thought the Bulldogs, who had been 7–3–1 in Dooley's first season, would have no chance for a win against Paul "Bear" Bryant's defending national champion team. I had to watch.

Georgia played valiantly but still trailed 17–10 with just a few minutes left in the game. Then Dooley called a play that remains as fresh in my mind today at age forty-six as it was that Saturday afternoon in my living room. Quarterback Kirby Moore dropped back and threw to tight end Pat Hodgson, who was falling to his knees when the ball hit his hands. Hodgson pitched the ball to running back Bob Taylor, who had been trailing the play. Taylor outran the Alabama secondary for a seventy-three-yard touchdown to make the score 17–16. The television announcers called it a "flea-flicker." I called it sheer madness.

I started screaming and running around the house. My mother was convinced that her eldest son had lost his mind.

"Georgia is going to tie Alabama," I yelled.

"That's nice, dear," she said, returning to her ironing.

Georgia coach Vince Dooley, aloft his players' shoulders, shakes hands with Bear Bryant after an 18–17 upset against Alabama (photo courtesy of Georgia SID).

Then, yet another magical thing happened. Instead of kicking the extra point to tie the game, Dooley elected to go for a two-point conversion. Moore found Hodgson open in the back of the end zone and Georgia won 18–17.

The game had stirred something in me. So when I arrived at Sanford Stadium the next Saturday to watch Georgia battle Vanderbilt, I was already a little excited and very curious. That day, something inside me changed forever.

In 1965, the capacity of Sanford Stadium was only forty-five thousand (today it is over eighty-six thousand), but the energy in that place was unlike anything I had ever felt before. There were bright colors. There were bands. There were pretty girls—lots of them.

When Preston Ridelhuber ran a punt back eighty-two yards for a touchdown, the stadium exploded with emotion. Georgia won the game 24–10. On the way home I couldn't exactly put my finger on what it was I had felt, but I knew I had witnessed something special.

Thirty-five years have passed since I saw my first live college football game. I have been a reporter for the last twenty-five of those years, during which my job has been to travel the United States and watch that same kind of scene played out in Auburn, Alabama; Knoxville, Tennessee; Chapel Hill, North Carolina; Ann Arbor, Michigan; State College, Pennsylvania; and too many other college hamlets to count.

Shortly after I came to the *Atlanta Journal-Constitution* in 1984, it became my goal to write a book that would capture the feelings I had experienced that day thirty-five years ago, a book that would attempt to explain the special relationship between the people of the South and college football. Over the years, so many people have shared with me how important college football is to them and their families. They view it as much more than a game. They have formed an emotional bond with college football that I have not seen in any other part of the country or with any other sport. I wanted to write a book that would pay tribute to that emotion and to the rich history of college football in the South.

Writing this book was a humbling experience on a lot of fronts, especially because it revealed to me just how many people have touched my life in a positive fashion. Each of them helped make this book possible. I am certain that I will forget some of them, and to those I apologize in advance. But the following people deserve thanks, for they all played a role in this book.

First, to my own coaches in what was a short but enjoyable athletic career. My first basketball coach, Charles "Red" Piland, taught me that discipline is the key to success in everything. C. S. Veazey, the head football coach at Greene County High School, taught me to love and respect the game. He was and always will be a second father to me. Harold Hammontree, Mack Poss, Dennis Fordham, and Joe McDaniel all taught me lessons I would later put to good use. And Georgia's Vince Dooley, although he was never my coach, taught me so much about the game in the fall of 1984, when I talked with him on a daily basis as a beat reporter for the *Atlanta Journal-Constitution*. For that I am grateful.

Also to the many college football coaches who have taken me into their confidence over the years and have given me special insight into the game, such as Vince Dooley; Jim Donnan; Erk Russell; Pat Dye; Steve Spurrier; Mike DuBose; Bill Curry; Terry Bowden; Tommy Tuberville; Phillip Fulmer; Johnny Majors; Jackie Sherrill; Gerry DiNardo; Bobby Bowden; Mack Brown; Chuck Amato; Bill Dooley; George O'Leary; Bill Lewis; Dick Sheridan; Jerry Claiborne; Steve Sloan; Danny Ford; Al Groh; Billy Brewer; Tommy West; Mike O'Cain; Ray Goff; and Carl Franks. The assistant coaches who have helped me are too numerous to mention, but Jim Collins at Florida and Steve Greer and Joe Tereshinski at Georgia have supported me since the beginning of my career. Thanks, guys.

My friends at the *Atlanta Journal-Constitution*, who have been understanding and supportive of me in every way, also deserve many thanks. One of the proudest days of my life was September 22, 1984, the day I sat between Jesse Outlar and Furman Bisher at the Georgia-Clemson game in Athens. As a boy, these men were my heroes. As an adult, they became close friends and trusted colleagues. Assistant Managing Editor for Sports Don Boykin is not only my boss but also my friend. Sports Editor Robert Mashburn offered me so much encouragement when I desperately needed it. Photo

Editor John Glenn gave me unlimited access to the newspaper's photo archives, and his assistant Connie Woods relentlessly tracked down photos and kept me organized. Without them, this book never would have happened. To David Davidson, Norman Arey, Leo Willingham, Jack Wilkinson, the late Tom McCollister, and the other members of the staff who have been so supportive, I will always be grateful.

I must also thank Ed Hinton, a former *Atlanta Journal-Constitution* staff member who loves the game and everything it means to people in the South. He taught me to love Ole Miss even though I didn't go to school there. He, more than anybody, knows what this book is about.

I am grateful also to friends who have published books on college football and who were quick to offer their expertise and encouragement. They are:

- Marty Mule of the *New Orleans Times-Picayune*, who wrote the definitive books on LSU and Tulane football.

- Bob Bradley, who knows more about Clemson and its rich history than anyone on the planet. Mr. Bradley is one of my favorite people in the whole world.

- Matt Fulks, whose *Sportscasters Dozen* was tremendously helpful to me in my effort to capture an important aspect of the southern game.

- Bill Cromartie, whose *Clean Old-Fashioned Hate* is the best book ever written about the rivalry between Georgia and Georgia Tech.

- Loran Smith and the late Lewis Grizzard, whose book on Georgia's National Championship season, *Glory, Glory*, set the standard for all

Photo sequence of the famous "Flea Flicker" play (Moore to Hodgson to Taylor), which helped Georgia beat Alabama 18–17 in the final minutes of a 1965 game (photos courtesy of Georgia SID).

books on college football. I wish Lewis could be here for one more tail-gating party. Loran's other book on Georgia football, *Between the Hedges*, is also a classic.

- Keith Dunnavant, whose book on Bear Bryant, *Coach*, is both well written and well researched.
- Al Browning, whose *Third Saturday in October* and *Bowl, Bama, Bowl* should be required reading for fans of Alabama and Tennessee.
- Tom Price, whose books on South Carolina football are rich with detail. When I was writing this book Tom was always willing to listen to me and offer advice.
- Norm Carlson and Buddy Martin, whose work on the Florida Gators is second to none. They are friends as well as great resources.
- Wayne Hester, whose books on the football histories of Alabama and Auburn are extraordinary pieces of work.

I cannot accurately measure the vast contributions to this book by the South's sports information directors, who are ultimately responsible for making sure that the history of the game is recorded properly for posterity.

From the SEC office: I wish to thank Commissioner Roy Kramer; Executive Associate Commissioner Mark Womack; and Charles Bloom of the league's information office. Also, Sports Information Directors Larry White (Alabama); Kent Partridge and Meredith Jenkins (Auburn); Rick Shaeffer (Arkansas); John Humenik, Norm Carlson, and Jeff Kamis (Florida); Claude Felton (Georgia), my friend for twenty-five years and simply the best in

the business; Tony Neely (Kentucky); Herb Vincent (LSU); Langston Rogers (Ole Miss); Mike Nemeth (Mississippi State); Kerry Tharp, Brian Bennette, and Tom Price (South Carolina); Bud Ford and Haywood Harris (Tennessee); and Rod Willams (Vanderbilt).

From the ACC office: I wish to thank Commissioner John Swofford; Assistant Commissioner Tom Mickle; and Brian Morrison, Marvin "Skeeter" Francis, and Barb Dery of the information office. Also, Sports Information Directors Tim Bourrett, Bob Bradley, and Sam Blackman (Clemson); Mike Cragg and Jon Jackson (Duke); Rob Wilson (Florida State); Mike Finn, Allison George, and Mike Stamus (Georgia Tech); Herb Hartnett and Chuck Walsh (Maryland); Steve Kirschner and Rick Brewer (North Carolina); Annabelle Vaughn, Ed Seeman, and Jim Pomerantz (N.C. State); Rich Murray (Virginia); and John Justus (Wake Forest).

Also, to the South's top athletic directors, who have been a tremendous resource. They include Auburn's David Housel, a friend and one of the most honorable men I know; Arkansas's Frank Broyles; Warner Alford and John Shafer of Ole Miss; Mississippi State's Larry Templeton; LSU's Joe Dean; Georgia's Vince Dooley; Florida's Jeremy Foley and his able assistant and my former classmate, Greg McGarity; South Carolina's Mike McGee; Tennessee's Doug Dickey; Vanderbilt's Todd Turner; Kentucky's C. M. Newton; Florida State's Dave Hart; and Georgia Tech's Homer Rice and Dave Braine.

And to my friends in the business, who supported me and assured me that I wasn't (totally) crazy to try this, such as: Ivan Maisel of *Sports Illustrated*; Gene Wojciechowski of *ESPN, The Magazine*, who taught me how to write a book proposal; Mark Blaudschun of *The Boston Globe*; Rich Rosenblatt of the Associated Press; Steve Weiberg of *USA Today*; Andy Bagnato and Malcolm Moran of the *Chicago Tribune*; Chris Dufresne of the *Los Angeles Times*; Steve Richardson of the Football Writers Association of America; Dick Weiss of the *New York Daily News*; Craig Barnes of the *Ft. Lauderdale Sun-Sentinel;* and Rick Franzman, who gave me my first job at the *Red & Black* at the University of Georgia in 1975.

To the gang at ESPN, who made me a part of their family from day one, including: the "Game Day" boys, Chris Fowler, Lee Corso, and Kirk Herbstreit, who are the best in the business; producers Barry Sacks, Steve Vecchione, and Stuart Barbara, who always encouraged me; Mr. Mo Davenport, who had faith in me and gave me a chance six years ago; Chris Raymond of *ESPN, The Magazine*; Ron Franklin, Mike Gottfried, and Adrian Karsten, who were always good listeners; and Mr. Len DeLuca, who is both a gentleman and a scholar. I must also thank the incomparable Keith Jackson of ABC, whose voice is and will always be the voice of college football. Nobody does it better.

Thanks also to my publisher, Triumph Books. When everybody else in the publishing world said this idea would never fly, they believed in me. Publisher Mitch Rogatz took a chance on this project, and for that I will forever be grateful. Editor Heidi Hill, a fellow Georgia grad, put up with me, and for that she deserves some kind of medal.

And to some special friends who lent me their support and encouragement during the process, such as: Gene Corrigan; Woody Durham; Tim Brando; Tricia Patterson; Wes Durham; M. L. Wray; Larry Munson; Bill Hartman; Chuck Dowdle; Freddy Jones; M. J. Park; B. B. Branton of Sewanee; Kim King; and Ray Goff, who remains the best veer quarterback I ever saw.

Thank you to my two best friends in the world, Carl Brantley and Tom McMillen. College brought us together and college football has helped keep us together. Their support and encouragement has been priceless.

Thanks also to Mr. Don Wilder, who gave me my first paying newspaper job, at the South Carolina *Union Daily Times* in 1976; the late Smith Barrier, who gave me my first big break when he hired me at the Greensboro, North Carolina, *News & Record* in March of 1977; Wilt Browning and Irwin Smallwood, who became my mentors in Greensboro and gave me the confidence that I could be successful in this business; and Van McKenzie, who allowed me to live out my dream by bringing me to the *Atlanta Journal-Constitution* in 1984.

Also to my teachers at Greene County High School and the University of Georgia, who believed in me before I believed in myself. A special thanks to Tommie Ward, my high school English teacher and friend. She convinced me that I could dare to dream of writing for a living.

Finally, I want to thank my family for all the sacrifices they have made that allowed me to pursue my dreams. Over the years Maria and Sara Catherine have spent a lot of time apologizing for my absence from things that "normal" people do. You guys are my foundation. My brother, David, was my first playmate and therefore the first to compete against me on the athletic field. I don't say it enough, but I love and respect him. My mother, Sara, is still my hero and the smartest person I know. She taught me how to read and how to dream, the two cornerstones of writing. My dad, Bobby, passed away in July of 1999. When he and I couldn't talk about anything else, we could still talk about sports. I wish he were here so that we could watch one last ball game together.

I have always felt that the best way to thank your mother and father for their extraordinary sacrifices is to do something with your life that makes them proud. I hope I have done that.

—T. B., Atlanta, 2000

SOUTHERN FRIED FOOTBALL

The History, Passion, and Glory of the Great Southern Game

INTRODUCTION

It's Always Been More Than a Game

"In the East, college football is a cultural exercise . . .
On the West Coast, it is a tourist attraction . . .
In the Midwest, it is cannibalism . . .
But in the South it is religion . . .
And Saturday is the holy day."

—Marino Casem, Southern University

"College football is not a matter of life and death . . .
It's much more important than that."

—sign behind the desk of a Southern football coach

Save some Southerners' unshakable belief that the Civil War was in fact the War of Northern Aggression, nothing is more ingrained in the Southern psyche than the love of Southern college football—not as a game or a mere diversion, but as a way of life.

Think about it. What other institution makes an otherwise normal, intelligent individual bark like a dog, wear red bib overalls, or paint his face (and other assorted body parts) with orange tiger paws? What other activity makes seemingly sane people rise at the crack of dawn on Saturday, drive for six hours, sit in the hot sun for three hours, and then drive six hours home so that they can make it to church on Sunday morning? At what other event will you see the president of the Junior League, dressed in her very best, hurl at a nineteen-year-old running back a string of obscenities that would make a sailor blush?

"The folks up north and in other places around the country play college football and they enjoy it," says former Auburn coach Pat Dye. "That's fine. But down here we don't play college football. We live it. And we live it every day."

Clemson's Gary Cooper celebrates with fans during a 1987 game with Georgia Tech (photo courtesy of the *Atlanta Journal-Constitution*/Frank Nemeier).

Only Southern college football games inspire such behavior, and each fall for more than one hundred years the people of the South have planned weddings, births, and even funerals around those very special fall Saturdays.

"Every spring I get calls from people wanting to double check our schedule for the fall so that they don't plan anything when we have a home game," says Sue Hall, Florida State coach Bobby Bowden's longtime secretary. "One woman said she had to change the date of her wedding because none of her bridesmaids were going to show up. They were all going to be at the game."

In the South, even childbirth has to work around the college football schedule. When Deborah Ford, the wife of Clemson coach Danny Ford, was pregnant, she was expected to give birth on the Saturday of a Tigers home football game. Instead, labor was induced and the baby was born on the Friday night before the game.

"I just figured it was part of being a coach's wife," she said.

To unbelievers, who may see all of this as merely an extreme exercise in Southern pride, I issue the following challenges: Visit Athens, Georgia; Tuscaloosa, Alabama; Knoxville, Tennessee; Gainesville, Florida; Chapel Hill, North Carolina; or any of the other sleepy college towns that are magically transformed when they welcome thousands of energetic fans into their midst on those fall Saturdays.

If you can get a ticket—and that's a big if, because tickets for college football games in the South go fast—don't watch the action on the field. Instead, study the people in the seats. You'll see on the faces of these fans what it is that connects them so deeply to the sport. While the people in South Bend, Indiana, Ann Arbor, Michigan, and Columbus, Ohio, dearly love the game of college football, in the South, love just ain't good enough. In that part of the world, when the subject is college football, the operative word is *passion*.

This passion, which grips the South not just in the fall but all year long, is the central character in *Southern Fried Football*.

For those who still believe that college football is just a game to the people of the South, I suggest you pull up a chair. You're about to get an education.

When Florida and Florida State battle for supremacy in the Sunshine State, when Georgia and Florida meet in Jacksonville for "The World's Largest Outdoor Cocktail Party," when Alabama and Auburn square off in the mother of all rivalries, a rivalry that not only divides families but also an entire state—on these special Saturdays, it's not about whose state or whose school has the better football team. The stakes are much higher than that.

A fan put it best a few years ago prior to a big game between Clemson and Georgia. "It's simple," he said. "It's our way of life against theirs."

* * * * *

The 2000 season will mark the 121st year that college football, in some form, has been a part of the Southern landscape. Having entered the twenty-first century, it is a good time to reflect on how far the game has come from its humble beginnings and how the people of the South have maintained their special relationship with college football.

College football has come a long way from the very first games, when fans traveled by horse and buggy and passed the hat to pay the teams' expenses. It has evolved into a multibillion-dollar enterprise; where once the small but curious crowds stood along the sidelines to watch teams play, today Southern college football is played before tens of thousands of fans in pastoral stadiums, plus millions more via worldwide television.

The players, once adventurous college boys just looking for a way to work off some excess energy, are now carefully trained and aggressively recruited to play the game. Some of these young men become Southern icons before they are old enough to shave. Coaches, who at one time would take money from their own pockets to pay their team's expenses, now command million-dollar salaries. For several generations, football coaches in the South have been treated with the respect and deference usually reserved for heads of state—but only if they win, of course. Few men are more powerful than a winning Southern college football coach.

But if a Southern football coach makes a habit of losing, he will awaken one Sunday morning to find a moving van parked in front of his house, as Tennessee's Bill Battle did in 1976. Southern college football fans are a lot of things. Subtle, they ain't.

In celebration of these glorious past 121 years, I offer you *Southern Fried Football*. It is not a dry, dusty recitation of facts and trivia, but a sentimental journey filled with special people, places, and moments, all of which have been frozen in time.

Professors George Petrie of Auburn (above) and Charles Herty of Georgia organized the first game between the two schools in 1892 (photo courtesy of Auburn SID).

People Like:

College professors Charles Herty of Georgia and George Petrie of Auburn, who learned about the game of football when they were classmates at Johns Hopkins University. In 1892, Herty and Petrie decided to field teams at their respective schools and play a game. Two thousand fans showed up at Atlanta's Piedmont Park to watch the first game ever played between Auburn and Georgia. In 2000, the schools will meet for the 104th time. More than eighty-five thousand fans will attend the game in person while millions more watch it on television.

John Heisman, the legendary coach for whom college football's most famous award is named. Heisman left Ohio in 1895 and came to the South, where he built winning programs at Clemson, Auburn, and Georgia Tech and had a profound effect on the development of the game.

His favorite saying was "Better to have died as a small boy than to fumble this football."

He coached Georgia Tech's infamous 222–0 win over Cumberland College in 1916. At half time, with his team up 136–0, he told his players: "Be careful of that team from Cumberland. There's no telling what they have up their sleeves."

Georgia Tech coach John Heisman (far right) with three unidentified players in 1919 (photo courtesy of the *Atlanta Journal-Constitution*).

Dan McGugin, the most successful coach in Vanderbilt history. In 1910 McGugin took his team to Yale. The Civil War, which had ended forty-five years earlier, was still fresh on the minds of all Southerners. In his pregame speech, McGugin reminded his players that many of their grandfathers were buried in Northern cemeteries and that the grandfathers of the Yale players across the way had put them there. Vanderbilt went out and tied Yale 0–0 in what was considered a huge upset at the time.

Vanderbilt coach Dan McGugin (photo courtesy of Vanderbilt SID).

McGugin forgot to mention one thing in his speech: his own grandfather had served under Union general William T. Sherman during Sherman's infamous and destructive March to the Sea across Georgia.

Places Like:

The Grove, a pastoral, tree-lined area on the University of Mississippi campus where fans gather to tailgate prior to the games in Oxford, Mississippi. Two hours before kickoff, the Ole Miss team walks single file through a human corridor of cheering fans in The Grove. It is an awe-inspiring moment.

"If you ain't ready to play after walking through The Grove," said former coach Billy Brewer, "you're probably dead."

LSU's Tiger Stadium, located in Baton Rouge, Louisiana, and host to some noisy Saturday night games. On October 8, 1988, when LSU scored to beat Auburn in the closing seconds of the game, the explosion of sound was so great that it registered on the seismograph at the LSU Geology Department.

The Esso Club, located in Clemson, South Carolina. Tiger fans from all walks of life gather at this gas station turned watering hole to enjoy a cold one before watching their beloved team take the field.

Moments Like:

Halloween night in 1959, when LSU's Billy Cannon ran his way to immortality by returning a punt eighty-nine yards for a touchdown and leading the Tigers to a 7–3 upset of Ole Miss. Cannon was awarded the Heisman Trophy that year. More than forty years after Cannon's heroic Halloween run, it remains one of the defining moments in college football history.

December 2, 1989, when, for the first time, Alabama played at Auburn's Jordan-Hare Stadium. Since 1902, the Alabama-Auburn game had always been played in Birmingham, which was considered to be a Crimson Tide stronghold. Legendary Alabama coach Bear Bryant and his successor, Ray Perkins, swore that Alabama would never stoop so low as to bring its team to Auburn. But after years of bitter negotiations, the day finally arrived.

Prior to the game, more than twenty thousand Auburn fans lined Donahue Drive, the road that runs between the school's athletic dormitory and the stadium, for the traditional "Tiger Walk." As the players walked through the waves of cheering fans, grown men cried.

"After years of bondage, our people were finally delivered to the Promised Land," said David Housel, the Auburn athletics director.

Auburn won the game, upsetting No. 2 Alabama 30–20.

November 18, 1961, when the football rivalry between Georgia Tech and Alabama turned ugly. During a 10–0 win by Alabama in Birmingham, Georgia Tech's Chick Graning suffered a broken nose and a broken jaw and lost five teeth after receiving an elbow to his face from Darwin Holt of the Crimson Tide. The incident touched off a war of words between the major newspapers in the two states. When the two teams met in Atlanta the following year, Tech fans in the stands threw so many things at Alabama coach Bear Bryant that he had to wear a helmet onto the field.

But Bryant still had his sense of humor. When a liquor bottle bounced at his feet, Bryant picked it up and said, "I thought Tech people drank a better brand of whiskey than this."

* * * * *

We know that Southerners love the game of college football, but why, after all these years and after all the changes that have taken place in the South, does the game still pull so strongly on Southern heartstrings? Sociologists say that college football has thrived in the South because the game pushes all the hot buttons of its people: war, regional pride, race, and politics.

Georgia, coached by Vince Dooley, posted a huge upset over Michigan in 1965 (photo courtesy of the *Atlanta Journal-Constitution*).

War

Even today, more than 130 years after the surrender at Appomattox, the South remains haunted by the Civil War. For many generations of fans, football has been a way to vicariously regain the ground lost in that epic struggle.

"The lost cause of the Civil War has never really gotten out of our souls," says Dr. David Sansing, the former director of the Center for the Study of Southern Culture at the University of Mississippi. "Football, with all of its battle-related language, has long been an expression of our Southern militarism. To some, football elevates war to a higher art with its marching bands and the large crowds. It's like sitting on the hillside looking down on the battle of Gettysburg."

Regional Pride

Beyond healing the wounds of the Civil War, winning in football has always been a way for the South to compensate for a long-standing regional inferiority complex. The South was left behind in the economic expansion after World War II, but by winning in football the South could prove its worth to the industrialized North. Southerners knew that many Northerners looked down on them as uneducated hicks. Football was one area in which the South could be superior.

Vince Dooley, the head coach at Georgia from 1964 to 1988, remembers the emotional reaction his team received from Southern fans when the Bulldogs won at Michigan in 1965. When the team returned to Athens, several thousand people greeted the Bulldogs at the airport.

"I didn't just hear from Georgia people, but from people all over the South," says Dooley. "To go up there and invade the North and come back a winner was the greatest thing for a lot of people. It was as if we had had a chance to go to Gettysburg again."

On January 1, 1981, Georgia had another opportunity to emerge victorious from a battle against a Northern team. The Bulldogs went to the Sugar Bowl in New Orleans and won their first national championship by beating the ultimate symbol of Northern superiority—the University of Notre Dame. The postgame celebration began in the Super Dome and carried on into the streets of New Orleans. It was one of the most emotional celebrations people in the region had ever seen.

"The celebration that day was about some feelings that dated all the way back to 1865," says Jim Minter, a former editor of the *Atlanta Constitution*.

For Georgia, winning the national championship was sweet, but beating Notre Dame, or any Northern school for the honor, made the experience simply divine.

Race

Perhaps the biggest indicator of how strongly Southerners feel about college football is that eventually their love for the sport proved to be stronger than the long-held prejudices many of them had on the subject of race.

Most of the major Southern colleges did not begin to recruit blacks to play football until the late 1960s and early 1970s. Some Southern schools would not play teams that had black players. While the first black college football players played in the South as early as the mid-1960s, the defining moment for the integration of Southern college football came on September 12, 1970, in Birmingham, Alabama.

Alabama coach Paul "Bear" Bryant, who had won three national championships in the 1960s with all-white teams, saw his Crimson Tide embarrassed 42–21 by the University of Southern California at Legion Field. The Trojans were led by their black fullback, Sam "Bam" Cunningham, who ripped through Alabama's defense to score two touchdowns.

That day Bryant realized that signing black players at the University of Alabama was no longer an issue of conscience: it was now a matter of winning. After the game Bryant told his closest friends that he would begin recruiting black players. With a newly integrated program, Alabama went on to become college football's dominant team in the 1970s with a record of 103–16–1, eight SEC titles, and three national titles.

Once Bryant had opened the door, other Southern schools quickly began bringing black athletes to their campuses, paving the way for greater understanding between the races.

In 1962, racial tensions were at a flash point on the Ole Miss campus when James Meredith became the first black man to enroll at the University of Mississippi. Thirteen years later Ben Williams, a black defensive tackle on the Ole Miss football team, was voted the school's Colonel Rebel, the highest honor that can be bestowed to any male student at the school.

"Ultimately Southerners said that football was more important than race," says Dr. Sansing. "Football turned out to be a bridge across the great divide of race. In the long run it has had a great effect."

Alabama coach Bear Bryant huddles with players (photo courtesy of Alabama SID).

Politics

More than one Southern politician has found that the best way to please constituents is to be supportive of college football. To this end, some politicians have gone to extremes.

In 1934, Louisiana governor Huey Long heard that sales for an LSU football game in Baton Rouge were lagging because the circus was coming to town the same night. In an effort to boost sales for the game, Long contacted Barnum & Bailey officials and informed them of an obscure state law that ordained that animals couldn't be washed on Saturdays in Baton Rouge. The circus show was canceled and ticket sales for the LSU game soared.

Sometimes the line between college football and politics becomes a bit fuzzy. In 1955 Fob James of Auburn led the SEC in rushing. Later he led the state of Alabama as governor. As icons of Southern culture, college football players and coaches already enjoy the respect and adoration of many Southerners, and thus can easily parlay their success as coaches into political careers. When Vince Dooley retired as head football coach at Georgia in 1988, he contemplated running for governor. In any other region of the country, the idea that a football coach could run a state office would have been laughable. But given the status accorded college football coaches in the South, the transition from football coach to governor seemed entirely logical.

Bill Curry with former Georgia Tech coach Bobby Dodd in 1983 (photo courtesy of the *Atlanta Journal-Constitution*/Charles Pugh).

* * * * *

Today, when competition for the entertainment dollar is fiercer than in any other time in our history, the South embraces and supports college football more than ever.

In the most recent statistics released by the National Collegiate Athletic Association (NCAA), nine of the top fourteen schools in college football attendance during the 1999 season were from the South. Tennessee, which averaged 106,839 fans per game, was No. 2 behind Michigan, followed by Georgia (5), Florida (6), Alabama (7), Auburn (9), Florida State (11), LSU (12), Clemson (13), and South Carolina (14).

Ticket demand for college football games is clearly the greatest in the South. During the 1999 season the SEC averaged more than one hundred percent capacity (100.4 percent) in its twelve stadiums. The Big 12 was a distant second at 93.8 percent; the ACC, another Southern conference, was fourth at 85.7 percent.

For the eighteenth straight year, the SEC led all major conferences in total attendance in 1999 with over 5.5 million. The SEC's average attendance of 70,521 per game in 1999 was an all-time high.

That college football is still gaining in popularity more than one hundred years after it began in the South comes as no surprise to Bill Curry. Curry played at Georgia Tech in the 1960s and has been the head coach at Georgia Tech, Alabama, and Kentucky. As a young boy Curry spent Saturdays with his grandmother, who lived and had raised her family in the shadow of Georgia's Sanford Stadium, in Athens, Georgia, watching fans heading to and from the games.

"I really didn't understand what was going on in that stadium, but I knew that when those people came back, they were either very happy or very sad," says Curry. "I figured it must be pretty important."

That's how Curry began his love affair with a game that is as much a part of Southern living as pecan pie and Wednesday night prayer meetings. And like that old-time religion, once Southern college football gets into your blood, you cannot be cured. You're hooked forever. "In the South, college football isn't just a game," Curry says. "It's who we are."

For Southerners, traveling to that first college football game is the first step on a journey that will last a lifetime. This book is a celebration of that journey.

A CHRONOLOGY OF SOUTHERN FRIED FOOTBALL

The Major Events That Shaped the Landscape of Southern College Football

1880: The first college football game in the South was played in Lexington, Kentucky, between Centre College and Kentucky University (now Transylvania University).

1881: The University of Kentucky, then known as Kentucky State College or State University of Kentucky, beat Kentucky University 7¼–1 in the school's first football game. After the three-game season, football did not return to Kentucky until 1891.

1888: On October 18 North Carolina and Wake Forest played a game in Raleigh, North Carolina, the first college football game to be played in the state. Wake Forest won 6–4.

On November 27 Trinity College (which later became Duke) defeated North Carolina 16–0 in Trinity's first football game.

Virginia also played its first football game that year, beating Pantops Academy 20–0.

1890: In January, after a player suffered a broken collarbone, North Carolina's faculty voted to discontinue football at the school. The ban lasted for only one season.

1891: On November 21 Tennessee played its first football game, losing to Sewanee 24–0.

1892: On February 20 Georgia and Auburn played before two thousand fans at Atlanta's Piedmont Park in a game that would kick off the first college football rivalry in the deep South. Professors Dr. Charles Herty of Georgia and Dr. George Petrie of Auburn, who had learned about the game while they were classmates at Johns Hopkins University, organized the event. Auburn won 10–0.

Georgia Tech played its first game on November 5 against Mercer in Macon, Georgia, and lost 12–6.

On November 11 Alabama played its first football game at a baseball park in Birmingham, beating a group of players from Birmingham High School 56–0.

On Thanksgiving Day a team of Mississippi A&M (now Mississippi State) faculty members challenged a group of students to a game of football, the first on that campus. The faculty won 4–0.

1893: LSU played its first football game, a 34–0 loss to Tulane.

On February 22 Alabama and Auburn played the first game in their storied rivalry, which Auburn won 32–22. Auburn, eager to win the first game it played against Alabama, had hired former Penn State player F. M. Balliet to coach Auburn's team for that one game.

On November 11 the University of Mississippi (Ole Miss) played its first football game, a 56–0 win over Tennessee's Southwest Baptist University.

North Carolina A&M (now N.C. State) played its first college game against Tennessee in Raleigh, winning 12–6.

1894: On December 22 representatives from seven Southern schools met in Atlanta to form the South's first college football conference, the Southeastern Intercollegiate Athletic Association (SIAA). The league would eventually grow to include as many as thirty schools.

Auburn beat Georgia Tech 94–0, but then scored only twelve points in its remaining three games to finish 1–3.

1895: Auburn hired John Heisman to coach the school's football team. Heisman led the school to a 2–1 record, including a 48–0 win over Alabama.

Glenn "Pop" Warner began his coaching career at Georgia. He stayed for only two seasons but went on to earn 319 career victories as the coach of various college football teams.

1896: On October 28 Clemson played its first football game, beating Furman 14–6 in Greenville, South Carolina.

At Mississippi A&M the student body raised three hundred dollars to hire J. B. Hildebrand, the school's first full-time coach. However, a yellow fever epidemic and the outbreak of the Spanish-American War soon halted the school's attempts to create a winning football program.

1897: On October 30 Georgia player Richard Vonalbade Gammon died from injuries he sustained in a game against Virginia. The Georgia state legislature passed a bill making it illegal to play football at state institutions, but Gammon's mother, Rosalind, who knew of her son's love for football, wrote a letter to Governor W. Y. Atkinson begging him not to sign the bill. The bill was not signed and football continued.

Georgia's Richard Vonalbade Gammon died playing football in 1897 (photo courtesy of the *Atlanta Journal-Constitution*).

1898: Because of the Spanish-American War, Tennessee did not field a team in this year.

1899: A team representing the University of the South, which is located in Sewanee, Tennessee, pulled off the greatest Iron Man feat in the history of college football. Beginning on November 9, 1899, Sewanee won 5 games in six days, all against national powers (Texas, Texas A&M, Tulane, LSU, and Mississippi) and by a combined score of 91–0. Sewanee went on to finish 12–0 and was declared the Southern football champion.

On December 8 John Heisman left Auburn to become the head coach at Clemson.

1900: Kentucky defeated Louisville YMCA 12–6 without running a single offensive play. The Wildcats kicked on first down on every possession and scored on a pair of YMCA fumbles in the end zone.

1901: Four years after the school's first attempt, Mississippi State made a second attempt to field a football team. On October 28 the school won the first game in its history, a 17–0 victory over Mississippi.

On October 5, in a game that was shortened to thirty minutes, Clemson, coached by John Heisman, beat Guilford 122–0.

Coach John Heisman, who built programs at Clemson, Auburn, and Georgia Tech (photo courtesy of the *Atlanta Journal-Constitution*).

1903: On November 26 John Heisman was hired as Georgia Tech's first full-time coach. Heisman remained until 1919, posting a record of 102–29–7. He might have stayed longer, but in a divorce settlement he agreed that he would not live in the same city as the one in which his ex-wife lived. She chose Atlanta and Heisman returned to Pennsylvania, his alma mater.

Vanderbilt hired Dan McGugin as its head coach. McGugin went on to build one of the South's greatest college football dynasties. In thirty years at Vanderbilt, he posted a record of 197–55–19.

1907: From November 4 through November 9, Clemson played—and lost—three games in less than a week's time. The Tigers lost to Auburn (12–0) on November 4, to Georgia (8–0) on November 7, and to Davidson (10–6) on November 9.

On Christmas Day in Havana, Cuba, LSU beat the University of Havana 56–0 in front of ten thousand fans.

Alabama and Auburn played to a 6–6 tie in Birmingham. Because of various disagreements between the two schools, they did not meet again until 1948.

Some Southern college teams, frustrated with Vanderbilt's dominance under coach Dan McGugin, began bringing in paid professionals, or "ringers," to play for their teams.

1908: Clemson's hopes for a winning season were dashed when several football players were expelled along with three hundred other students for stealing a Civil War cannon from the Pendleton town square and bringing it back to Clemson. The Tigers went 1–6 that season.

1909: Kentucky adopted "Wildcats" as its official team name.

1912: On January 1, in the first and only game the team has played outside the United States, Mississippi A&M defeated Club Atletico de Cuba 12–0 in Havana.

1913: Students built the original west stands of Georgia Tech's Grant Field, which seated five thousand people. Today it is known as Bobby Dodd Stadium, and it remains the oldest on-campus Division I stadium in the country.

Having earned an 8–0 record, Auburn won its first SIAA championship.

1915: Vanderbilt's "point-a-minute" team averaged 51 points per game, scoring 514 points in 510 minutes. The Commodores gave up only thirty-eight points, thirty-five of those in a 35–10 loss to Virginia, Vanderbilt's only defeat of the season.

1916: On October 7 Georgia Tech defeated Cumberland 222–0 in the most lopsided game ever played in the history of college football. At half time, Tech coach John Heisman told his players to watch out for those Cumberland players, because "there's no telling what they have up their sleeves." Tech was leading 126–0 at the time.

Kentucky dedicated its playing field as Stoll Field.

1917: Georgia Tech went 9–0 and won the first of its four national championships. The Yellow Jackets outscored their opponents 491–17 but declined a trip to the Rose Bowl so that many of their players could enlist and fight in World War I.

North Carolina did not field a team for two years because of the war.

1918: Vanderbilt did not field a team because of World War I.

1920: William Alexander succeeded John Heisman as head coach at Georgia Tech. In twenty-five years at Tech, Alexander posted a record of 134–95–15. He was the first coach to take teams to the Sugar, Cotton, Orange, and Rose bowls.

Representatives from the larger schools in the SIAA met in Gainesville, Florida, to form the Southern Conference.

Mississippi State students renamed the school's football field Scott Field, in honor of track star and Olympian Don Scott, a football letterman at Mississippi in 1915 and 1916.

1921: On September 21 Tennessee played its first game at Shields-Watkins Field, which would later become Neyland Stadium. The capacity at the field was 3,200. Tennessee beat Emory & Henry 27–0.

1922: A record crowd of 24,300 people turned out for a game between Auburn and Georgia Tech in Atlanta. The gate of $45,000 was the largest ever for a college football game in the South.

After winning 99 games in eighteen seasons, Mike Donahue left Auburn to become the head coach at LSU, where he was only 23–19–2 in five years.

1926: In the biggest win of Curley Byrd's career as Maryland's coach, the Terps upset heavily favored Yale 15–0 in New Haven, Connecticut.

After Tennessee had lost 18 of its first 21 games against Vanderbilt, school officials hired Captain Robert R. Neyland as the school's head football coach. Neyland's teams went on to beat Vanderbilt in 16 of the next 19 games.

1927: After a riot broke out at the end of the 1926 Ole Miss-Mississippi State football game, Ole Miss honor society Sigma Iota recommended that the two schools ease tensions by playing for a trophy, a golden football that later became known as the Golden Egg.

On November 12 North Carolina opened Kenan Stadium with a 27–0 win over Davidson.

1929: On January 1 Georgia Tech beat California 8–7 in the Rose Bowl to top off an undefeated record and win its second national title. The most memorable moment of the game was when California's Roy Riegels picked up a fumble and ran toward the Tech goal line. He was eventually tackled by his own teammates.

On October 12 Georgia defeated mighty Yale 15–0 in the inaugural game at Sanford Stadium.

1930: On March 6 Wallace Wade agreed to leave Alabama and become the head coach at Duke. Wade remained at Alabama for the 1930 season, leading the Crimson Tide to a 10–0 record, a win in the Rose Bowl, and the national championship.

On July 15 Frank Thomas, a former Notre Dame player and the running backs coach at Georgia, was named the new head coach at Alabama.

1932: On October 15, in one of the greatest punting duels ever, Alabama beat Tennessee 7–3 in Birmingham. Alabama's Johnny Cain averaged forty-eight yards on nineteen kicks; Tennessee's Beattie Feathers averaged forty-three yards on twenty-one kicks.

Mississippi A&M was officially renamed Mississippi State.

1933: At a meeting on February 13, thirteen charter members formed the Southeastern Conference. Alabama won the conference's first championship with a 5–0–1 record.

1934: Alabama went 10–0 and beat Stanford 29–13 in the Rose Bowl to share the national championship with Minnesota. Two ends on that Crimson Tide team—Don Hutson and Paul "Bear" Bryant—were destined for the Hall of Fame.

Suffering from health problems, Coach Dan McGugin retired after thirty seasons as the head coach at Vanderbilt. Over the course of those years he won 197 games and had only one losing season.

1935: Tackle Frank "Bruiser" Kinard of Ole Miss defined the term "Iron Man" when he played 708 out of 720 possible minutes. The Rebels posted a 9–3 season.

1936: Dan McGugin, who presided over the most successful period in Vanderbilt football history, died at the age of fifty-six.

Ole Miss adopted "Rebels" as the official name of the school's athletic teams.

Paul "Bear" Bryant was an end on Alabama's 1934 Rose Bowl team (photo courtesy of the *Atlanta Journal-Constitution*).

1937: In the first bowl game played outside the continental United States, Auburn and Villanova played to a 7–7 tie in the Bacardi Bowl in Havana, Cuba. The game was the climax to Cuba's National Sports Festival and was almost canceled when dictator Fulgencio Batista, who had just assumed power, did not find his picture in the game program. A quick trip to the printer solved the problem and the game went on.

1938: Duke had posted a 9–0 regular season without giving up a point. The Blue Devils were forty seconds from perfection when they gave up a touchdown to Southern California in the waning moments of the Rose Bowl and lost 7–3. That team, the school's most famous ever, became known as the "Iron Dukes."

1939: Georgia named Wally Butts, the Little Round Man from Milledgeville, Georgia, its head coach. In twenty-two seasons Butts won 140 games and four SEC titles.

In 1941, Tennessee coach Robert Neyland returned to military duty where he would serve for five years (photo courtesy of the *Atlanta Journal-Constitution*).

Tennessee posted a 10–0 regular season during which it did not give up a single point. Without starting players Bob Suffridge and George Cafego the Volunteers lost to Southern California 14–0 in the Rose Bowl.

On November 30 Auburn played its first game in the school's on-campus stadium against Florida. Seating capacity for what later became Jordan-Hare Stadium was 7,500.

1940: SEC charter member Sewanee, after being unable to win a conference game in eight seasons, withdrew from the conference.

On January 1, in Clemson's first bowl appearance, the Tigers beat Boston College 6–3 in the Cotton Bowl.

On January 10 Jess Neely resigned as Clemson's head coach and accepted the head coaching position at Rice. The next day, Frank Howard was named Clemson's head football coach, a position he would hold for thirty years.

1941: On January 1 Mississippi State won its first bowl game, a 14–7 win over Georgetown in the Orange Bowl. That fall, Mississippi State won its first and only SEC title.

On November 15 Grambling's Eddie Robinson, who would later become the winningest coach in the history of NCAA football, won his first game, a 37–6 win over Tillotson College.

America's involvement in World War II began, and Tennessee coach General Robert Neyland was recalled to active duty. John Barnhill took over the program until Neyland returned for the 1946 season.

1942: Because of the bombing of Pearl Harbor on December 7, 1941, large crowds were banned on the West Coast. As a result, the Rose Bowl on January 1 was moved from Pasadena, California, to Durham, North Carolina, where Duke hosted Oregon State. Oregon State won the game 20–16 before fifty-six thousand fans.

Georgia won its first SEC championship, led by the dream backfield of Frank Sinkwich and Charley Trippi.

On September 19 Clemson opened Memorial Stadium. The seating capacity was twenty thousand.

1943: At the height of World War II, seven of the twelve members of the Southeastern Conference did not field teams. Those schools were Alabama, Auburn, Florida, Kentucky, Mississippi, Mississippi State, and Tennessee. The University of Louisville did not field a team from 1943 to 1945.

1944: With many players still fighting in the war, some schools fielded teams with freshmen and "4-Fs," men who were not physically able to serve in battle. Alabama fielded such a team, nicknamed the "War Babies" by Coach Frank Thomas. That team, led by future Hall of Famer Harry Gilmer, went 5–2–2 and lost to Duke 29–26 in the Sugar Bowl.

1945: After fourteen seasons as an assistant to head coach William Alexander, Bobby Dodd accepted the head coaching position at Georgia Tech. He was only the third head coach in Georgia Tech history and remained for twenty-two seasons, posting a record of 165–64–8.

Maryland hired Paul "Bear" Bryant as head coach. It was Bryant's first head coaching job. He put together a team of players from his Navy preflight squads and went 6–2–1.

1946: Georgia went 11–0 and won its second SEC title under Wally Butts.

After one year at Maryland, Bear Bryant left for Kentucky, where he coached for eight seasons.

After sixteen years and 115 victories, poor health forced Frank Thomas to resign as head coach at Alabama. He was replaced by Harold "Red" Drew.

John Vaught (left) takes over for Red Drew at Ole Miss in 1947 (photo courtesy of the *Atlanta Journal-Constitution*).

1947: On January 1 Georgia played North Carolina in the Sugar Bowl. The game featured a matchup between two of the best players of that era: Georgia's Charley Trippi and North Carolina's Charlie Justice. Trippi led the Bulldogs to a 20–10 win over North Carolina and Justice in New Orleans.

Florida State, which had been a women's college until the 1940s, fielded its first football team. The Seminoles went 0–5.

On January 14 Ole Miss hired John Vaught as its head coach. Vaught's team won an SEC championship in his very first season. Over the next twenty-four years, Vaught led the Rebels to 190 wins, six SEC titles, and three national championships.

On December 6 Kentucky played in the first and only Great Lakes Bowl, defeating Villanova 24–14 before 14,908 at Cleveland Municipal Stadium.

Maryland hired Jim Tatum as its head coach.

George Petrie, the man who brought football to Auburn in 1892, died.

1948: On December 4 Alabama and Auburn played each other for the first time since 1907. Alabama won the game 55–0 in Birmingham. Paul "Bear" Bryant, Kentucky's head coach and the future head coach at Alabama, attended the game.

1949: Broadcaster Lindsey Nelson, with the support of Tennessee coach Robert Neyland, formed the Volunteer Radio Network.

1950: On September 30 Maryland dedicated Byrd Stadium with a 35–21 win over its arch rival, Navy.

In a classic game played in the cold and snow, Tennessee defeated eventual SEC champion Kentucky 7–0 in Knoxville. It would be the only loss all season for coach Bear Bryant's team.

1951: After three awful years under Earl Brown, Auburn hired Ralph "Shug" Jordan as its head football coach. Jordan stayed for twenty-five years and became the school's all-time winningest coach.

Alabama met Tennessee in Birmingham to play the first televised game in the deep South.

On January 1 Kentucky capped off its 1950 SEC championship season by beating No. 1 Oklahoma 13–7 in the Sugar Bowl, snapping the Sooners' 31-game winning streak. Also on January 1, No. 4 Tennessee upset Texas 20–14 in the Cotton Bowl, setting the stage for the Volunteers' 10–0 regular season and national championship win that fall.

An internal study at Virginia recommended that the school should drop football and discontinue all athletics scholarships. This recommendation came in the middle of an 8–1 football season and so no action was taken.

The Southern Conference banned teams from playing in bowl games and limited squads to just forty players for conference games.

1952: On January 1 Maryland completed its first undefeated season with a 28–13 upset of No. 1 Tennessee in the Sugar Bowl. That fall, however, Ole Miss upset No. 3 Maryland, a twenty-point favorite, 21–14 in Oxford to break the Terps' 22-game winning streak.

Georgia Tech went 12–0 to win its third national title and its first under coach Bobby Dodd.

General Robert Neyland, Tennessee's legendary coach, was forced to retire due to poor health and left with a career record of 173–31–12. Neyland coached the season finale with Vanderbilt but stepped down before the Cotton Bowl. Harvey Robinson was named Tennessee's head coach.

Brothers Dick and Ed Modzelewski helped Maryland upset Tennessee in the 1952 Sugar Bowl (photo courtesy of the *Atlanta Journal-Constitution*).

Clemson and Maryland were declared ineligible for the Southern Conference championship after both schools went against the wishes of the conference and accepted bowl bids in 1951.

Mississippi State quarterback Jackie Parker set an SEC scoring record for a single season with 120 points.

1953: Bear Bryant, having grown tired of dueling with Adolph Rupp, Kentucky's dictatorial basketball coach, left the Wildcats to become the head coach at Texas A&M. Bryant realized his value at Kentucky when, during an athletics award ceremony, alumni gave him a cigarette lighter and Rupp a new Cadillac. Bryant was replaced by Blanton Collier.

Upset by limitations on their football programs, seven of the larger schools in the Southern Conference met in Greensboro, North Carolina, to form the Atlantic Coast Conference.

Maryland (10–1) finished ahead of Notre Dame in the final Associated Press poll for the national championship.

1954: On January 1 at the Cotton Bowl, Alabama's Tommy Lewis made a play that will live in infamy. Rice University was leading 7–6 in the second quarter when running back Dickie Moegle broke free and ran up the Alabama sideline for an apparent touchdown. But before he could score on the run, Alabama's Lewis, who had been sitting on the sidelines, jumped into the field of play and tackled Moegle. The officials awarded Moegle a ninety-five-yard touchdown run and Rice won the game 28–6. Lewis became such a national celebrity that Ed Sullivan called him from New York and asked him to appear on his show.

On February 1 Darrell Royal, who would later go on to fame as the head coach at Texas, was named the head coach at Mississippi State. At thirty, he was the youngest head coach in the SEC. He would spend two years in Starkville and leave with a record of 12–8.

1955: After a disagreement with Maryland officials concerning the funding of the football program, Jim Tatum left College Park to become the head coach at North Carolina, his alma mater.

Bowden Wyatt, a former star player at Tennessee, became the Vols' head coach.

On October 15 Auburn beat Georgia Tech 14–12 in Atlanta, its first win over the Yellow Jackets in fifteen seasons.

Tennessee coach Bowden Wyatt celebrates with his players after the Vols beat Georgia Tech in 1956 (photo courtesy of the *Atlanta Journal-Constitution*).

1956: Tennessee went 10–0 before losing 13–7 to Baylor in the Sugar Bowl. Vols halfback Johnny Majors finished second to Notre Dame's Paul Hornung for the Heisman Trophy.

On January 1 Ole Miss rallied from a 13–0 deficit to beat TCU 14–13 in the Cotton Bowl. It was the Rebels' first major bowl win.

On November 13 in Atlanta, No. 3 Tennessee beat No. 2 Georgia Tech 6–0 in what many consider one of the classic games in Southern football history.

1957: Auburn won the AP national championship with a 10–0 record and a defense that posted six shutouts and allowed only twenty-eight points. The Tigers closed out that successful season with a 40–0 win over Alabama on November 30. As a result of this loss, a delegation of Alabama movers and shakers traveled to Texas A&M. Three days later, on December 3, Paul "Bear" Bryant was officially named the new head football coach of the Crimson Tide. When asked why he left Texas A&M when he had seven years left on his contract, Bryant simply said: "Mama called."

On October 19 Queen Elizabeth and Prince Phillip attended the Maryland–North Carolina football game at College Park.

LSU coach Paul Dietzel (right) accepts the 1958 national championship trophy (photo courtesy of the *Atlanta Journal-Constitution*).

On November 23 N.C. State's Dick Christy had the best individual game in ACC history. In a game against South Carolina, Christy scored all of N.C. State's points with four touchdowns, two extra points, and a forty-six-yard field goal scored with no time remaining. The 29–26 win over South Carolina gave N.C. State its first ACC championship.

1958: LSU, led by running back Billy Cannon and a defensive unit known as the "Chinese Bandits," posted the school's first undefeated season in fifty years and won the national championship.

Only a 7–7 tie with Georgia Tech kept Auburn (9–0–1) from recording its second straight undefeated season.

1959: LSU's Billy Cannon wrapped up the Heisman Trophy on a gloomy Halloween night in Baton Rouge. Cannon electrified the crowd with an eighty-nine-yard punt return to beat Ole Miss 7–3. In the final poll of 1959, four SEC teams—Ole Miss (3), LSU (4), Georgia (5), and Alabama (10)—were ranked in the Top 10.

The 1959 Ole Miss team went on to avenge its only loss to LSU by beating the Tigers 21–0 in the Sugar Bowl. That Ole Miss team was later named the SEC Team of the Decade.

On September 26 Auburn lost to Tennessee 3–0, snapping its string of 24 straight games without a loss.

North Carolina coach Jim Tatum died suddenly of Rocky Mountain Spotted Fever.

1960: Ole Miss, led by quarterback Jake Gibbs, went 10–0–1 and was declared the national champion by the Football Writers Association of America.

1961: In his fourth year at Alabama, Bear Bryant won his first of six national championships and his first of thirteen SEC titles for the Crimson Tide.

On November 22 Georgia Tech's Chick Graning lost five teeth and suffered a broken jaw as a result of a hit from Alabama's Darwin Holt. The incident touched off a war of words between the newspapers in Atlanta and Birmingham.

1962: On March 28 General Robert R. Neyland, the most successful coach in Tennessee history, died in Knoxville.

1963: The Saturday Evening Post published an article that claimed that Bear Bryant and former Georgia coach Wally Butts conspired to fix the 1962 Georgia-Alabama game, which Alabama won 35–0. Both coaches later sued the magazine and won substantial judgments.

Georgia Tech's Billy Lothridge finished second to Navy's Roger Staubach in the Heisman Trophy voting.

On October 12 Florida upset No. 3 Alabama 10–6 in Tuscaloosa. It was one of the biggest wins of the Ray Graves era at Florida. Alabama would not lose another game at home until 1982.

On November 22 N.C. State beat Wake Forest to earn a share of the ACC title. The game was overshadowed by the assassination of President John F. Kennedy in Dallas.

On November 30 Georgia Tech played its final game as a member of the SEC, a 14–3 win over Georgia.

On December 4 Vince Dooley, a thirty-one-year-old assistant football coach at Auburn, was named the head coach at Georgia.

Doug Dickey, a top assistant at Arkansas, was hired as the head coach at Tennessee.

1964: On November 21 the University of Florida played at Florida State for the first time in college football history. Florida State won the game 16–7. After earning six straight wins over the Seminoles, Florida wore the words "Go for Seven" across the fronts of their jerseys.

On June 1 Georgia Tech officially withdrew from the SEC and became an Independent.

On October 17 Arkansas upset Texas 14–13 thanks to Ken Hatfield's eighty-one-yard punt return for a touchdown. The Razorbacks won a share of the national championship.

Frank Broyles led Arkansas to a national championship in 1964 (photo courtesy of the *Atlanta Journal-Constitution*).

On November 14 Alabama beat Georgia Tech 24–7 in the last the game the two old rivals would play until 1979.

1965: On September 18, using the now legendary "flea-flicker" play from Kirby Moore to Pat Hodgson to Bob Taylor, Georgia upset defending national champion Alabama 18–17 in Athens. Alabama still won its second straight national title.

Alabama quarterback Joe Namath signed the largest pro contract ever—for $400,000 to play with the New York Jets.

On October 18, two days after a 7–7 tie with Alabama, three Tennessee assistant coaches—Bill Majors, Bob Jones, and Charles Rash—were killed when an automobile collided with a train.

Kentucky's Nat Northington became the first African-American football player to sign with an SEC school. In 1967 he would be the first black player to play in an SEC game.

On November 13 N.C. State played its last game in Riddick Stadium, beating Florida State 3–0.

1966: On January 1 LSU upset Arkansas 14–7 in the Cotton Bowl, snapping the Razorbacks' 22-game winning streak.

Florida quarterback Steve Spurrier won the Heisman Trophy. Spurrier was the first winner from a Southern school since LSU's Billy Cannon won the trophy in 1959.

Georgia won its first SEC championship since 1959 and its first for third-year coach Vince Dooley.

On June 1 Tulane withdrew from the SEC.

Florida quarterback Steve Spurrier (photo courtesy of the Associated Press).

1967: On January 1, after a 9–1 regular season, Bobby Dodd ended his legendary coaching career at Georgia Tech with a 27–12 loss to Florida in the Orange Bowl. The Florida team was led by quarterback Steve Spurrier.

On October 7, led by quarterback Jim Donnan and the "White Shoes" defense, N.C. State went on the road and upset No. 2 Houston 16–6.

1968: Tennessee became the first team in the South to install artificial turf in its football stadium. On September 14 Georgia and Tennessee played to a 17–17 tie in the first game on the new surface. Georgia went on to win the SEC championship.

Lester McClain and Albert Davis became the first African-Americans to play for Tennessee.

1969: On October 5 Alabama defeated Mississippi 33–32 at Birmingham's Legion Field in one of the great quarterback duels in the history of Southern college football. Archie Manning of Ole Miss completed thirty-three of fifty-two passes for 436 yards and had 540 yards of total offense. Alabama's Scott Hunter completed twenty-two of twenty-nine passes for 300 yards.

On December 6, with President Richard Nixon looking on, No. 1 Texas beat No. 2 Arkansas 15–14 in Fayetteville, Arkansas. Afterward, Nixon went to the Texas locker room and proclaimed the Longhorns the national champions.

On December 10 Frank Howard resigned as Clemson's head football coach after thirty seasons.

Eddie McAshan, first black quarterback at Georgia Tech (photo courtesy of the *Atlanta Journal-Constitution*).

Florida A&M coach Jake Gaither won the final game of his career when the Rattlers defeated Grambling 23–19 in the Orange Blossom Classic. At the time, Gaither (203–36–4) had the best winning percentage (84 percent) in all of college football.

1970: Quarterback Eddie McAshan became the first black man to play football at Georgia Tech. A year later, Georgia signed its first black player, running back Horace King from Athens.

On September 12, in Alabama's season opener against Southern California, the Trojans' Sam Cunningham ran for 135 yards and two touchdowns. That game convinced Bear Bryant to begin recruiting black players.

On January 6 Archie Manning of Ole Miss received the Walter Camp Award as the nation's best college football player.

In June, Brian Piccolo, the former ACC Player of the Year at Wake Forest in 1964 and a running back with the Chicago Bears, died of cancer.

Doug Dickey suddenly left Tennessee to become the head coach at Florida, his alma mater. Dickey was replaced by Bill Battle, a twenty-eight-year-old assistant coach and a former player at Alabama.

1971: On January 13 John Vaught retired after twenty-four seasons as the head coach at Ole Miss.

Alabama coach Bear Bryant and his coaching staff spent the summer with Darrell Royal of Texas, learning the Wishbone offense. By the end of the seventies, Alabama had won eight SEC titles and three national titles and had posted a 103–16–1 record.

After retiring in 1970, John Vaught returned as the coach at Ole Miss midway through the 1973 season (photo courtesy of the *Atlanta Journal-Constitution*).

On November 13 Auburn quarterback Pat Sullivan wrapped up the Heisman Trophy with a memorable performance in a 35–20 win over Georgia in Athens.

On November 24 thirty-four-year-old Lou Holtz was named the head coach at N.C. State.

South Carolina dropped out of the ACC and became an Independent.

On December 11 Ben Williams and James Reed became the first black players to sign with Ole Miss.

On December 31, in a battle between brothers, coach Vince Dooley of Georgia beat coach Bill Dooley of North Carolina 7–3 in the Gator Bowl.

1972: On December 2 in the final minutes of the Auburn-Alabama game, Auburn's Bill Newton blocked two Alabama punts, and both were returned for touchdowns by David Langer. Auburn won 17–16, and the phrase "Punt, Bama, Punt!" was forever etched in SEC lore.

With Terry Beasley (88) and Pat Sullivan (7) Auburn coach Shug Jordan went 9–2 in 1971 (photo courtesy of the *Atlanta Journal-Constitution*).

Tennessee's Condrege Holloway became the first black quarterback in SEC history.

Virginia Tech's Don Strock led the nation in passing with 3,170 yards.

1973: On September 23, after a 17–13 loss to Memphis State left Ole Miss with a 1–2 record, coach Billy Kinard and athletics director Bruiser Kinard were fired. The next day, John Vaught came out of retirement to coach the rest of the 1973 season. Ole Miss won 5 of its final 8 games. On December 21 Vaught announced his second retirement as coach.

1974: On January 1 No. 3 Notre Dame gambled and threw out of its own end zone, preserving a 24–23 upset of No. 1 Alabama in the Sugar Bowl. Alabama (11–1) was still declared the 1973 national champion by United Press International.

On September 14 Alabama coach Bear Bryant returned to Maryland for the first time since 1945, when he was the Terps' head coach. His Crimson Tide won the game 21–16 before 54,412 fans, the largest crowd ever to see a game at Byrd Stadium in College Park.

Ray Goff led Georgia to the SEC Championship in 1976 (photo courtesy of the *Atlanta Journal-Constitution*).

On September 28 Georgia Tech played at Clemson for the first time. All previous games between the two schools had been held at Grant Field in Atlanta.

1975: On January 1 Alabama was 11–0 for the second straight year when it met Notre Dame, this time in the Orange Bowl. Notre Dame's players, determined to send coach Ara Parseghian out a winner in his last game, beat the Crimson Tide 13–11.

At a hastily called press conference on April 9, Shug Jordan announced that the 1975 season would be his last as Auburn's head coach. Jordan retired after twenty-five seasons with 176 wins. Assistant Doug Barfield took over as head coach.

1976: Led by quarterback Ray Goff, Georgia won its third SEC tile for coach Vince Dooley. The Bulldogs then lost to national champion Pittsburgh in the Sugar Bowl.

Bobby Bowden was hired as head coach at Florida State.

Tennessee coach Bill Battle resigned under pressure and was replaced by Johnny Majors, the former Volunteer star, who had just coached Pittsburgh to the national title.

On November 26 in Atlanta, Georgia Tech upset No. 11 Notre Dame 23–14 without attempting a single pass.

1977: On September 17 Clemson won at Georgia 7–6 in the Tigers' first win in Athens since 1914.

On October 27 Prince Charles of Wales traveled to Athens, Georgia, to see his first game of American football. It was not a good day for the home team as Kentucky beat Georgia 33–0.

In one of the biggest upsets in the school's history, Ole Miss beat No. 3 Notre Dame 20–13 in Jackson. It would be the only loss all season for Notre Dame, which went on to win the national championship.

Georgia Tech's Eddie Lee Ivery set an NCAA record with 356 yards rushing against Air Force in 1978 (photo courtesy of the *Atlanta Journal-Constitution*).

1978: On November 11 Georgia Tech's Eddie Lee Ivery set an NCAA record by rushing for 356 yards against the Air Force Academy.

On December 4 Charley Pell resigned as Clemson's head coach to become the head coach at Florida.

On December 29, in Danny Ford's first game as Clemson's head coach, the Tigers beat Ohio State 17–15 in the Gator Bowl. During that game, Ohio State coach Woody Hayes struck Clemson player Charlie Bauman. Soon after the incident Hayes was forced out as coach.

On January 2 Arkansas posted one of the biggest upsets in the history of the

Orange Bowl. Although coach Lou Holtz had suspended his top two rushers and Arkansas was given no chance to beat No. 2 Oklahoma, Arkansas dominated the Sooners on the way to a 31–6 victory.

In January Bill Dooley resigned as head coach at North Carolina to become the head coach/athletic director at Virginia Tech. Dooley was replaced by Dick Crum of Miami of Ohio.

1979: On January 1 Alabama defeated Penn State 14–7 at the Sugar Bowl to win the national championship.

On February 12 Emory Bellard, the inventor of the Wishbone offense, was named the head coach at Mississippi State. He would remain there until January 15, 1986.

Coach Vince Dooley with Georgia's 1980 National Championship trophy (photo courtesy of the *Atlanta Journal-Constitution*).

On October 20 former Alabama coach Harold "Red" Drew died at the age of eighty-four.

1980: On January 1 Alabama defeated Arkansas 24–9 in the Sugar Bowl to win the 1979 national championship, its third of the decade.

South Carolina running back George Rogers won the Heisman Trophy, the first ever for the school.

In July former Auburn coach Shug Jordan died.

On November 1 Mississippi State posted the biggest upset in the school's history, a 6–3 win over No. 1 Alabama in Jackson, Mississippi.

On November 8, 1–7 Georgia Tech stunned the football world by tying No. 1 Notre Dame 3–3 in Atlanta. On the same day, No. 2 Georgia rallied from behind in the final minutes to beat Florida 26–21 on a miracle ninety-three-yard touchdown pass from Buck Belue to Lindsay Scott. Georgia was ranked No. 1 in the next polls and stayed there. The Bulldogs, led by freshman tailback Herschel Walker, finished the regular season 11–0 and won their first SEC title since 1976.

On December 1 Doug Barfield resigned as Auburn's head coach with a record of 29–25–1. Auburn pursued Georgia's Vince Dooley, an Auburn grad, but Dooley declined the job offer.

On December 23 Pat Dye, who had interviewed at Auburn, resigned from his post at Wyoming without knowing if he would get the Auburn job.

1981: On January 1, with president and Georgia native Jimmy Carter looking on, Georgia defeated Notre Dame 17–10 in the Sugar Bowl for the school's first consensus national championship.

On January 2 Pat Dye, a former All-America at Georgia and an assistant coach at Alabama, was named the head coach at Auburn.

On September 18 Auburn played its first regular-season night game against North Carolina neighbor Wake Forest.

On November 7 in Chapel Hill, Clemson defeated North Carolina 10–8 in the first battle between two Top 10 teams in ACC history. Clemson would go on to post an 11–0 season and win the ACC title.

On November 28 Alabama defeated Auburn 28–17 to give coach Paul "Bear" Bryant his 315th career win, which broke the Division I record held by Amos Alonzo Stagg.

1982: On January 1 Clemson beat Nebraska 22–15 in the Orange Bowl to win its first national championship.

On October 16 Ole Miss added the name of former coach John Vaught to its stadium.

In the fall of the 1982 season, Alabama started out 7–1 before losing its final 3 games. On December 15 Bear Bryant announced that he would retire after the Liberty Bowl. On December 29 Bryant won his 323rd and final game as a coach, a 21–15 win over Illinois.

Georgia's Herschel Walker won the Heisman Trophy. He was only the second Bulldog player to be so honored.

Alabama's Bear Bryant died just twenty-eight days after coaching his final game (photo courtesy of the *Atlanta Journal-Constitution*).

1983: On January 26, just forty-two days after he had announced his retirement as head coach, Alabama's Bear Bryant died at the age of sixty-nine. He was replaced by former player Ray Perkins.

Georgia Tech, which had been an Independent since 1964, joined the ACC.

Georgia's Herschel Walker gave up his final year of eligibility and signed with the New Jersey Generals of the USFL.

On November 12 Auburn beat Georgia 13–7 in Athens to clinch its first SEC championship since 1957.

1984: On January 1 Al Del Greco kicked a nineteen-yard field goal with only a few seconds remaining to lead Auburn to a 9–7 defeat of Michigan in the Sugar Bowl. The Tigers finished 11–1 with a final No. 3 ranking in Pat Dye's third season as head coach.

Florida finished first in the SEC but gave up the title as part of an NCAA probation.

After fourteen years with an artificial surface, Ole Miss' Vaught-Hemingway Stadium switched to natural grass.

1985: On October 5 Grambling coach Eddie Robinson became the winningest coach in NCAA history when his team defeated Prairie View 27–7. Robinson's 324 wins surpassed Bear Bryant's 323 wins. Bryant remained the leading winner among Division I coaches.

Auburn's Bo Jackson won the Heisman Trophy, the first for the school since Pat Sullivan won it in 1971.

1986: On September 27 Ole Miss retired the No. 18 jersey of quarterback Archie Manning. It remains the only number the school has ever taken out of competition.

On December 31 Ray Perkins resigned as Alabama's head coach to become the head coach of the NFL's Tampa Bay Buccaneers.

1987: On January 3 Bobby Ross was hired as Georgia Tech's eighth coach. Ross, a former coach at Maryland, would remain at Tech for five seasons.

On January 4 Bill Curry, a former player and the former head coach at Georgia Tech, was officially named the head coach at Alabama. He was not a popular choice among many Crimson Tide fans.

Tulane's Mack Brown replaced Dick Crum as the head coach at North Carolina.

1988: On October 8 Ole Miss upset Alabama 22–12 in Tuscaloosa on Alabama's homecoming. It was the Rebels' first win ever over the Crimson Tide in the state of Alabama and it spoiled the dedication of the Bear Bryant Museum. Later, a disgruntled Alabama fan threw a brick through the office window of coach Bill Curry.

That same day LSU's Tommy Hodson threw an eleven-yard touchdown pass to Eddie Fuller with 1:41 remaining to beat Auburn 7–6. The explosion of sound was so loud that it registered as a small earthquake on the seismograph at the LSU Geology Department.

1989: On January 1 at the Gator Bowl, Georgia defeated Michigan State 34–27 in Vince Dooley's last game as coach. Dooley's final record in twenty-five seasons was 201 wins, six SEC titles, one national title, and twenty bowl appearances. The next day at a press conference in Jacksonville, Dooley was replaced by Ray Goff, a former Bulldog quarterback.

On December 2, second-ranked Alabama played at Auburn's Jordan-Hare Stadium for the first time in college football history. A crowd of 85,319, the largest football crowd ever in the state, watched as Auburn upset Alabama 30–20.

Duke won the ACC title under coach Steve Spurrier, who would leave on December 31 to become the head coach at Florida, his alma mater.

1990: Despite having led Alabama to a 10–2 record in 1989 and having been named the SEC Coach of the Year, Bill Curry could not win the hearts of the majority of Alabama's fans. After the school offered him a new contract that would limit his power to run the football program, Curry resigned and on January 8 became the head coach at Kentucky.

On January 11 Gene Stallings, a former player for Bear Bryant at Texas A&M, was named the new head coach at Alabama.

On January 18 Danny Ford resigned as Clemson's head coach after eleven seasons. Three days later Ken Hatfield became the head coach.

On November 3 Scott Sisson kicked a thirty-seven-yard field goal with seven seconds left to lead Georgia Tech to an upset of No. 1 Virginia, 41–38. Georgia Tech then beat Nebraska in the Citrus Bowl to finish 11–0–1 and win the UPI national championship.

On December 9 Jackie Sherrill, a former Alabama player and the former head coach at Pittsburgh and Texas A&M, became the thirtieth head coach in the history of Mississippi State.

1991: On May 6 Ole Miss football player Roy Lee "Chucky" Mullins, who had been paralyzed from the neck down after a collision in a 1989 game against Vanderbilt, died in a Memphis hospital.

Steve Spurrier led Florida to its first SEC championship in 1991 (photo courtesy of the *Atlanta Journal-Constitution*).

On July 1 South Carolina and Arkansas officially joined the SEC, and Florida State became a member of the ACC.

On November 16 Florida beat Kentucky 35–26 to win the school's first official SEC title. The Gators, under coach Steve Spurrier, would go on to win five SEC championships in six seasons.

1992: Miami's Gino Torretta won the Heisman Trophy.

Alabama defeated Florida 28–21 in the first SEC championship game played at Legion Field in Birmingham.

On Thanksgiving Day, after a 17–0 loss to Alabama, Pat Dye resigned as Auburn's football coach.

Tennessee coach Johnny Majors missed 4 games due to heart surgery. Assistant coach Phillip Fulmer went

4–0 as the interim coach. When Majors resigned at the end of the season Fulmer became Tennessee's head coach.

1993: On January 1 Alabama defeated No. 1 Miami 34–13 in New Orleans to win the school's twelfth national championship.

Florida State quarterback Charlie Ward won the Heisman Trophy while Tennessee quarterback Heath Shuler finished second.

Auburn, under first-year coach Terry Bowden, went 11–0. The Tigers could not play in a bowl game because of an NCAA probation.

1994: On January 1 Florida State defeated Nebraska 18–16 in the Orange Bowl for the school's first national championship.

Georgia coach Vince Dooley was inducted into the College Football Hall of Fame.

On September 3 Kentucky and Louisville resumed their football rivalry after a seventy-year hiatus.

Tennessee's Neyland Stadium went back to natural grass after twenty-seven years of using artificial turf.

1995: Grambling's Eddie Robinson became the first coach in college football history to win 400 games.

Kentucky's Moe Williams posted 429 all-purpose yards in a 35–30 win at South Carolina. The total is the highest in SEC history and the second highest in NCAA history.

On November 2 in Charlottesville, Virginia, No. 2 Florida State was upset by Virginia 33–28. It was the Seminoles' first loss in the 30 ACC games the team had played since joining the conference in 1992.

1996: Florida won its fourth straight SEC championship, one short of the record held by Alabama.

Tennessee's Neyland Stadium expanded to 102,854 and became the nation's second-largest on-campus football stadium.

Charlie Conerly, one of the greatest quarterbacks in Ole Miss history, died on February 13 after a lengthy illness.

Frank Howard, Clemson's legendary coach from 1940 to 1969, died at his home in Clemson.

Florida quarterback Danny Wuerffel won the Heisman Trophy.

1997: On January 2 Florida defeated Florida State 52–20 in the Sugar Bowl for the school's first national championship.

Grambling's Eddie Robinson coached his final season.

Tennessee quarterback Peyton Manning, who would leave college football as the SEC's all-time total offense leader (11,020 yards), finished second to Michigan's Charles Woodson for the Heisman Trophy. He is the fourth Tennessee player to have finished second for the award.

On December 5, after a 10–1 regular season, Mack Brown resigned from North Carolina to become the head coach at Texas. He was replaced by defensive coordinator Carl Torbush.

Tennessee's Peyton Manning, son of Archie Manning (photo courtesy of Tennessee SID).

1998: In Knoxville, before 107,653 fans, the largest crowd ever at a football game in the South, Tennessee defeated Florida 20–17 in overtime. It was Tennessee's first win over Florida since 1992.

In April Tennessee's Peyton Manning was the No. 1 pick in the NFL draft by the Indianapolis Colts.

On October 23, midway through the season, Terry Bowden resigned as Auburn's head coach and was replaced by Bill Oliver.

On November 28 Tommy Tuberville left Ole Miss to become Auburn's head coach.

1999: Two Southern teams, Tennessee and Florida State, played in the Fiesta Bowl for the national championship on January 4. Tennessee won 23–16 in Tempe, Arizona, for its first national championship since 1951.

On October 23 Florida State's Bobby Bowden became only the fifth Division I coach in college football history to win 300 games. Bowden beat his son, Tommy, the head coach at Clemson, 17–14 for win No. 300.

On December 7 Georgia running back Herschel Walker, Alabama lineman John Hannah, Arkansas wide receiver Chuck Dicus, and former Kentucky coach Jerry Claiborne were inducted into the College Football Hall of Fame.

Former N.C. State and Notre Dame coach Lou Holtz, who had been hired to rebuild the troubled program at South Carolina, went 0–11 in his first season.

Alabama won its first SEC championship since 1992.

Florida State went 11–0 and won its eighth straight ACC championship.

2000: On January 4 No. 1 Florida State defeated No. 2 Virginia Tech 46–29 for coach Bobby Bowden's second national championship. The 1999 season was also Bowden's first undefeated season (12–0).

Florida State, ranked No. 1 in the preseason, became the first team to stay on top of the polls wire to wire since the Associated Press preseason poll began in 1950.

SOUTHERN FRIED **FOOTBALL** FROM **A** TO **Z**

AUBIE THE TIGER: Before Aubie was Auburn's award-winning mascot, a cartoon version of the tiger, drawn by artist Phil Neel of the *Birmingham Post-Herald*, appeared in a 1959 game program. Since 1979, a student dressed in a tiger costume has filled the role.

ARTIFICIAL TURF: When Tennessee installed an artificial playing surface in its stadium for the 1968 season, it was the first school in the South to do so. The first game the Volunteers played on the new field in Knoxville, on September 14, resulted in a 17–17 tie with Georgia. Tennessee tied the game with a two-point conversion with no time left. After Tennessee's success on its artificial surface, many more Southern schools had them installed. But eventually coaches concluded that they caused more injuries than grass fields did, and schools with grass fields began to use this to their advantage when recruiting players. In the 1990s schools with artificial turf fields began returning to natural grass fields. Tennessee finally replaced its artificial turf with natural grass in 1994.

BEER BARREL: Painted orange and blue and filled with beer, this barrel once went to the winner of the annual Tennessee-Kentucky game. The tradition was discontinued in 1999 after a Kentucky football player died tragically in an alcohol-related automobile accident.

BOURBON BARREL: This barrel is presented each year to the winner of the Kentucky-Indiana game. The series between the two schools began in 1893 but is not played every year; the 2000 game will be the thirtieth in the series.

CHARLEY BAUMAN: Ohio State coach Woody Hayes struck this Clemson player during the final minutes of the Buckeyes, 17–15 loss to the Tigers in the 1978 Gator Bowl. Hayes was forced to resign as a result of the incident.

BACARDI BOWL: Played on January 1, 1937, in Havana, Cuba, between Auburn and Villanova, this game was the first and only bowl game to be played outside the United States. The game, which ended in a 7–7 tie, was considered a flop because only nine thousand people paid to see it. Among the spectators was dictator Fulgencio Batista, who watched the game with his armed guards.

BIG THURSDAY: From 1896 to 1959, rivals Clemson and South Carolina played their traditional game during the State Fair in Columbia, South Carolina, on the third Thursday of October. Clemson fans eventually grew tired of playing such an important game on the road every year, so in 1960, at the insistence of Tiger coach Frank Howard, the Tigers' home games were moved back to Clemson's campus. Clemson won the last Big Thursday game 27–0.

BETWEEN THE HEDGES: This reference to the English privet hedges surrounding the field at Georgia's Sanford Stadium was supposedly coined by legendary sportswriter Grantland Rice, who is believed to have been the first to say that Georgia had an advantage any time it played its opponent "between the hedges." The hedges were only a foot tall when the stadium was dedicated in a game against Yale in 1929. In late 1995, the original hedges were removed in order to make room for the Olympic soccer events that would be held there in 1996. New hedges, which were grown from cuttings of the originals, were replanted that fall and today are stronger than ever.

Mississippi State's famed Cowbells (photo courtesy of Mississippi State SID).

COWBELLS: This noise-making device is a favorite among Mississippi State fans. Although in 1974 the SEC banned the use of cowbells during conference games because opposing coaches complained of the noise and thought it gave Mississippi State an unfair advantage, determined Bulldog fans still manage to sneak them into games both at home and on the road.

CHECKERBOARD END ZONE: The end zones at Tennessee's Neyland Stadium feature a checkerboard design comprised of a series of orange and white blocks. This design was first used when Doug Dickey arrived as coach in 1964 and was discontinued in 1968 when Tennessee installed artificial turf in its stadium. The tradition was reinstated at Tennessee in 1989 and is considered one of the school's trademarks.

CHIEF OSCEOLA: Since 1978, Chief Osceola has been Florida State's official mascot. Before each game, an FSU student chosen for the honor rides to the middle of the field on an Appaloosa named Renegade. In front of the opposing bench, Chief Osceola plants a fiery spear into the turf of Doak Campbell Stadium, signifying that the battle is about to begin.

CHINESE BANDITS: LSU coach Paul Dietzel gave this nickname to one of the defensive units on his 1958 national championship team. The name came from a "Terry and the Pirates" comic strip that referred to the Chinese Bandits as "the most vicious people in the world." The unit became so famous that the players were featured in Life magazine wearing Chinese masks.

DEATH VALLEY: This nickname for Clemson's Memorial Stadium was popularized by Lonnie McMillian, a former coach at Presbyterian College, who remarked that his teams always seemed to get killed there. Ironically, a cemetery is located just outside the stadium.

ESSO CLUB: Located just across the street from the Clemson campus, this converted gas station serves as a popular gathering place for fans to sing, dance, and have a cool one before and after Tiger games.

GATOR GROWL: This entertainment extravaganza takes place each year on the Friday night before Florida's homecoming game and draws more than seventy-two thousand students and alumni.

GOLDEN EGG: After a near-riot at the 1926 Mississippi–Mississippi State game, an Ole Miss honor society proposed that the two teams play for a trophy each year, and the tradition is still going strong today. The trophy, a gold-plated football on a pedestal, eventually became known as the Golden Egg.

"GOOD OLD SONG": Sung to the tune of "Auld Lang Syne," this song has served as Virginia's unofficial alma mater since 1893.

H-BOYS: This name was given to the Ole Miss backfield of Junie Hovious and Merle Hapes, who became two of the biggest names in college football from 1939 to 1941.

CONDREDGE HOLLOWAY: When Holloway lined up for Tennessee in 1972, he became the first black quarterback in the history of the SEC. He turned down an opportunity to play baseball for the Montreal Expos and an $85,000 dollar signing bonus to stay at Tennessee. After leaving Tennessee, Holloway went on to have a successful career in the Canadian Football League.

Bear Bryant and his houndstooth hat (photo courtesy of the *Atlanta Journal-Constitution*).

HOUNDSTOOTH HAT: This was the preferred headwear of Paul "Bear" Bryant, Alabama's legendary coach from 1958 to 1982.

HOWARD'S ROCK: Located at the top of a grassy hill on the east end of Clemson's Memorial Stadium, this rock was originally given to former Tiger coach Frank Howard by a friend who had picked it up in Death Valley, California. Howard placed the rock on a pedestal on top of the hill on September 24, 1966, prior to a game with Virginia, and then each Clemson player touched the rock and ran down the hill for good luck. Clemson won the game 40–35, and the tradition of running down the hill after touching Howard's Rock was born.

ICE BOWL: The 1947 Cotton Bowl between LSU and Arkansas was nicknamed the Ice Bowl when a storm hit Dallas and the city was pelted with ice, sleet, and snow. Fans had to build fires in the stands so they could stay and watch the game. LSU was led by quarterback Y. A. Tittle and Arkansas was led by future Hall of Famer Clyde Scott. LSU dominated the game fifteen first downs to one but could not score. The game ended in a 0–0 tie.

IRON BOWL: When rivals Auburn and Alabama played their annual game in the Iron City of Birmingham, it was referred to as the Iron Bowl. A dispute between the two schools led to the discontinuation of the series after the 1907 game. When the annual tradition was resumed in 1948, every game was played in Birmingham's Legion Field, considered an Alabama stronghold, until 1989, when Alabama played at Auburn for the first time. Now the game is played on the school's respective campuses in Auburn and Tuscaloosa.

IRON DUKES: Duke University's most famous team, known as the "Iron Dukes," earned this nickname after playing the entire 1938 regular season without giving up one single point. The Blue Devils could have enjoyed complete perfection that season, but Southern California scored a touchdown on them with forty seconds left in the Rose Bowl and won 7–3.

KOOL KOYOTES: The players on the 1967 N.C. State team are best known for painting their black shoes white as a sign of their determination not to let any opposing team cross the white goal line. The team's "White Shoes" defense gave the school recognition, as did the N.C. State students who, assigned the duty of buying a live wolf to serve as the school's mascot, were duped into buying a coyote by a dishonest animal dealer. *Sports Illustrated* published an article on the incident, and the nickname stuck.

MIKE THE TIGER: This real, honest-to-goodness Bengal tiger prowls in his cage on the sidelines during LSU's games in Baton Rouge. Before the game, Mike's cage is parked near the opponents' dressing room so that the players are forced to walk past his imposing presence as they go to and from the field. LSU began using a live mascot in 1935, and the latest mascot, Mike V, began his reign in April of 1990.

1A and 1B: Bear Bryant established this numbering system to identify twins Harry and Larry Jones, who played at Kentucky from 1950 to 1952. Harry wore 1A and Larry wore 1B. Harry led the Wildcats in all-purpose yardage in 1951 while Larry led them in kick-off returns in 1952.

"PUNT, BAMA, PUNT": This phrase identifies what was perhaps the most famous game of the storied series between Alabama and Auburn. Trailing 16–0 going into the fourth quarter, Auburn's Gardner Jett got a field goal to make the score 16–3. Then the incredible happened. Auburn's Bill Newton blocked an Alabama punt and David Langer returned it twenty-five yards for a touchdown. Three minutes later, Newton blocked another punt and again Langer returned it for a touchdown, this time from twenty yards out, and Auburn won 17–16. The phrase was soon found on bumper stickers throughout the state.

Auburn's Bill Newton (left) and David Langer were heroes against Alabama in 1972 (photo courtesy of the *Atlanta Journal-Constitution*).

RAMBLIN' WRECK: This restored 1930 Model A Ford Sport Coupe leads the Georgia Tech football team onto the field before the beginning of each home game. It is also the name of one of the most famous fight songs in the history of college football. (For the words, see the section on Georgia Tech, pages 166–169 in the Game Day chapter.)

"ROCKY TOP": It's not Tennessee's official fight song, but it is the most popular. Released in 1967, this song is played almost continuously during a Tennessee game by the Pride of the Southland Band. (For the words, see the section on Tennessee, pages 169–172, in the Game Day chapter.)

SMOKEY: This bluetick hound dog serves as Tennessee's mascot. Smokey I was adopted in 1953, and Smokey VII now roams the Tennessee sidelines.

SOD CEMETERY: In Bobby Bowden's early days as Florida State's head coach, he had to play the nation's toughest teams on the road in order to build a name for his program. When Florida State would win one of those big road games, someone would gather a piece of the opposing field, bring it back to Tallahassee, and plant it in the "Sod Cemetery" near the Florida State practice field. A brass plate bearing the game's final score is placed next to each burial site, signifying another Florida State "Sod Game."

TESTUDO: This diamondback turtle became Maryland's official mascot on May 23, 1933. Tetsudo is not a live turtle, but a student dressed in costume.

TEXTILE BOWL: The annual game between Clemson and N.C. State is called the Textile Bowl because both North Carolina and South Carolina are states noted for their textile manufacturing and because Clemson and N.C. State have two of the best textile schools in the world.

THE AMAZIN'S: In 1972, after the departure of Heisman Trophy winner Pat Sullivan and receiver Terry Beasley, Auburn was picked to finish seventh in the SEC. But the Tigers went 10–1, a record that included a 17–16 win over Alabama. "The Amazin's," as they became known, finished fifth in the Associated Press poll.

THE AWARD-WINNING, FIGHTING CAVALIER INDOOR/OUTDOOR PRECISION MARCHING PEP BAND AND CHOWDER SOCIETY-REVUE, UNLIMITED: Also known as the University of Virginia Pep Band.

THE GROVE: This ten-acre plot of land in the middle of the Mississippi campus in Oxford is where fans traditionally go to tailgate prior to Ole Miss games. In 1985 Rebels coach Billy Brewer began marching his players through the Grove on their way to Vaught-Hemingway Stadium so that they could enjoy the tradition as well. Fans now line up on either side of the team and cheer their heroes on as they march to the field.

THE IMMORTALS: Unbeaten (7–0), untied, and unscored upon, W. R. Bass's formidable 1898 Kentucky Wildcats team, also known as the Immortals, outscored the opposition 180–0.

THE RAG: At one time this rag went to the winner of the LSU-Tulane game. Half of the rag was decorated in LSU's purple and gold, and the other half was decorated in Tulane's green and white. The victorious school held the rag for an entire year, but it was eventually misplaced and its current whereabouts are unknown.

THE SWAMP: When Steve Spurrier took over as head coach of the Gators in 1990, he assigned this nickname to Florida's Ben Hill Griffin Stadium. Spurrier liked the name because "only Gators can survive a trip to the Swamp." Going into the 2000 season, Florida is 57–4 at home under Spurrier.

THE THIRD SATURDAY IN OCTOBER: On this date Alabama and Tennessee play their traditional game, which both schools consider a measuring stick for their respective teams. Over the years, when Alabama and Tennessee coaches have been asked about the quality of their teams in the fall, they simply say, "I'll let you know after the third Saturday in October."

THE THIN THIRTY: When football coach Blanton Collier left Kentucky in 1962, Charlie Bradshaw, a disciple of Paul "Bear" Bryant, took over. Bradshaw pushed that first team so hard that more than fifty players quit. The remaining thirty, who posted a record of 3–5–2, were nicknamed The Thin Thirty. This team turned out to be the most famous team Bradshaw fielded at Kentucky, where he was 25–41–4 in seven seasons.

THE WRECK TECH PAJAMA PARADE: This tradition began in 1896 and lasted for ninety-two years. The night before their 1896 game with Georgia Tech, Auburn students greased the railroad tracks on which the train carrying the Tech team would be traveling the next day. When the train neared its stop, it could not stop and skidded for ten miles. Although Auburn students never played that trick again, each year before their team played Tech the students marched in their pajamas to celebrate the event. The two teams have not played since 1987.

TIGERAMA: More than 35,000 people come to Clemson's Memorial Stadium for this combination pep rally, beauty pageant, and fireworks display, which is held each year on the Friday night before Clemson's homecoming game.

TIGER WALK: About two hours before every home game, Auburn's players walk down Donahue Drive from Sewell Hall, where most of the football players live, to Jordan-Hare Stadium. Fans form a human corridor on either side of the players and cheer them on as they make their way to the stadium. In 1989, prior to the historic Auburn-Alabama game, more than twenty thousand people turned out for the Tiger Walk.

TOOMER'S CORNER: This corner, located where the university campus meets the town of Auburn at the intersection of College Street and Magnolia Avenue, has long been a gathering place for fans to celebrate after games. After big victories, students and fans roll the trees and other objects with toilet paper. In 1995 students rolled Toomer's Corner when rival Alabama was placed on NCAA probation.

UGA, Georgia's mascot (photo courtesy of Dan Evans/University of Georgia).

UGA: This purebred English bulldog is the official mascot of the University of Georgia. Georgia's first mascot, UGA (pronounced ugh-uh) I, made its first appearance in the fall of 1955, and today UGA VI carries on the tradition. UGA V, who retired before the 1999 season, was the most recognized of all the UGAs, having appeared on the cover of the April 28, 1997, issue of Sports Illustrated as college football's best mascot. Later that year he had a cameo in Clint Eastwood's movie *Midnight in the Garden of Good and Evil.*

VOLUNTEER NAVY: In 1962 radio broadcaster George Mooney found a way to get to Tennessee's Neyland Stadium without having to navigate the notorious Knoxville traffic. He took his small boat down the Tennessee River and docked near the stadium. His secret caught on and today more than two hundred boats make the trip prior to Tennessee home games.

WAHOOS: This nickname for the University of Virginia is one of several and the one most commonly used by students and fans.

"WAR EAGLE!": Auburn's battle cry is more than one hundred years old. According to the legend, a former Civil War soldier who had become a member of Auburn's faculty attended the first game between Auburn and Georgia in Atlanta in 1892. With the man was the eagle he had raised after the war. When Auburn scored the first touchdown, the eagle broke free and began to soar above the field. The Auburn crowd saw the eagle flying overhead and shouted, "War Eagle!" and a tradition was born.

THE WORLD'S LARGEST OUTDOOR COCKTAIL PARTY: Until 1933, the annual Georgia-Florida game had been played in several different locations, including Macon, Athens, and Savannah in Georgia and Tampa, Jacksonville, and Gainesville in Florida. That year officials from both schools decided to permanently move the game to Jacksonville to provide a late fall vacation for both sets of fans. The game's nickname was adopted because of the tendency of the fans to party to excess.

WRONG WAY RIEGELS: Georgia Tech won the 1929 Rose Bowl and the national championship thanks to one of the most famous blunders in college football history. In the second quarter of the game, Georgia Tech fumbled on its own 36-yard line, and Roy Riegels, the captain of the California football team, picked up the ball and began running the wrong way. His teammates tried to get him to turn around, but he would not listen. He was finally tackled near the goal line. When California tried to punt, Tech blocked the kick for a safety, earning the winning points in an 8–7 Georgia Tech victory.

XEN C. SCOTT: In 1919, Alabama hired Scott, a Cleveland sportswriter, as its head football coach. Scott, a tiny man (5'6", 135 pounds) who had played at Cleveland's Western Reserve, coached Alabama for four seasons, winning 29 games.

ZIPP NEWMAN: This former sports editor of the Birmingham News is generally given credit for creating Alabama's nickname "The Crimson Tide" in 1919. Sportswriters previously had referred to Alabama's team, which wore crimson uniforms, as the "Thin Red Line."

THE PLAYERS

If Southerners view college football as battle, then it stands to reason that the players are their gladiators, their Saturday afternoon heroes. And nowhere have college football players performed more heroically or been held in higher esteem than in the South.

Still, much of the history of these men is unknown. Did you know, for example, that of the sixty-five Heisman Trophies awarded by New York's Downtown Athletic Club, eleven have gone to players from the South? These Southern Heisman winners range from Georgia's Frank Sinkwich, who wore his Marine Corps uniform to accept the trophy in 1942, to Florida's Danny Wuerffel, the son of a Presbyterian minister, who won in 1996.

What may be more compelling and less widely known is how many Southern players have finished second in the voting for the Heisman Trophy. Georgia's Charley Trippi finished second to Army's great Glenn Davis in 1946. North Carolina's Charlie "Choo Choo" Justice finished second in the Heisman voting twice, in 1948 (to Doak Walker, SMU) and in 1949 (to Leon Hart, Notre Dame). A total of thirteen Southern players have finished second in the Heisman voting, including a father-son team of near-Heisman winners. Ole Miss quarterback Archie Manning finished third in 1970, and his son, Peyton, finished second to Michigan's Charles Woodson in 1997.

These, of course, were the glamour boys of Southern college football. But the South has produced more than its share of bruisers—the rough and tough men who, while their names weren't always in the headlines, gave the Southern game its rugged flavor.

Men Like:

Auburn's Zeke Smith, who was so good that in 1958, when he was a junior, a professional team from Canada offered him a contract, which was unheard of in that day. Smith turned down the money to stay at Auburn.

Ole Miss' Frank "Bruiser" Kinard, the ultimate Iron Man. During the 1935 season, Kinard was on the field for 708 out of the 720 minutes his team played.

Tennessee defensive tackle Doug Atkins, who never won a major award but was still named the SEC's Player of the Quarter Century (1950–75). Atkins went on to become a member of both the college and pro football halls of fame.

The efforts of Southern college football players past and present are frozen in time and will remain forever etched in the hearts and minds of those who love the great Southern game. Many of these players are gone, and most of those who remain have watched their once-powerful bodies submit to the inevitable changes of time. But as long as someone remembers what these special men did on those wonderful Saturdays long, long ago, they will remain forever young. These are their stories.

The Heisman Winners

Every year since 1935 the Downtown Athletic Club in New York has presented the Heisman Trophy to college football's most outstanding player. Eleven of the sixty-five Heismans awarded from 1935 to 1999 have gone to players from the South, and most Southern fans argue that the number should be much higher. Those eleven who did win college football's highest honor, however, have earned a special place in the history of Southern college football.

Georgia, 1942—Heisman Trophy winner Frank Sinkwich led the Bulldogs to the Rose Bowl (photo courtesy of the *Atlanta Journal-Constitution*).

Frank Sinkwich, Georgia, 1942

To this day, two images of Sinkwich, the South's first Heisman winner, are seared into the collective consciousness of college football fans. The first image is of Sinkwich, wearing a protective mask that covered half his face, running and passing down the field in 1941. Sinkwich wore the mask to protect his jaw, which had been broken during a pileup in a game against South Carolina. The picture went nationwide and fans everywhere started buzzing about "Flatfoot Frankie," Georgia's triple threat at halfback. Despite his injured jaw, junior Sinkwich put on one of the greatest performances in bowl history when he ran for 139 yards and passed for 243 yards and three touchdowns in the 1942 Orange Bowl. That total offense record of 382 yards still stands.

As a senior, Sinkwich led Georgia to an 11–1 record, an SEC championship, and a berth in the 1943 Rose Bowl, in which the Bulldogs beat UCLA. The other image that fans will always remember is of Sinkwich, dressed in his Marine

Corps uniform, picking up his Heisman Trophy before he left for Pasadena. He entered the service shortly after the Rose Bowl.

Sinkwich played several years of professional football and coached briefly at Tampa before becoming a wholesale beer distributor. He was inducted into the College Football Hall of Fame in 1954 and died on October 22, 1990.

Billy Cannon, LSU, 1959

At 6'1", 210 pounds, Billy Cannon possessed a deadly combination of speed and power. He led LSU to an undefeated season and a national championship in 1958, but his career, and perhaps his life, has been defined by a few seconds on Halloween night in 1959.

LSU's Billy Cannon, the 1959 Heisman Trophy winner (photo courtesy of the *Atlanta Journal-Constitution*).

LSU, undefeated and ranked No. 3, trailed Ole Miss, ranked No. 1 and also undefeated, 3–0 on that foggy Saturday night in Baton Rouge. With about ten minutes left in the game, Cannon dropped back to receive a punt. He took the ball on a bounce at his 11-yard line. The old films show that eight Mississippi players got at least one hand on Cannon, but he was able to elude them all, including Rebel All-American Jake Gibbs, who was the punter and the last man to miss Cannon. Cannon scored on the eighty-nine-yard run, and LSU won the game 7–3.

While many people know of Cannon's run, few remember that Ole Miss almost came back to win the game. The Rebels drove down to the one-yard line, where Cannon and Warren Rabb tackled the ball carrier and stopped the drive with eighteen seconds left in the game.

Cannon went on to play eleven years of professional football before enrolling in dental school at Tennessee. He is now an orthodontist in Baton Rouge, Louisiana.

Florida quarterback Steve Spurrier won the Heisman Trophy in 1966 (photo courtesy of Florida SID).

Steve Spurrier, Florida, 1966

Whatever Steve Spurrier may have lacked in physical ability, he more than made up for in confidence. This son of an East Tennessee minister had total belief in his ability to lead football teams to victory. It is a trait that has served him well throughout his life.

Spurrier's confidence was never more evident than on October 29, 1966, when he made the play that would launch him to the Heisman Trophy. Florida was undefeated and ranked No. 7 going into a big game with Auburn. Thanks to the work of Florida sports information director Norm Carlson, the press box that Saturday was full of national writers wanting to see Spurrier. He played a brilliant game, throwing for 259 yards and punting for a 47-yard average. But with the score tied at 27–27, Florida faced a fourth and long at the Auburn 25-yard line.

Florida called time out and Coach Ray Graves pondered his options. He knew that the forty-two-yard field goal was out of the range of Florida's regular kicker and that going for the first down against the Auburn defense was a long shot. Then Spurrier jogged over and said, "Coach, let me give it a shot."

The request didn't register with Graves, who was deep in thought. Spurrier asked again, this time more forcefully. Graves then looked at him and yelled, "Go kick it, Orr!" calling Spurrier by his middle name. He made the field goal and Florida won 30–27. The Heisman voters awarded him a lopsided victory over Purdue's Bob Griese.

Spurrier went on to play for ten years in the NFL before becoming a coach. After a three-season stint as Duke's head coach, he returned to Florida in 1990 and won five SEC championships in his first seven seasons as the coach of the Gators. Spurrier was inducted into the College Football Hall of Fame in 1986.

Pat Sullivan, Auburn, 1971

Like Steve Spurrier, Auburn's Pat Sullivan delivered one of his greatest performances to earn the Heisman Trophy. Undefeated and sixth-ranked Auburn played at undefeated and seventh-ranked Georgia on November 13, 1971, to an overflowing crowd at Sanford Stadium, all watching to see who would win and challenge Alabama for the SEC championship.

Pat Sullivan (photo courtesy of the *Atlanta Journal-Constitution*).

The fans also came to see if Sullivan could do something to overtake Cornell's Ed Marinaro in the Heisman Trophy race. Handsome running back Marinaro, who would later become an actor, was perceived to have an edge over the low-key Southern quarterback from Birmingham, Alabama. But Sullivan defied the odds-makers, throwing for an impressive 248 yards and four touchdowns. He made one of his completions, a twenty-seven-yarder to wide receiver Dick Schmaltz, as he was falling to the ground. He simply threw the ball side-armed up the field. Auburn went on to win the game 35–20.

"What I remember most is that time after time we had him, but he always found a way to make the play," says former Georgia coach Vince Dooley. "He was a super player having a super day. We tried everything we could to stop him but nothing worked. That day he was the best quarterback I had ever seen."

Sullivan's performance gave him the edge over Marinaro, and he won the Heisman by only 152 points. Once he left Auburn, Sullivan played briefly in the NFL. He returned to Auburn in 1986 as an assistant coach and was named head coach at Texas Christian six years later. After leaving TCU, Sullivan returned to Birmingham and entered into private business. He then joined the staff at the University of Alabama–Birmingham in 1998. Sullivan was inducted into the College Football Hall of Fame in 1991.

South Carolina running back George Rogers won the 1980 Heisman Trophy (photo courtesy of South Carolina SID).

George Rogers, South Carolina, 1980

Few players have had to overcome more obstacles on the way to greatness than George Rogers. Born into poverty in tiny Duluth, Georgia, Rogers was only six years old when his parents divorced. Hard times soon fell on the family. He had two brothers and two sisters, and his mother had no money. His father had gone to prison for killing a woman with whom he had been involved. "What I remember most is that we moved about eight times, just to stay ahead of the bills," says Rogers. "Kids would taunt me because of my old clothes. You don't forget things like that."

Football would be his way out. In junior high, Rogers lied about his age and joined a labor pool, working for $1.80 an hour to earn the two-dollar fee for team insurance. In high school, Rogers moved out of the Atlanta housing projects to live with his aunt, who would only allow him to play football if he did his schoolwork and helped around the house. The structure and discipline worked. Rogers enrolled at Duluth High School, where he would be named the Georgia Class AA Player of the Year in both of his final two seasons.

At South Carolina, Rogers had three straight seasons of more than 1,000 yards, and in 1980 he led the nation with 1,781 yards rushing. He had 21 consecutive games of one hundred yards or more. "He was the most complete back I ever coached," says former South Carolina coach Jim Carlen. "He could run around people or over people. And once he got ahead of them, he could outrun them."

Rogers was the No. 1 pick by New Orleans in the 1981 NFL draft. He finished his pro career with the Washington Redskins in 1988 and was inducted into the College Football Hall of Fame in 1997.

Herschel Walker, Georgia, 1982

While most of the Southern Heisman winners forged their legends as seniors, Georgia's Herschel Walker became a star in his very first college game.

Georgia was trailing Tennessee 15–2 in the 1980 opener for both teams on a steamy Saturday night in Knoxville, Tennessee. Walker, a true freshman, had come to Georgia after one of the most publicized recruiting battles in the history of college football. Coach Vince Dooley was hesitant to throw such a young player into the fire, but assistant coach Mike Cavan, who had recruited Walker out of Wrightsville, Georgia, pleaded with Dooley to give the kid a chance.

Herschel Walker (photo courtesy of the *Atlanta Journal-Constitution*).

"I just told Coach Dooley that I didn't see any way we were going to win the game if we didn't give the ball to Herschel," says Cavan. Trailing by thirteen points with time running out in the third quarter, Georgia decided to give the ball to Walker. He scored his first college touchdown by running over Tennessee safety Bill Bates for sixteen yards. Then, early in the fourth quarter, Walker scored again from nine yards out, giving the Bulldogs a 16–15 victory.

That game launched Walker's storybook career and carried Georgia to a 12–0 season and the 1980 national championship. Over the next three years Georgia just kept giving the ball to Walker, who rushed for a total of 5,097 yards, an NCAA record for total yards in three seasons. With Walker, Georgia won 32 games and lost only 2 while posting three straight SEC championships. Walker finished third in the Heisman voting in 1980 and second to Marcus Allen in 1981. In 1982 he won the award, finishing ahead of Stanford's John Elway.

After his junior season Walker left Georgia to sign with the New Jersey Generals of the now-defunct United States Football League. He was inducted into the College Football Hall of Fame in 1999.

Vincent "Bo" Jackson, Auburn, 1985

At times during his brilliant career (1982–85), Vincent "Bo" Jackson's athletic talents simply defied description. The 6'1", 222-pound running back possessed the speed and power to either run around or run over defenders. As a baseball player at Auburn, he had a career .335 average and twenty-eight homers. He could have been a world-class track star if he had made up his mind to do it. As it was, Jackson ran for 4,303 yards in four seasons and led Auburn to SEC championships in 1983 and 1985.

"If you're lucky, you get to coach one like him in a lifetime, and I was lucky," says Pat Dye, his former coach at Auburn.

Auburn's Bo Jackson won the Heisman Trophy in 1985 (photo courtesy of the *Atlanta Journal-Constitution*).

Jackson earned his nickname as a youngster because he was wild (like a wild "boar"), and even Jackson's mother predicted that he would eventually end up in jail if he didn't change his wild ways. Jackson did change when he arrived at Auburn in 1982. He had enjoyed a brilliant, multisport high school career and had been taken in the second round of the amateur baseball draft by the New York Yankees. But he deferred his dream of playing in the major leagues so that he could play football for Auburn.

After rushing for 1,213 yards and leading the Tigers to an SEC championship as a sophomore in 1983, Jackson was a leading candidate for the Heisman in 1984. Then a shoulder injury all but knocked him out for the season.

When Jackson returned to the field for the 1985 season, he played with a vengeance, rushing for 1,786 yards and seventeen touchdowns and leading Auburn to another SEC title. Jackson won the Heisman Trophy by a mere forty-five points, the narrowest margin ever, over Iowa quarterback Chuck Long. When Jackson left Auburn the following spring, he was the SEC's first three-sport letterman (football, baseball, and track) in thirty years.

Jackson went on to become an NFL All-Pro and a baseball All-Star. In 1991 his professional athletic career was cut short by a hip injury, but he will always be remembered as one of the greatest athletes to have ever put on a college uniform.

Vinny Testaverde, Miami, 1986

To some, a dream delayed is a dream denied. But not to Vinny Testaverde, who endured one roadblock after the next to fulfill his dream. Since Testaverde's birth in November of 1963, his father, Al, had dreamed that his son would someday win the Heisman Trophy. Testaverde was but a few days old when "Big Al" placed a football in his son's crib.

But after a brilliant high school career in Elmont, New York, Testaverde's insufficient grades kept him from being accepted to college. So Testaverde spent a year at Fork Union

Military Academy in Virginia to improve his grades and further hone his athletic skills. In 1982, Testaverde's first year at the University of Miami, he played behind Jim Kelly, who would go on to an All-Pro career in the NFL. Then, in 1983, Testaverde lost the battle for the position of quarterback to Bernie Kosar, who would lead the Hurricanes to a national championship. Testaverde redshirted that season and backed up Kosar in 1984.

Miami's Vinny Testaverde (photo courtesy of Miami SID).

Testaverde finally got his chance to quarterback in 1985 when Kosar left school early to play in the NFL. In his very first start, against Florida, the Hurricanes lost 35–23. But this first loss would turn out to be the only regular season loss Testaverde would experience as Miami's quarterback. The Hurricanes went 10–1 that season before losing to Tennessee in the Sugar Bowl. Testaverde finished fifth in the Heisman voting.

The next season Testaverde led the Heisman race from the beginning and beat Temple's Paul Palmer by 1,541 points. Miami had an undefeated regular season but was stopped short of the national championship by Penn State in the Fiesta Bowl. Testaverde finished his college career with 6,058 yards passing and forty-eight touchdowns. He was the No. 1 overall pick in the 1987 NFL draft, by Tampa Bay.

Gino Torretta, Miami, 1992

The list of great quarterbacks from the University of Miami reads like a who's who of college football: Jim Kelly, Vinny Testaverde, Bernie Kosar, Steve Walsh, Craig Erickson. But Gino Torretta won more games (26) and passed for more yards (7,690) than any of them. Torretta was the least physically gifted of the bunch, slow of foot with suspect arm strength. Nevertheless, as a high school junior he promised his mother that he would someday win the Heisman Trophy.

A native of tiny Pinole, California, where his father, Al, ran a tavern, Torretta defied the critics at every turn. Al Torretta had taught his son that he could do anything he put his mind to. While Torretta's statistics were not always impressive, he invariably found a way to help his team win whenever the game was on the line.

Gino Torretta, Heisman winner (photo courtesy of Miami SID).

In 1991, although he led the Hurricanes to a national championship, he barely had a presence in the Heisman Trophy voting. But in 1992 Torretta played brilliantly, particularly in the big games. In a 19–16 win over Florida State, in what was billed "The Game of the Century," Torretta made every big completion down the stretch to allow the Hurricanes to hold on to a victory. When asked what made the difference in the tightly fought game, Florida State's Bobby Bowden gave a one-word answer: "Torretta."

That year Torretta beat out San Diego State's Marshall Faulk for the Heisman Trophy, and the people at Al Torretta's packed Antler's Tavern in Pinole were in a jovial mood. The only person missing was Al Torretta, who had died in 1988.

Charlie Ward, Florida State, 1993

Even though the rest of the Florida State staff, including head coach Bobby Bowden, disagreed with him, Wayne McDuffie was adamant. He was convinced that Ward, a skinny kid from Thomasville, Georgia, could play quarterback in Division I. McDuffie jumped on his chair and said that the meeting would not end until they all agreed to sign Ward. The coaches finally relented, perhaps for no other reason than to calm McDuffie down.

McDuffie, who later joined the coaching staff at Georgia and died in 1995, will always be remembered as the coach who insisted that Florida State sign Charlie Ward, who went on to win the 1993 Heisman Trophy and lead the Seminoles to their first national championship.

Ward's journey to greatness, however, was not an easy one. He sat out a year to work on his grades, and when he arrived at Florida State so many good quarterbacks were on the team already that he had to redshirt. He got on the field, but only as a punter, and the following year he was a little-used backup

As a junior in 1992, Ward finally earned the starting quarterback position but struggled early, throwing eight interceptions in his first 2 games. Against Clemson, Ward's four interceptions were a major reason why the Seminoles were trailing 24–20 with only a few minutes left in the game. Then, in an outstanding turnaround, Ward led FSU on a seventy-seven-yard drive and won the game with a nine-yard touchdown pass.

"After that I knew that there was no way to rattle this guy," says Bowden. "It never occurred to Charlie to quit. All he cared about was winning."

But it was during the next week's game against Georgia Tech that the legend of Charlie Ward was born. Florida State was trailing 21–7 in the second half when assistant coach Brad Scott convinced Bowden to put Ward into a no-huddle, fast break offense that they had worked on during the week. It turned out to be the perfect outlet for Ward's skills. Florida State came back to win 29–24 and continued to use that offense for the rest of the season.

Quarterback Charlie Ward led Florida State to the 1993 National Championship (photo courtesy of the *Atlanta Journal-Constitution*/Jonathan Newton).

As a senior, Ward completed almost 70 percent of his passes and threw only four interceptions. Florida State went 10–1 that season and earned a berth against Nebraska in the Orange Bowl to win the national championship. Ward capped off a tremendous college career with his performance in the Orange Bowl. With his team trailing 16–15, Ward led the Seminoles down the field in the closing seconds of the game and set up a field goal that earned Florida an 18–16 victory and the national championship.

Before that game Ward picked up the Heisman Trophy, having beaten Tennessee's Heath Shuler by the second-largest margin in the history of the award. Only O. J. Simpson in 1968 was a more overwhelming choice.

Ward ended his football career with a 23–2 record, 2,647 yards passing, and twenty-two touchdowns. "It was a great ride for all of us," says Bowden. "We just appreciated the fact that Charlie let us go along."

Ward, who was also a starter on the Florida State basketball team, was a first-round pick of the New York Knicks and played in the 1999 NBA finals.

Danny Wuerffel, Florida, 1996

The most praiseworthy statement ever said about Danny Wuerffel came from his coach, Steve Spurrier. "Danny is a better person than he is a quarterback," Spurrier said. "And Danny is a great, great quarterback."

Danny Wuerffel won the Heisman Trophy and led Florida to a national title in 1996 (photo courtesy of the *Atlanta Journal-Constitution*).

Spurrier often argued that despite Wuerffel's unconventional throwing style, which made him look more like a man tossing a shot put than one passing a football, Wuerffel should be considered the greatest quarterback in the history of college football.

Wuerffel's numbers certainly back up that claim. When he left Florida after the 1996 season, he was the most efficient quarterback in NCAA history with a career rating of 163.6. He led the Gators to four straight SEC championships (1993–96) and a national championship in 1996, when he was a senior. He was 32–3–1 as a starting quarterback with a record of 27-1 in the rugged Southeastern Conference. But invariably, the discussion of Danny Wuerffel always turned away from his numbers and to his character, which was outstanding.

The son of a Presbyterian minister (like Spurrier), Wuerffel played four years of college football at the highest level and was never affected by the hype or the glamour. During his college career he held Bible study classes on Tuesdays and hosted the Fellowship of Christian Athletes meetings on Wednesdays. He graduated with a 3.75 grade point average and is the only Heisman Trophy winner in history to also win the Draddy Award, which is awarded each year to college football's top scholar-athlete.

"I enjoy football, but it has never been the most important thing in my life," Wuerffel said in a 1996 interview.

Running Spurrier's sophisticated passing system to near perfection, Wuerffel became only the second quarterback in NCAA history (BYU's Ty Detmer was the first) to throw more than one hundred touchdown passes. In the big games, Wuerffel was at his best. In 19 games against Top 25 teams, he threw for 5,683 yards and fifty-six touchdowns. In 1996, Wuerffel won the Heisman Trophy over Iowa State running back Troy Davis. After college, Wuerffel was drafted by the NFL's New Orleans Saints.

Close but No Trophy: The South's Heisman Runnersup

Tennessee's Fabulous Four

Tennessee has made a lot of college football history over the past one hundred years, but here's a distinction the Volunteers do not necessarily enjoy: Tennessee is the only school to have had four players finish second for the Heisman Trophy while never having had a winner. Only one other school, Southern California, has had four Heisman runnersup, but it has also had several winners. Following is a look at the four men who came so close to college football's biggest award.

In 1951 tailback HANK LAURICELLA led Tennessee to a 10–0 regular season, an SEC championship, and the school's first consensus national championship. Despite an impressive season, Lauricella could not overcome Princeton's Dick Kazmaier, who led the Tigers to a 22-game winning streak and won the Heisman in a lopsided vote, 1,777 points to Lauricella's 424.

In 1956 tailback JOHNNY MAJORS led the Volunteers to a 10–0 regular season and an SEC championship. No player in the country could match Majors's versatility on the football field, but his talent was no match for the good looks and star power of Notre Dame's Paul Hornung, who won the Heisman despite having played on a 2–8 team.

In 1993 quarterback HEATH SHULER led Tennessee to a 10–1 regular season while throwing for twenty-five touchdowns. Shuler was a big, powerful man from the hills of North Carolina who could beat teams with his arm as well as with his feet. But nobody was going to beat out Florida State quarterback Charlie Ward, who won the Heisman and led the Seminoles to the national championship.

Tennessee's first three Heisman second-place finishes may have been disappointing to fans, but when PEYTON MANNING finished behind Michigan defense back Charles Woodson in 1997, it was a bitter pill to swallow for everyone in Big Orange Country.

No player in school history was more revered than Manning, the son of former Ole Miss quarterback Archie Manning. When he passed up million-dollar offers from the NFL so that he could return for his senior season, Tennessee fans were convinced that the Heisman would be his. But despite having led Tennessee to an 11–1 regular season record and the SEC championship, Manning finished second to Woodson, who had had several big performances in key nationally televised games.

Tennessee fans angrily accused the news media, particularly the television networks, of showing bias toward Woodson. To this day, many Volunteer fans are still angry that the team does not yet have a Heisman Trophy winner.

You Call This Justice?

While Tennessee holds the distinction of four Heisman runnersup, North Carolina's Charlie Justice is the only player in college football history to have finished second in the Heisman Trophy race twice. In 1948 Justice, North Carolina's all-purpose halfback, finished second to SMU's Doak Walker. In 1949 he came in second to Notre Dame's Hall of Fame end, Leon Hart. Justice finished his career with 4,883 yards of total offense. As a punter, he had a 42.6-yard career average.

Charlie Justice (photo courtesy of the *Atlanta Journal-Constitution*).

Another Charley Comes Close

Georgia has had two Heisman Trophy winners (Frank Sinkwich, 1942; Herschel Walker, 1982), but Charley Trippi is still considered to be the best all-around athlete to have played football for the Bulldogs. An all-purpose halfback like North Carolina's Justice, Trippi played in the same backfield with Sinkwich on Georgia's 1942 Rose Bowl team. He spent the 1943 and 1944 seasons in the Air Force and then returned to play the last 5 games of the 1945 season and lead Georgia to an SEC championship in 1946. That year Trippi finished second in the Heisman race to Army Hall of Famer Glenn Davis.

Charley Trippi, All-American (photo courtesy of the *Atlanta Journal-Constitution*).

Still No Heisman at Georgia Tech

John Heisman enjoyed his greatest success as a coach during his sixteen years (1904–19) at Georgia Tech. It is one of college football's greatest ironies that the school so associated with the famous coach has never won a Heisman Trophy. The closest Georgia Tech has come to the prize was in 1963 when Billy Lothridge finished second to Navy's Roger Staubach, and in 1999 when Joe Hamilton finished second to Wisconsin running back Ron Dayne.

Lothridge did it all for Georgia Tech. Not only was he a great quarterback who could run and throw, he was also the team's punter, placekicker, and kickoff man. In 1963 Lothridge threw for 1,017 yards and ran for 1,240 more. He averaged forty-one yards punting, made twelve of seventeen field goals, and was responsible for twenty-three touchdowns. He finished ninth in the Heisman voting in 1962. Florida coach Ray Graves called him "the greatest quarterback we've ever faced."

Georgia Tech All-American quarterback Billy Lothridge with Center Bill Curry, 1963 (photo courtesy of the *Atlanta Journal-Constitution*).

In 1999 Hamilton became the ACC's all-time total offense leader. But it wasn't quite enough to catch Dayne, who won the Heisman Trophy and gave the Yellow Jackets their second runnerup.

A Tough Break for a Terp

Maryland was one of the dominant teams in all of college football in the early 1950s because coach Jim Tatum had found the perfect quarterback for his Split-T offense: Jack Scarbath. In three years as the Terps' starter, Scarbath posted a record of 24–4–1, which included a 22-game winning streak. Scarbath's biggest victory came after the 1951 season when Maryland upset undefeated and No. 1–ranked Tennessee, which had already been declared the national champion, 28–13 in the Sugar Bowl.

After that 10–0 season, Scarbath was a strong favorite for the Heisman going into the 1952 season. But in their eighth game Maryland's winning streak ended with a 21–14 loss at Mississippi. Maryland didn't go to a bowl that year and the Heisman went to Billy Vessels of Oklahoma.

A Close Call for Stovall

When Jerry Stovall arrived at LSU in 1960, he had some big shoes to fill—those belonging to halfback Billy Cannon, the 1959 Heisman Trophy winner—and he came close to matching most of Cannon's achievements. A rugged, two-way player, Stovall was a two-time All-American on offense, but among coaches he was considered one of the best defensive backs in the country, which he would prove later as an All-Pro with the St. Louis Cardinals. In 1961 he led the Tigers to a 10–1 record and an SEC championship. The next year he finished second in the Heisman race to Terry Baker of Oregon State in what was at that time the closest voting ever: 707 points to 618.

LSU quarterback Jerry Stovall finished second in competition for the Heisman Trophy in 1962 (photo courtesy of the *Atlanta Journal-Constitution*).

Casey Weldon (photo courtesy of the *Atlanta Journal-Constitution*).

Mighty Casey Finishes Second to Howard

Casey Weldon grew up in Tallahassee, Florida, wanting nothing more than to play quarterback for the hometown Florida State Seminoles. In 1989 Weldon finally got his wish, and in 1991 he threw for 2,527 yards and twenty-two touchdowns, leading Florida State to a 10–2 finish and a No. 4 ranking in the final Associated Press poll. He won the Johnny Unitas Golden Arm Award, which goes to the nation's best quarterback, but in the Heisman voting he finished second to Michigan wide receiver Desmond Howard.

Heisman Runnersup

While eleven Southern players have won the Heisman Trophy, thirteen others have finished second and ten have finished third. But for fate or timing any of these men could have won college football's highest honor.

Second in Line for the Heisman

Name	Position	School	Year	Winner
Charley Trippi	HB	Georgia	1946	Glenn Davis, Army
Charlie Justice	HB	North Carolina	1948	Doak Walker, SMU
Charlie Justice	HB	North Carolina	1949	Leon Hart, Notre Dame
Hank Lauricella	RB	Tennessee	1951	Dick Kazmaier, Princeton
Jack Scarbath	QB	Maryland	1952	Billy Vessels, Oklahoma
Johnny Majors	RB	Tennessee	1956	Paul Hornung, Notre Dame
Jerry Stovall	HB	LSU	1962	Terry Baker, Oregon State
Billy Lothridge	QB	Georgia Tech	1963	Roger Staubach, Navy
Herschel Walker	RB	Georgia	1981	Marcus Allen, USC
Casey Weldon	QB	Florida State	1991	Desmond Howard, Michigan
Heath Shuler	QB	Tennessee	1993	Charlie Ward, Florida State
Peyton Manning	QB	Tennessee	1997	Charles Woodson, Michigan
Joe Hamilton	QB	Georgia Tech	1999	Ron Dayne, Wisconsin

Third in Line for the Heisman

Clint Castleberry	RB	Georgia Tech	1942	Frank Sinkwich, Georgia
Babe Parilli	QB	Kentucky	1951	Dick Kazmaier, Princeton
Billy Cannon	HB	LSU	1958	Pete Dawkins, Army
Jake Gibbs	QB	Mississippi	1960	Joe Bellino, Navy
Archie Manning	QB	Mississippi	1970	Jim Plunkett, Stanford
Herschel Walker	RB	Georgia	1980	George Rogers, South Carolina
Garrison Hearst	RB	Georgia	1992	Gino Torretta, Miami
David Palmer	WR	Alabama	1993	Charlie Ward, Florida State
Steve McNair	QB	Alcorn State	1994	Rashaan Salaam, Colorado
Danny Wuerffel	QB	Florida	1995	Eddie George, Ohio State

The Southern Fried Football Hall of Fame: One Hundred More Players Who Made a Difference

1. Don Hutson, WR, Alabama: The first Heisman Trophy was awarded in 1935. But if it had been given in 1934, it surely would have gone to Alabama's Hutson. In the 1935 Rose Bowl, Hutson caught six passes for 165 yards and touchdowns of 59 and 54 yards. Hutson went on to NFL glory with the Green Bay Packers and is a member of both the college and pro football halls of fame. Frank Thomas, his coach at Alabama, called Hutson "the best player I ever coached."

Ole Miss coach John Vaught with Archie Manning prior to 1968 Liberty Bowl (photo courtesy of the *Atlanta Journal-Constitution*).

2. Archie Manning, QB, Mississippi: Manning finished fourth in the Heisman voting as a junior in 1969 and third behind Stanford's Jim Plunkett and Notre Dame's Joe Theismann in 1970. He still holds the SEC record for total offense in a single game with 540 yards against Alabama in 1969. Manning went on to a long NFL career with the New Orleans Saints and the Minnesota Vikings. Two of his sons, Cooper and Eli, played football at Ole Miss, and his son

Peyton was an All-American quarterback at Tennessee, the runnerup for the Heisman Trophy in 1997, and the No. 1 pick in the 1998 NFL draft.

3. Doug Atkins, E, Tennessee: A big, rugged defensive end, Atkins was an All-American in 1952 and a key player on Tennessee's 1951 national championship team. The Football Writers Association of America selected Atkins as the SEC Player of the Quarter Century. He went on to have a successful pro career with the Chicago Bears, who took him in the first round of the 1953 draft. Atkins is in both the college and pro football halls of fame.

4. "Bullet" Bill Dudley, HB, Virginia: Dudley was one of the most versatile players in college football. As a nineteen-year-old senior in 1941, he was responsible for 206 of the 279 points scored by the Cavaliers and finished fifth in the Heisman race.

5. Babe Parilli, QB, Kentucky: Parilli finished fourth in the Heisman race in 1950 and third in 1951. In three seasons, Parilli threw for fifty touchdowns and led the Wildcats to the Orange, Sugar, and Cotton bowls.

Charlie Conerly led Ole Miss to an SEC championship in 1947 and went on to star with the New York Giants (photo courtesy of the *Atlanta Journal-Constitution*).

6. Charlie Conerly, QB, Mississippi: Charlie Conerly finished fourth in the Heisman race in 1947, just ahead of Alabama's Harry Gilmer (see number 9). Conerly led the Rebels to their first SEC championship in 1947 and went on to enjoy NFL fame with the New York Giants.

As a pro, Conerly led the Giants to four NFL championship games, winning the title in 1956.

7. Lee Roy Jordan, LB, Alabama: Jordan may be the best inside linebacker in the history of college football. A two-time All-American, Jordan recorded an unheard-of thirty-one tackles in Alabama's 17–0 win over Oklahoma in the 1963 Orange Bowl. He was Alabama's Player of the Decade in the 1960s and went on to an All-Pro career with the Dallas Cowboys.

8. Jake Gibbs, QB, Mississippi: Gibbs finished third in the Heisman voting in 1960 having led Ole Miss to a 10–0–1 season and a national championship. After a distinguished college football career, Gibbs signed with the New York Yankees, with whom he would play for seven seasons.

9. Harry Gilmer, QB, Alabama: Gilmer was one of the most versatile players the South has ever produced. As a sophomore in 1945, Gilmer was an All-American and the SEC Player of the Year. He was voted MVP after leading the Crimson Tide to a 34–14 win over Southern California in the Rose Bowl. In 1946 he led the Crimson Tide in passing, rushing, interceptions, punt returns, and kickoff returns. His total of fifty-two career touchdowns is still an Alabama record.

Clint Castleberry (photo courtesy of the *Atlanta Journal-Constitution*).

10. Clint Castleberry, RB, Georgia Tech: When Castleberry finished third in the Heisman voting as a freshman in 1942, fans expected him to enjoy a great career in college football. But six weeks after he played in the 1943 Cotton Bowl, Castleberry enlisted in the service as a member of the Army Air Corps. On November 7, 1944, his plane disappeared off the West African coast, and he was never found.

11. Tucker Fredrickson, HB/DB, Auburn: Fredrickson finished sixth in the Heisman voting in 1964 but was the first player picked in the NFL draft. Auburn coach Shug Jordan called Frederickson, who was both a great runner and a great defensive back, the most complete player he had ever seen.

12. Tommy Casanova, WR/DB, LSU: In 1970 Casanova returned two punts for touchdowns in a win over Ole Miss that earned LSU the SEC championship. Casanova did not fare well in the 1971 Heisman voting, but he should have. In an era of two-platoon football, Casanova played offense and defense and returned punts.

13. Bob Gain, T, Kentucky: Gain was a two-time All-American and a three-time All-SEC pick. In his four years as a tackle under coach Paul "Bear" Bryant, from 1947 to 1950, Kentucky went 33–10–2 and won an SEC title.

14. Dick Modzelewski, DL, Maryland: When Modzelewski claimed the Outland Trophy in 1952, he became Maryland's first winner of a major award. A three-time All-American, he led a Maryland defense that gave up a touchdown only four times in 29 games.

15. Gene McEver, RB, Tennessee: McEver led the nation in scoring in 1929, and Tennessee coach Robert Neyland, who was not known for idle praise, called McEver the best player he had ever coached. McEver was elected to the College Football Hall of Fame in 1954.

16. Zeke Smith, OG/LB, Auburn: Smith, who played both offensive guard and linebacker, won the Outland Trophy as a junior in 1958 and was an All-American in 1959. He was so good that the Baltimore Colts drafted him after his junior season. A Canadian Football League team also offered him a $15,000 signing bonus, but he turned down both offers so that he could return to Auburn in 1959.

17. Vaughn Mancha, C, Alabama: Mancha started his first game as a freshman in 1944 and never gave up the spot over the course of a brilliant four-year career. He played in one Rose Bowl and two Sugar Bowls and was a consensus pick for All-America in 1945. He was elected to the College Football Hall of Fame in 1990.

18. Walter Payton, RB, Jackson State: After he finished an outstanding career on the small-college level, this native of Columbia, Mississippi, was picked fourth overall in the 1975 NFL draft by the Chicago Bears. Payton went on to become the NFL's all-time leading rusher with 16,726 yards in thirteen seasons. In 1999 Payton died of a rare liver disease. He is in both the college and pro football halls of fame.

North Carolina Hall of Famers Charlie Justice (22) and Art Weiner (50) in 1949 (photo courtesy of the *Atlanta Journal-Constitution*).

19. Steve DeLong, MG, Tennessee: Tennessee's team struggled in 1964, but that didn't keep DeLong from becoming one of the nation's most dominant defensive players. He was a two-time All-American and the No. 6 pick in the first round of the 1965 NFL draft. In 1993 DeLong was inducted into the College Football Hall of Fame.

20. Art Weiner, E, North Carolina: A two-time All-American, Weiner was one of the greatest two-way ends in the history of college football. He led the nation in receiving with fifty-two catches in 1949 after having been ranked seventh in the nation the year before with thirty-one catches. Weiner, a three-time

All-Southern-Conference player, was picked by the New York Bulldogs in the second round of the 1950 NFL draft.

21. Bill Stanfill, DE, Georgia: Stanfill was a quick and rangy defensive end whom other teams simply could not block. He led the Bulldogs to an SEC championship in 1968 and later starred in the Super Bowl with the Miami Dolphins. Stanfill was inducted into the College Football Hall of Fame in 1998.

22. Frank "Bruiser" Kinard, T, Mississippi: Kinard was a two-time All-American in 1936–37. His name should have been "Iron Man," for during the 1935 season he was on the field for 708 of the 720 minutes his team played.

Frank "Bruiser" Kinard of Ole Miss was an All-American in 1936 and 1937 (photo courtesy of the *Atlanta Journal-Constitution*).

23. Jack Youngblood, DE, Florida: The definitive defensive end and an All-American in 1970, Youngblood was named to the All-SEC quarter century team for 1950–74. Youngblood, a first-round pick of the Los Angeles Rams in 1971, was twice named the NFL's Defensive Player of the Year. He was inducted into the College Football Hall of Fame in 1992.

24. Bob Suffridge, G, Tennessee: Suffridge was Tennessee's first three-time All-American, having played on the great 1938, 1939, and 1940 Volunteers teams. The hometown boy from Knoxville, Tennessee, was elected to the College Football Hall of Fame in 1961.

25. Randy White, DT, Maryland: White forever changed the position of defensive lineman. Although he was big, he was considered one of the quickest linemen ever to play the game. In 1974 he won every major award for linemen, including the Outland Trophy and the Lombardi Award, and was a first-round pick of the Dallas Cowboys in the NFL draft. He is in both the college and pro football halls of fame.

26. Terry Bradshaw, QB, Louisiana Tech: Bradshaw played far from the bright lights of national publicity but put up some impressive numbers during his four years at Louisiana Tech (1966–69). Over the course of his college career, Bradshaw completed 52.5 percent of his passes for 7,149 yards and forty-two touchdowns. He was the first player taken in the 1970 NFL draft when he was picked by the Pittsburgh

Steelers. He led the Steelers to four Super Bowl titles and was voted MVP in Super Bowls XIII and XIV. When he retired after the 1983 season, he had a career 27,989 yards passing. Bradshaw was inducted into the Pro Football Hall of Fame in 1989 and the College Football Hall of Fame in 1996.

27. Bruce Smith, DT, Virginia Tech: Smith was the first player from the state of Virginia to win the Outland Trophy (Corey Moore of Virginia Tech became the second in 1999). He was the most dominant lineman in college football for four seasons, accounting for 504 yards in losses, more than five times the length of a football field. He was the first player taken in the 1985 NFL draft.

28. Mike McGee, G, Duke: McGee won the Outland Trophy in 1959 despite having played on a 4–6 team. He was a second-round draft pick by the St. Louis Cardinals and finished third in the NFL Rookie of the Year balloting. After his playing career was cut short by an injury, McGee started coaching and eventually became involved in athletics administration. As of the 2000 season, McGee is the athletic director at South Carolina.

Georgia coach Wally Butts with quarterback Fran Tarkenton in 1959 (photo courtesy of the *Atlanta Journal-Constitution*).

29. Fran Tarkenton, QB, Georgia: Possessing a unique ability to scramble, Tarkenton led the Bulldogs to an SEC championship in 1959 and went on to become a record-setting quarterback in the NFL. He played in three Super Bowls over the course of a seventeen-year pro career. He is a member of the College Football Hall of Fame.

30. Jim Ritcher, C, N.C. State: Ritcher, one of only three players in ACC history to win the Outland Trophy, is considered one of the best centers to have ever played college football. A two-time All-American, Ritcher won the Outland Trophy in 1979 and spent his thirteen-year professional career with the Buffalo Bills.

31. Tracy Rocker, DT, Auburn: As a freshman, Rocker led the SEC in tackles for a down lineman. A three-time All-

Tracy Rocker of Auburn (photo courtesy of the *Atlanta Journal-Constitution*).

SEC player and a two-time All-American, in 1988 he became the first player in SEC history to win both the Outland Trophy and the Lombardi Award.

32. Johnny Mack Brown, HB, Alabama: Brown was All-Southern Conference in 1924 and 1925 but is best remembered for his performance in the 1926 Rose Bowl. He caught passes for fifty-eight and sixty-two yards, setting up Alabama touchdowns in the historic 20–19 win that gave the Crimson Tide a national championship. After playing in the Rose Bowl, Brown remained in California and eventually became a cowboy movie star.

33. Buck Buchanan, DT, Grambling: Buchanan played for Eddie Robinson's Grambling Tigers from 1959 to 1962. A member of both the pro and college football halls of fame, Buchanan was the first player chosen by the Dallas Texans, who later became the Kansas City Chiefs, in the 1963 American Football League draft. He played his entire fifteen-year pro career with the Chiefs and appeared in two Super Bowls. He was inducted into the NFL Hall of Fame in 1990 and the College Football Hall of Fame in 1996.

34. George Cafego, RB, Tennessee: Nicknamed "Bad News," Cafego was an All-American tailback for the Volunteers in 1938 and 1939. Tennessee coach Robert Neyland discovered Cafego playing sandlot baseball in Cafego's native West Virginia. He had not planned to go to college but Neyland talked him into coming to Tennessee. The No. 1 pick in the 1940 NFL draft, Cafego was named to the College Football Hall of Fame in 1969.

35. Johnny Cain, FB, Alabama: Cain, the only sophomore starter on Alabama's 1930 national championship team, was a two-time All-America pick. Nicknamed "Hurry," Cain earned fame as a powerful left-footed punter. In a 1932 game against Tennessee, he averaged forty-eight yards on nineteen kicks in the driving rain. The native of Montgomery, Alabama, was named to the College Football Hall of Fame in 1973.

36. Ted Hendricks, DE, Miami: A three-time All-American (1966, 1967, 1968), Hendricks defined the position of defensive end as a collegian and then perfected it in a brilliant NFL career. The second Miami player named to the College Football Hall of Fame (Jim Otto was the first), Hendricks, the only player in Miami history to be named to three All-America teams, finished fifth in the Heisman Trophy voting in 1968.

37. Jimmy Hitchcock, HB, Auburn: Known as the "Phantom from Union Springs," Hitchcock became Auburn's first All-America player in 1932 when he led the Tigers to a 9–0–1 record and the Southern Conference championship. He was a triple threat as a runner, passer, and punter. In a 1932 game against Tulane, Hitchcock returned an intercepted pass sixty yards for a touchdown. Later in the game, he picked up an errant snap on a punt attempt and ran sixty-three yards for another score in a 19–7 win. Hitchcock was also an All-American in baseball and later played in the Major Leagues.

38. Beattie Feathers, HB, Tennessee: Feathers was a three-year starter (1931–33) at tailback for the Volunteers and was voted the Most Valuable Player in the SEC in 1933. The native of Bristol, Virginia, was the second Tennessee player to be elected to the Hall of Fame when he was inducted in 1954. He later went on to have a career in coaching.

Miami defensive tackle Russell Maryland (photo courtesy of the *Atlanta Journal-Constitution*).

39. Russell Maryland, DT, Miami: In 1990 Maryland became the first player in Miami history to win the Outland Trophy, which goes to the nation's best interior lineman. He was the first player chosen in the 1991 NFL draft, by the Dallas Cowboys.

40. Bobby Dodd, QB, Tennessee: Dodd is one of only three men in the College Football Hall of Fame as both a player and a coach. Tennessee was 27–1–1 in Dodd's three years at quarterback (1928–30) and the native of Kingsport, Tennessee, was named an All-American in 1930. He left Tennessee to become an assistant coach at Georgia Tech in 1931 and later served as head coach at Tech from 1945 to 1966.

41. Charlie Flowers, FB, Mississippi: Flowers was an All-American and the captain of the Ole Miss team in 1959, which the SEC named its Team of the Decade. Flowers led the SEC in rushing in 1957 and in rushing and scoring in 1959. That year he also finished fifth in the Heisman Trophy voting. The native of Marianna, Arkansas, was elected to the College Football Hall of Fame in 1997.

42. Reggie White, DT, Tennessee: White, a big but fast tackle who could run around blockers or through them, was an All-American in 1983 when he led the Vols to a 9–3 season. He went on to have an All-Pro career with the Green Bay Packers.

43. Jackie Parker, QB, Mississippi State: In 1952 Parker led the nation in scoring and set an SEC record for points in a season with 120, which was an even greater accomplishment because Parker played on a 5–4 team. Parker, a junior college transfer, played only two seasons at Mississippi State but is still considered the best quarterback in Mississippi State history. He was inducted into the College Football Hall of Fame in 1976.

44. John Hannah, OG, Alabama: Hannah is considered by many to be the finest offensive lineman in the history of football, pro or college. A two-time All-America pick (1971, 1972), Hannah was named to Alabama's Team of the Century and ESPN's all-time college football team. He went on to enjoy an All-Pro career with the New England Patriots and was elected to the NFL Hall of Fame. In 1999 he was inducted into the College Football Hall of Fame.

45. Walter Gilbert, C/LB, Auburn: After 108 years of football Gilbert remains Auburn's only three-time All-American (1934, 1935, 1936). In an era of one-platoon football, Gilbert was considered by many to be the best at both center and linebacker. His 1936 team went 7–2–1 and played in the school's first bowl game, the Bacardi Bowl in Havana, Cuba. He was elected to the College Football Hall of Fame in 1956.

46. Herman Hickman, G, Tennessee: In Hickman's three years at guard (1929–31), the Volunteers won 27 games and lost only 1. He was an All-American in 1931 and was named by the Football Writers Association of America to the all-time SEC team. In 1959 he was inducted into the College Football Hall of Fame.

47. Bob McWhorter, HB, Georgia: McWhorter was an All-Southern-Conference performer for four consecutive years (1910–13) and was the Bulldogs' first-ever All-American player. With McWhorter in the backfield, Georgia won 25 out of 34 games in four years, the first real sustained success in the team's history. One of seven members of the McWhorter family to play at Georgia, he was inducted into the College Football Hall of Fame in 1954.

48. Doug Williams, QB, Grambling: Williams threw for 8,411 yards and ninety-three touchdowns in his brilliant career (1974–77) with Eddie Robinson's Tigers. He led Grambling to a 35–5 record in four seasons and finished fourth in the Heisman race in 1977. He was picked in the first round of the 1978 NFL draft by Tampa Bay and was later traded to the Washington Redskins, where he enjoyed the pinnacle of his football career, leading his team to a 42–10 victory over Denver in Super Bowl XXII. Williams was named the Most Valuable Player in that game. In 1998 Williams replaced Robinson as the head coach at Grambling.

49. Barney Poole, E, Ole Miss: Poole, recognized today as one of the greatest ends in SEC history, played for Ole Miss in 1942 and was then called away to serve in World War II. While in the service Poole played for West Point, but after the war he wanted to return to Ole Miss to finish out his college career. Army coach Earl Blaik, however, would not release him. So Poole purposely flunked out of the academy and returned to Ole Miss for the 1947 and 1948 seasons. He teamed up with another Hall of Famer, quarterback Charlie Conerly, to lead the Rebels to an SEC championship in 1947.

50. Fred Sington, T, Alabama: Sington was such a dominating lineman that no less an expert than Notre Dame's Knute Rockne called him "the greatest lineman in the county." A member of Phi Beta Kappa as well as an All-American, Sington played from 1928 to 1930 and was a leader on the 1930 Alabama team that went undefeated and beat Washington State in the Rose Bowl. A native of Birmingham, Alabama, Sington was named to the College Football Hall of Fame in 1955.

Georgia Tech All-American George Morris, 1952 (photo courtesy of the *Atlanta Journal-Constitution*).

51. George Morris, C/LB, Georgia Tech: Morris was one of the cornerstones of Georgia Tech's 1951 SEC championship team and its undefeated 1952 national championship team. The native of Vicksburg, Mississippi, was an All-America selection in 1952, the same year he was named the SEC's Most Valuable Player. Morris was a second-round draft choice of the San Francisco 49ers. He was inducted into the College Football Hall of Fame in 1981.

52. Bill Hartman, FB, Georgia: Hartman capped off a dynamic college career (1934–37) by being named captain of Georgia's 1937 team. In that same year he was named All-SEC and All-America. Hartman went on to a pro career with the Washington Redskins, and after his retirement from pro football he returned to Georgia as an assistant coach. When he left full-time coaching to enjoy a successful career in the insurance business, he remained at Georgia as a part-time coach of the Bulldogs' kickers. He was inducted into the College Football Hall of Fame in 1984.

53. Bert Jones, QB, LSU: An All-American in 1972, Jones was a strong-armed leader who had a knack for winning. He led the Tigers to an SEC championship as a sophomore and ended his career with a 26–6 record and three bowl appearances. He is best remembered for throwing a touchdown pass to Brad Davis as time expired in a 17–16 win over Ole Miss in 1972. Jones finished fourth in the Heisman race in 1972 and was later the No. 1 pick in the NFL draft, by the Baltimore Colts.

54. Bob Johnson, C, Tennessee: Johnson was a two-time All-American in 1966–67, a member of Tennessee's SEC championship team in 1967, and a member of the all-time All-SEC football team. He was also an academic All-American in 1967.

55. Ron Simmons, NG, Florida State: Still considered the greatest defensive player in Florida State history, Simmons was the Seminoles' first two-time consensus All-American (1979–80), leading Florida State to a pair of Orange Bowl appearances. He posted twenty-five quarterback sacks in his career, which still stands as a school record going into the 2000 season. He was the first Florida State player in the school's history to have his jersey (No. 50) retired.

56. Condredge Holloway, QB, Tennessee: Holloway didn't break the color barrier at Tennessee; that honor went to wide receiver Lester McClain. But Holloway was the first black man to play quarterback in the SEC. As a sophomore in 1972 Holloway led the Vols to a 10–2 record. After he left Tennessee in 1974, Holloway played professional football in Canada.

Tennessee's Condredge Holloway, the first black man to play quarterback in the SEC (1972–74) (photo courtesy of the *Atlanta Journal-Constitution*).

57. Emmitt Smith, RB, Florida: From the first day he walked onto the Florida campus Smith was a star. He was the national freshman of the year in 1987 and the SEC Player of the Year in 1989, finishing ninth in the Heisman race as a freshman and seventh as a junior. After only three seasons he left Florida with fifty-eight school records, including a career rushing mark of 3,928 yards. He was a first-round pick of the Dallas Cowboys, where he has had a brilliant career, and became the first

Emmitt Smith, University of Florida (photo courtesy of the *Atlanta Journal-Constitution*).

back in NFL history to rush for more than 1,400 yards in five consecutive seasons (1991–95). He was the NFL's MVP in 1993 and the MVP of Super Bowl XXVIII.

58. Gaynell "Gus" Tinsley, E, LSU: When Tinsley was named All-American in 1935 and 1936, he became the first player in LSU history to earn the honor. Playing both offense and defense, Tinsley led the Tigers to two SEC championships and berths in three Sugar Bowls. After he ended his pro career with the Chicago Cardinals, Tinsley returned to LSU to serve as head coach from 1948 to 1954.

59. Ed Molinski, G, Tennessee: Another standout on the great Neyland teams of 1938–40, Molinski was an All-American in 1939 and 1940. The native of Massilon, Ohio, was named to the College Football Hall of Fame in 1990.

60. Ozzie Newsome, WR, Alabama: Next to Don Hutson, Newsome was the best receiver in Crimson Tide history. Beginning in 1974, he started 47 games for Alabama in a career that spanned four years. He averaged 20.3 yards per catch and helped the Crimson Tide win three SEC championships. After Newsome left Alabama he enjoyed a thirteen-year career with the NFL's Cleveland Browns. He was named to the College Football Hall of Fame in 1994.

61. Clyde Scott, HB/DB, Arkansas: Scott possessed tremendous speed for his era (1946–48); as a track star, he won a silver medal in the hurdles in the 1948 Olympics. After participating in the Olympics, he had an All-America season with the Razorbacks even though they went 5–5. Scott, who played both halfback and defensive back, made great plays on both sides of the ball. In the 1947 Cotton Bowl, he preserved a 0–0 tie with LSU by tackling Tiger wide receiver Jeff Odom at the Arkansas one-yard line. His 1,463 yards rushing was a record for Arkansas at the time. Nicknamed "Smackover," after his hometown in Arkansas, Scott was inducted into the College Football Hall of Fame in 1971.

62. Bowden Wyatt, E, Tennessee: Along with fellow Volunteer Bobby Dodd and Amos Alonzo Stagg, Wyatt is one of only three men in the Hall of Fame as both a player and a coach. He was an end on the undefeated Tennessee team of 1938 and later went on to become the head coach at Wyoming, Arkansas, and Tennessee.

63. Banks McFadden, HB, Clemson: McFadden was the most versatile athlete ever to perform at Clemson, or anywhere else for that matter. In 1938–39 McFadden was an All-American in both football and basketball. He led Clemson to its first basketball championship in 1939 and later that fall took the Tigers to their first bowl (the 1940 Cotton Bowl). The guy could kick too: in 1939 he had twenty-two punts of fifty yards or more. McFadden is the only Clemson player in the College Football Hall of Fame and the only Clemson athlete in the school's history to have had both his football and basketball jersey retired.

64. Pooley Hubert, QB, Alabama: Hubert was the second All-America player in Alabama's history and a four-year letterman (1922–25) on Alabama teams that had a combined record of 31–6–2. As quarterback, he led Alabama to its first-ever Rose Bowl, in which the Crimson Tide beat Washington 20–19. The native of Meridan, Mississippi, was elected to the College Football Hall of Fame in 1964.

65. Jimmy Taylor, FB, LSU: Taylor rushed for 1,314 yards in two seasons as a starter for LSU and was considered one of the most complete players of his day. He shared the backfield with sophomore Billy Cannon and was an All-American in 1957 despite having played on a team that finished 5–5. Taylor went on to have a brilliant pro career with the Green Bay Packers and was inducted into the Pro Football Hall of Fame in 1976.

66. Lance Alworth, WR, Arkansas: The enormity of Alworth's talent was not fully realized until he reached the NFL, but he is still considered the greatest athlete to have ever put on a Razorback uniform. He played wingback at Arkansas, which made him both a runner and a receiver, and as a senior was an All-American when he led his team in rushing (516 yards), caught eighteen passes for 320 yards, led the nation in punt returns (17.1 average), and handled kickoff returns. He also served as the team's punter. In the three years with Alworth in the lineup (1959–61), Arkansas either won or shared the Southwest Conference championship. As if that wasn't enough, Alworth was on the SWC all-academic team and lettered in baseball. He set school records in the 100-yard dash (9.6 seconds) and the 220-yard dash (21.4 seconds). After college he had an outstanding pro career with the San Diego Chargers. He was inducted into the College Football Hall of Fame in 1984.

67. Dale Van Sickel, E, Florida: Van Sickel was Florida's first All-American and was considered one of the nation's best pass receivers in 1928, when he played on college football's highest scoring team (336 points in 9 games). After college, he worked as a successful stunt man in Hollywood for nearly five decades. He died as a result of injuries in the late 1960s.

68. Henry Goldthwaite "Diddy" Seibels, HB, Sewanee: Seibels was a four-year (1897–1900) star at Sewanee and the key player on the 1899 "Iron Man" team that went 12–0 and won 5 road games in six days, all by shutouts. A native of Montgomery, Alabama, Seibels came to Sewanee to play baseball but eventually became a three-sport star (baseball, football, and golf). During his last three seasons at Sewanee, the Tigers went 20–1–1. He died in 1967 at the age of ninety-one and was inducted into the College Football Hall of Fame in 1973.

69. Vernon "Catfish" Smith, E, Georgia: Smith had a solid college career (1929–31) but is best remembered for his incredible performance in Georgia's 1929 game against Yale, one of the college football powers of the era. It was at this game that Georgia dedicated Sanford Stadium. Few thought the Bulldogs had a chance, but Smith scored all of Georgia's points in a 15–0 win. As a senior, Smith was named an All-American. He was inducted into the College Football Hall of Fame in 1979.

70. Lou Michaels, T/K, Kentucky: A two-time All-America pick (1956–57), Michaels lettered for three years at Kentucky as a tackle, punter, and placekicker. He was voted Lineman of the Year in both 1956 (Birmingham TD Club) and 1957 (Atlanta TD Club). He had a successful post-college career as a kicker with the Baltimore Colts and was inducted into the College Football Hall of Fame in 1992.

71. Dixie Howell, QB, Alabama: Howell, who played from 1932 to 1934, is best remembered for his great performance in the 1935 Rose Bowl. A native of Hartford, Alabama, Howell rushed for 111 yards, passed for 160 more, and punted six times for a 43.8 average. Alabama, which went 10–0 and won the national championship that season, beat Stanford 29–13 in Pasadena. Howell was named to the College Football Hall of Fame in 1970 and to the Rose Bowl Hall of Fame in 1993.

72. E. G. "Doc" Fenton, RB/QB, LSU: Fenton led the Tigers to a 10–0 season in 1908 and is considered the first great football player in LSU history. The rangy Fenton, blessed with what was great speed for that day, scored 125 points in 10 games in an era in which a touchdown counted only five points. As of the 2000 season that record still stands at LSU. With Fenton, the 1908 team scored 442 points in 450 minutes of play and won the Southern Intercollegiate Association championship.

73. Steve Kiner, LB, Tennessee: Kiner burst onto the scene as a sophomore in 1967 and quickly gained a reputation as one of the toughest linebackers in the game. He was an All-American in 1968 and 1969 and went on to play professional football with four different NFL teams.

74. Ken Kavanaugh, E, LSU: An All-America pick in 1939, Kavanaugh, who also played baseball for LSU, was ahead of his time as a pass receiver. He led the nation in

Alabama coach Bear Bryant with quarterback Joe Namath in 1964 (photo courtesy of the *Atlanta Journal-Constitution*/Billy Downs).

receiving in 1939 with thirty catches for 467 yards and eight touchdowns and finished seventh in the Heisman race that season. After college he had an outstanding pro career with the New York Giants.

75. Parker Hall, HB, Mississippi: Hall was one of the better two-way players in Ole Miss history. In 1938 he led the nation in scoring (seventy-three points), yards per rush (6.46), touchdowns (twenty-two), and all-purpose yards per game (129.1). On defense Hall was second in the nation with seven interceptions and led the nation with the most yards in pass interception returns (128). He was named NFL Rookie of the Year in 1939 and was inducted into the College Football Hall of Fame in 1991.

76. Joe Namath, QB, Alabama: The legend from Beaver Falls, Pennsylvania, overcame discipline and knee problems to lead Alabama to a three-year (1962–64) record of 29–4, which included a national championship in 1964. As a sophomore, Namath led the Crimson Tide to a 10–1 record and a 17–0 victory over Oklahoma in the Orange Bowl. After missing several games at the end of the 1963 season due to disciplinary problems, Namath led Alabama to a 10–0 regular season and a spot in the Orange Bowl. Despite a knee injury, Namath threw for 255 yards in Alabama's 21–17 loss to Texas. He was named the game's Most Valuable Player.

77. Loyd Phillips, T, Arkansas: Phillips, who is still considered the best lineman in Arkansas history, was an All-American in 1965 and 1966, won the Outland Trophy in

1966, and was named to the All-Southwest-Conference team three times (1964–66). In Phillips's three years in the lineup, the Razorbacks were 11–0 in 1964 (and were named the national champions), 10–1 in 1965, and 8–2 in 1966. His total of 304 career tackles is ninth on the school's all-time list, and he still holds the Arkansas record for the most tackles by a lineman.

78. D. D. Lewis, LB, Mississippi State: Although he was a two-time (1966–67) All-SEC and All-America linebacker for the Bulldogs, Lewis did not get a lot of recognition as a collegian because Mississippi State never had a winning season while he played there. The Dallas Cowboys waited until the sixth round (the 159th pick overall) to take Lewis, who went on to become an All-Pro and play in five Super Bowls in a thirteen-year pro career.

79. Nate Dougherty, G, Tennessee: Dougherty was a standout in the early part of the century (1906–09) and played on the first two Tennessee teams (1907–08) to win 7 games in a season. The native of Scott County, Virginia, was named All-Southern Conference in 1907–08. Dougherty was elected to the College Football Hall of Fame in 1967.

80. Wilber Marshall, LB, Florida: Considered by many to be the best linebacker ever to play for the Gators, Marshall was an All-American in 1982 and 1983 and a finalist for the Lombardi Award both seasons. In 1983 he was named college football's national player of the year. The Chicago Bears took him in the first round of the 1984 NFL draft, and he was a starter on the Bears' 1985 Super Bowl championship team. Marshall was a three-time (1986, 1987, 1992) All-Pro selection.

81. John Michels, G, Tennessee: Michels helped anchor the Tennessee line in 1950, 1951, and 1952, a stretch during which the Volunteers won 29 games and lost only 4. The 1951 team was declared the national champion after an undefeated regular season. Michels, a native of Philadelphia, was named to the College Football Hall of Fame in 1956.

82. Jerry Rice, WR, Mississippi Valley: Rice is perhaps the best wide receiver to ever play the game, college or pro, though he didn't get the national recognition he deserved in college because he played at a Division II school. He played brilliantly as a senior, earning 1,845 receiving yards and twenty-eight touchdowns, and left Mississippi Valley after the 1984 season with 4,693 receiving yards and eighteen Division II records. Rice was the San Francisco 49ers sixteenth overall pick in the 1985 NFL draft. The 2000 season will be his sixteenth in the NFL, where he has totally rewritten the record books for receiving.

83. Abe Mickal, HB, LSU: Mickal, a native of Syria, came to the United States as a small boy after the outbreak of World War I. He considered going to Notre Dame but chose LSU after Notre Dame coach Knute Rockne was killed in a plane crash. Mickal led the Tigers to a 23–4–5 record from 1933 to 1935. The former president of the LSU student body, he went on after college to become a doctor. He was elected to the College Football Hall of Fame in 1967.

Florida State's incomparable Deion Sanders (photo courtesy of the *Atlanta Journal-Constitution*).

84. Bob Ward, G, Maryland: Ward was too small (165 pounds) to be a lineman, but he never got the message. He was an All-American middle guard in 1950 and an All-American offensive guard on Maryland's undefeated 1951 team. In Ward's four seasons at Maryland the Terps had a record of 32–7–1. He was named Southern Conference Player of the Year in 1951 and was inducted into the College Football Hall of Fame in 1980.

85. Deion Sanders, DB, Florida State: Sanders was the best defensive back to ever play at Florida State and one of only four Seminole players to have had his jersey (No. 2) retired. He won the Jim Thorpe Award, which goes to the nation's best defensive back, in 1988. Sanders, who also lettered in baseball and track for the Seminoles, left Florida State with fourteen career interceptions and the school's career record for punt return yardage (1,429 yards). He went to the NFL and played on Super Bowl championship teams in San Francisco and Dallas. He also played in the World Series for the Atlanta Braves.

86. Pat Trammell, QB, Alabama: Trammell, who played quarterback on Bear Bryant's first national championship team in 1961, is remembered both for the way he lived and the way he died. In 1961 Trammel led the Crimson Tide to a 10–0 regular season and then closed out his career by scoring the only touchdown in a 10–3 win over Arkansas in the Sugar Bowl. After college Trammell went to medical school and later began his practice in Birmingham. In 1968 he was diagnosed with a brain tumor, and the following year he died at the age of twenty-eight.

87. Jake Scott, DB, Georgia: Scott was one of the best defensive backs/punt returners to ever play in the South. In 1968 he intercepted ten passes, tying an SEC record that stood until 1982. That same season Scott was Georgia's primary return man, averaging 12.6 yards on thirty-five kick returns. His total of sixteen career interceptions in only two

Alabama's Cornelius Bennett was a three-time All-American (photo courtesy of the *Atlanta Journal-Constitution*).

seasons is seventh on the SEC's all-time list. When he left Georgia after the 1968 season, he went on to enjoy a successful pro career with the Washington Redskins and the Miami Dolphins. The four-time All-Pro was a member of the Dolphins' undefeated Super Bowl championship team of 1972.

88. George Mira, QB, Miami: A two-time All-American (1962–63), Mira was the first in what would be a long line of great quarterbacks at Miami. He led the nation in total offense (2,318 yards) as a senior despite having played on a 3–7 team. In 1962 he finished fifth in the Heisman Trophy voting, and in 1964 he was a second-round draft choice of the San Francisco 49ers. He played with four different NFL teams before his retirement and is one of only four Miami players to have had his jersey (No. 10) retired.

89. Cornelius Bennett, LB, Alabama: The winner of the 1986 Lombardi Award, Bennett was a three-time (1984–86) All-American for the Crimson Tide. Named the SEC Athlete of the Year in 1987, Bennett went on to have a successful NFL career and play in four Super Bowls for the Buffalo Bills.

90. Ray Beck, OG, Georgia Tech: One of the most dominating linemen in the history of Southern college football, Beck played a major role in Georgia Tech's 11–0–1 season when he was a senior in 1951. That same year he was named an All-American and the SEC's Most Valuable Player. The native of Cedartown, Georgia, was inducted into the College Football Hall of Fame in 1997.

91. Fred Biletnikoff, WR, Florida State: Biletnikoff was Florida State's first consensus All-America pick in 1964, the year he caught fifty-seven passes. After college he had a successful pro career with the Oakland Raiders, playing in six Pro Bowls and earning the honor of MVP in Super Bowl IX. He was inducted into the Pro Football Hall of Fame in 1988 and the College Football Hall of Fame in 1991.

92. Don McCauley, RB, North Carolina: The Tar Heels have had an NCAA-record twenty-four backs to run for more than one thousand yards in a season. McCauley was the first and perhaps the best. He was the ACC Player of the Year as a junior and a senior

(1969–70) and a consensus All-America pick in 1970. His 1970 total of 1,720 yards rushing broke the NCAA record at that time, which was held by Southern California's O. J. Simpson. McCauley led the nation in all-purpose running as a senior and his 126 points scored in 1970 still stands as the ACC record. McCauley was taken in the first round of the 1971 NFL draft by the Baltimore Colts, with whom he played for eleven seasons.

Larry Morris was an All-American center and linebacker in 1953 (photo courtesy of the *Atlanta Journal-Constitution*).

93. Jerry Butler, WR, Clemson: Butler was named first-team All-American for the Tigers in 1978 with 2,223 receiving yards. Along with quarterback Steve Fuller, in 1978 he helped lead the Tigers to an 11–1 season, the team's best ever up to that point. The Buffalo Bills picked him in the first round of the 1979 NFL draft, and he was named the AFC Rookie of the Year.

94. Carl Hinkle, C, Vanderbilt: The strongest of the famed Vanderbilt "Iron Men" of 1937, Hinkle, who played all sixty minutes in seven of Vanderbilt's games that season, led the Commodores to a 7–2 record. If not for a 9–7 loss to Alabama, Vanderbilt would have gone to the Rose Bowl, but Hinkle was still named the SEC's Most Valuable Player that season. After he left Vanderbilt, Hinkle attended West Point and was a highly decorated soldier in World War II. He was inducted into the College Football Hall of Fame in 1959.

95. Clarence "Ace" Parker, QB, Duke: From 1934 to 1936, Parker led Wallace Wade's Blue Devils to a combined record of 24–5. He was a first-team All-American and All-Southern-Conference that season. After he left Duke, Parker played seven seasons of professional football with the Brooklyn Dodgers and the Boston Yanks, leading the NFL in passing in 1938 with 865 yards. A charter member of the Duke Athletic Hall of Fame, Parker was inducted into the College Football Hall of Fame in 1955.

96. Larry Morris, C/LB, Georgia Tech: A four-year starter (1951–54) during the most successful period in Tech's history, Morris started as a true freshman in 1951 at linebacker on the Yellow Jackets' 11–0–1 team and as a sophomore on the 12–0 national championship team in 1952. Named the SEC lineman of the year in 1954, Morris was a first-round draft choice of the L.A. Rams. He was also named to the SEC quarter-century team for 1950–74. Morris was inducted into the College Football Hall of Fame in 1992.

97. Ted Brown, RB, N.C. State: Brown wasn't big (5'11", 190), but he was able to punch through ACC defenses for three 1,000-yard seasons and 4,602 career rushing yards, a conference career record that still stands. A consensus All-America pick as a senior in 1978, Brown was the NCAA's fourth all-time leading rusher at the end of his college career. He went on to play for seven years with the Minnesota Vikings.

98. George McAfee, QB, Duke: McAfee led the Blue Devils to a 24–4–1 record in three seasons (1937–39), which included an appearance in the 1939 Rose Bowl. McAfee's 1938 team, known as the "Iron Dukes," were undefeated and unscored upon during the regular season before losing to Southern California 7–3 in the Rose Bowl. In 1940 McAfee was a first-round choice of the Chicago Bears, with whom he played both offense and defense, posting twenty-one career interceptions. He is a member of both the college and pro football halls of fame.

99. Chuck Dicus, WR, Arkansas: A speedy wide receiver who was a generation ahead of his time, Dicus rewrote the Arkansas record books for receivers. Many of his records stood for more than twenty years, and his 118 career catches is still fourth on the school's all-time list. He was a three-year All-Southwest-Conference pick (1968–70) and an All-American in 1969 and 1970. Dicus, who had a reputation for coming up big in the important games, led the Razorbacks to a 16–2 win over Georgia in the 1969 Sugar Bowl with twelve catches for 169 yards. In the legendary game pitting No. 1 Texas against No. 2 Arkansas in 1969, Dicus caught nine passes for 146 yards and had a touchdown pass called back. He was inducted into the College Football Hall of Fame in 1999.

100. Ron Sellers, WR, Florida State: With all the great receivers who have played at Florida State, Sellers still remains the most prolific. From 1966 to 1968 Sellers caught 212 passes for 3,598 yards, an average of 119.9 yards per game. As a junior he had seventy catches for 1,228 yards, and as a senior he had eighty-six receptions for 1,496 yards. Sellers was inducted into the College Football Hall of Fame in 1988.

50 Honorable Mentions

1. **Bill Armstrong,** DB, Wake Forest (1973–76)
2. **Charles Alexander,** RB, LSU (1975–78)
3. **Bill Banker,** HB, Tulane (1927–29)
4. **Maxie Baughan,** C/LB, Georgia Tech (1927–29)
5. **Bobby Bryant,** DB, South Carolina (1964–66)
6. **Don Bosseler,** FB, Miami (1953–56)
7. **Hunter Carpenter,** HB, North Carolina/Virginia Tech (1900–05)
8. **Jack Cloud,** FB, William & Mary (1946–49)
9. **Josh Cody,** T, Vanderbilt (1914–19)
10. **Fred Crawford,** T, Duke (1931–33)
11. **Carroll Dale,** WR, Virginia Tech (1956–59)
12. **Jerry Dalrymple,** E, Tulane (1929–31)
13. **Bobby Davis,** T, Georgia Tech (1944–47)
14. **Al Derogatis,** C/T, Duke (1945–48)
15. **Joe Delaney,** RB, Northwestern State [Louisiana] (1977–80)
16. **Bill Fincher,** E/T, Georgia Tech (1916–20)
17. **Buck Flowers,** HB, Davidson/Georgia Tech (1916–20)
18. **William Fuller,** DT, North Carolina (1980–83)
19. **Roman Gabriel,** QB, N.C. State (1959–61)
20. **Bill George,** QB, Wake Forest (1948–51)
21. **Dan Hill,** C, Duke (1936–38)
22. **Sonny Jurgensen,** QB, Duke (1954–56)
23. **Gary "Big Hands" Johnson,** DT, Grambling (1971–74)
24. **Frank Juhan,** C, Sewanee (1908–1910)
25. **Les Lautenschlaeger,** QB, Tulane (1922–25)
26. **Bob Matheson,** LB, Duke (1964–66)
27. **Jack McDowall,** HB, N.C. State (1925–27)
28. **Bob Pellegrini,** C, Maryland (1953–55)
29. **Henry Phillips,** C, Sewanee (1900–05)
30. **Eddie Price,** FB, Tulane (1946–49)
31. **Peter Pund,** C, Georgia Tech (1926–28)
32. **Buster Ramsey,** G, William & Mary (1939–42)
33. **Gary Reasons,** LB, Northwestern State (1980–83)
34. **Jack Reynolds,** LB, Tennessee (1967–69)
35. **Randy Rhino,** DB, Georgia Tech (1972–74)

36. Wear Schoonover, E, Arkansas (1927–29)
37. Tom Scott, E, Virginia (1950–52)
38. Frank Lorio, DB, Virginia Tech (1965–67)
39. Monk Simons, RB, Tulane (1932–34)
40. Riley Smith, QB/FB, Alabama (1933–35)
41. Norm Snead, QB, Wake Forest (1958–60)
42. Bill Spears, QB, Vanderbilt (1925–27)
43. Ken Stabler, QB, Alabama (1965–67)
44. Joe Steffy, G, Tennessee (1944–47)
45. Everett Strupper, HB, Georgia Tech (1915–17)
46. Lynn Bomar, E, Vanderbilt (1921–24)
47. Eric Tipton, HB, Duke (1936–38)
48. Y. A. Title, QB, LSU (1944–47)
49. Don Whitmire, T, Alabama (1941–42)
50. Jim Youngblood, LB, Tennessee Tech (1969–72)

Players by Awards

Outland Trophy

The Outland honors the best interior lineman in the nation and was first presented in 1946 by the Football Writers Association of America. The award is named for its benefactor, Dr. John H. Outland. The Southern winners are:

Zeke Smith with coach Shug Jordan (photo courtesy of the *Atlanta Journal-Constitution*).

Bob Gain, Kentucky, 1950
Dick Modzelewski, Maryland, 1952
Bill Brooks, Arkansas, 1954
Zeke Smith, Auburn, 1958
Mike McGee, Duke, 1959
Steve DeLong, Tennessee, 1964
Lloyd Phillips, Arkansas, 1966
Bill Stanfill, Georgia, 1968
Randy White, Maryland, 1974
Jim Ritcher, N.C. State, 1979
Bruce Smith, Virginia Tech, 1984

Tracy Rocker, Auburn, 1988
Russell Maryland, Miami, 1990
Chris Samuels, Alabama, 1999

Maxwell Award

The Maxwell goes to the nation's outstanding football player and has been presented since 1937 by the Maxwell Memorial Football Club of Philadelphia. The award is named after Robert "Tiny" Maxwell, a Philadelphia native who played at the University of Chicago at the turn of the century. The Southern winners are:

Bill Dudley, Virginia, 1941
Charley Trippi, Georgia, 1946
Herschel Walker, Georgia, 1982
Vinny Testaverde, Miami, 1986
Gino Torretta, Miami, 1992
Charlie Ward, Florida State, 1993
Danny Wuerffel, Florida, 1996
Peyton Manning, Tennessee, 1997

Walter Camp **Award**

The Walter Camp Award goes to the nation's outstanding football player and was first presented in 1937 by the Walter Camp Football Foundation. The award is named after legendary coach Walter Camp, one of the innovators of American football. The Southern winners are:

Billy Dudley, Virginia, 1941
Frank Sinkwich, Georgia, 1942
Charley Trippi, Georgia, 1946
Babe Parilli, Kentucky, 1950
Bernie Faloney, Maryland, 1953
Billy Cannon, LSU, 1959
Jerry Stovall, LSU, 1962
Steve Spurrier, Florida, 1966
Archie Manning, Mississippi, 1969
Herschel Walker, Georgia, 1980
Gino Torretta, Miami, 1992
Charlie Ward, Florida State, 1993
Danny Wuerffel, Florida, 1996

Lombardi Award

Given to the outstanding lineman or linebacker of the year, the Lombardi Award is presented in the name of Vince Lombardi, the Hall of Fame coach of the Green Bay Packers. Since 1970, the award has been presented by the Rotary Club of Houston. The Southern winners are:

Randy White, Maryland, 1974
Cornelius Bennett, Alabama, 1986
Tracy Rocker, Auburn, 1988
Marvin Jones, Florida State, 1992
Warren Sapp, Miami, 1994
Corey Moore, Virginia Tech, 1999

Jim Thorpe **Award**

The Jim Thorpe Award was first presented in 1986 by the Jim Thorpe Athletic Club of Oklahoma City to the nation's best defensive back. The award is named after Olympic champion Jim Thorpe, a two-time All-American halfback at Carlisle. The Southern winners are:

Deion Sanders, Florida State, 1988
Terrell Buckley, Florida State, 1991
Antonio Langham, Alabama, 1993
Lawrence Wright, Florida, 1996

Davey O'Brien **Award**

The Davey O'Brien Award was first presented in 1977 to the outstanding player in the Southwest. Since 1981 the award has gone to the nation's best quarterback. The Davey O'Brien Education and Charitable Trust of Fort Worth, Texas, presents the award, which is named after the legendary quarterback from Texas Christian. The Southern winners are:

Vinny Testaverde, Miami, 1986
Gino Torretta, Miami, 1992
Charlie Ward, Florida State, 1993
Danny Wuerffel, Florida, 1995, 1996
Peyton Manning, Tennessee, 1997
Joe Hamilton, Georgia Tech, 1999

Butkus Award

The Butkus Award was first presented in 1985 by the Downtown Athletic Club of Orlando to the nation's best linebacker. The award is named after Dick Butkus, a two-time All-American from Illinois and a six-time All-Pro with the Chicago Bears. The Southern winners are:

Paul McGowan, Florida State, 1987
Derrick Thomas, Alabama, 1988
Marvin Jones, Florida State, 1992

Lou Groza **Award**

Since 1992 this award, which is sponsored by the Palm Beach County Sports Authority in conjunction with the Orange Bowl committee, has been presented to the nation's best kicker. It is named after the NFL Hall of Fame placekicker. The Southern winners are:

Judd Davis, Florida, 1993
Marc Primanti, N.C. State, 1996
Sebastian Janikowski, Florida State, 1998, 1999

Doak Walker **Award**

Since 1990 this award, which is sponsored by the GTE/Southern Methodist Athletic Forum in Dallas, Texas, has been presented to the nation's best running back. It is named after the three-time All-American from SMU. Georgia's Garrison Hearst won this award in 1992.

Bronco Nagurski **Award**

Since 1993 this award has been presented by the Football Writers Association of America to the nation's top collegiate defensive player. The award is named after the Hall of Fame tackle who played at Minnesota from 1927 to 1929. The Southern winners are:

Warren Sapp, Miami, 1994
Champ Bailey, Georgia, 1998
Corey Moore, Virginia Tech, 1999

THE COACHES

If the South looks upon its college football players as Saturday's soldiers, it only follows that the men who coach the game are treated with the respect and deference accorded great generals.

The men who shaped the great Southern game came from many different walks of life, but all of them had the same traits in common: an unshakable belief in themselves and their ability to do the job; a strong commitment to excellence, which they also demanded of those around them; and an utter contempt for losing and for those who were willing to tolerate it in any form. For the coaches who win, the rewards are significant. In the South, the successful college football coach is as powerful as any politician or university president.

Over the past one hundred years the Southern college football coach's job has evolved from a chore once handled by college professors in their free time to today's high-profile, demanding—and rewarding—career.

The Great Southern Coaches

In 1919 head coach John Heisman was at the height of his success at Georgia Tech. The same could not have been said of his marriage. As part of the divorce agreement, Heisman promised that he would not live in the same city as the one in which his wife lived, "in order to avoid any social embarrassment." Mrs. Heisman chose to stay in Atlanta and Heisman had to leave. Just like that, his career at Georgia Tech was over.

In 1942 at the age of fifty-two, Duke's Wallace Wade decided to leave the sidelines because he wanted to join the war effort. He fought in the Battle of Normandy and received the Bronze Star.

Despite his gruff exterior, Alabama's Bear Bryant had a sense of humor. And it popped up at the most interesting times.

In 1968, Alabama traveled to Knoxville to play Tennessee. Alabama's quarterback, sophomore Scott Hunter, was nervous about his first game against the Crimson Tide's big rival. Tennessee's mascot, a bluetick hound named Smokey, ran up to Hunter during warm-ups and nipped at him. Hunter reacted by kicking Smokey, sending the crowd at Neyland Stadium into a frenzy. A few seconds later, Hunter felt a powerful arm around his shoulders. It was Bryant. "Scaawtt," Bryant said, in his from-the-bottom-of-the-well drawl, "we got enough trouble up here without you trying to kick their damn dog." Tennessee won the game 10–9.

Now here's a closer look at some of the key men who helped put the passion into Southern college football.

Florida State's Bobby Bowden joined the three-hundred-win club with a 12–0 national championship team in 1999 (photo courtesy of the *Atlanta Journal-Constitution*).

Robert C. "Bobby" Bowden Samford, West Virginia, Florida State **1959–62, 1970–present**

In 1943, thirteen-year-old Bobby Bowden was stricken by rheumatic fever, and with it came one of the toughest ordeals a teenager could face: six months of bed rest followed by a year's confinement to ensure a complete recovery.

"There was no television, no video games, no computer," Bowden says. "Just me and my radio."

On the radio Bowden listened to what he would later call a "play-by-play" of World War II. The young Bowden would envision the battles and play out in his mind the strategies of the great generals who fought them. The interest in strategy Bowden developed during those months of confinement created the foundation that would later make him one of the most successful coaches in college football history.

The 2000 season will be Bowden's twenty-fifth at Florida State University and his thirty-fifth as a college football coach. He is one of only five NCAA Division I coaches to have won 300 games. On that short list, only Bowden and Penn State's Joe Paterno are still active coaches.

A native of Birmingham, Alabama, Bowden literally grew up in the shadow of historic Legion Field and fulfilled a lifelong dream when he played quarterback as a freshman for the University of Alabama. But Bowden found something he loved more than Alabama football, and that was the lovely Ann Estock, his childhood sweetheart. So after just one semester at Alabama, Bowden came back to Birmingham, married Ann, and transferred to Howard College, now Samford University.

He was only twenty-nine years old when he became the head coach at Samford, where he stayed for four seasons followed by six more at West Virginia. When he took over at Florida State in 1976, he inherited a program that had won just 4 games over the previous three seasons, including a 0–11 record in 1973. He later said that at that time he never imagined staying at Florida State for the long haul.

"I figured we would build the program up for a few years and then a bigger opportunity would come along," he says.

But things didn't go according to plan. In just his second year, Florida State won 10 games. In his fourth year, the Seminoles went 11–1 and earned a trip to the Orange Bowl. And in 1987 Bowden's teams began one of the most impressive strings of successful seasons in the history of the sport. Through the 1999 season, Florida State had posted thirteen straight years with 10 wins or more and thirteen straight finishes in the Final Associated Press Top Four.

It is likely that Bowden's 1999 season will go down in history as his best. He joined the three-hundred-win club on October 23 when his team beat Clemson, which was coached by his son Tommy. The Seminoles went on to an 11–0 regular season and a No. 1 ranking and then beat No. 2 Virginia Tech 46–29 in the Sugar Bowl to give Bowden his second national championship.

Bowden, who will turn seventy-one on November 8, 2000, shows no signs of slowing down. He says he will coach as long as his health holds out.

"After you retire, there's only one big event left," says Bowden. "And I ain't ready for that."

SCHOOL	YEARS	RECORD
Samford	1959–62	31–6–0
West Virginia	1970–75	42–26–0
Florida State	1976–present	231–53–4
Total	(through 1999)	304–85–4

ACC Championships: (8)—'92, '93, '94, '95, '96, '97, '98, '99
National championships: (2)—'93, '99

Paul W. "Bear" Bryant
Maryland, Kentucky, Texas A&M, Alabama **1945–82**

The end of the 1957 season represented one of the lowest points in the University of Alabama's proud football history. The Crimson Tide finished their fourth straight losing season with an embarrassing 40–0 loss to Auburn, their hated rival. Then, to add insult to injury, Auburn was declared the national champion. The tenure of Alabama coach J. B. "Ears" Whitworth—whose teams had recorded a 4–24–2 record in three seasons—had been a disaster. Something had to be done.

Alabama legend Paul "Bear" Bryant announces his retirement on December 15, 1982 (photo courtesy of the *Atlanta Journal-Constitution*).

That something happened three days after Alabama's loss to Auburn when Paul W. Bryant, who had been an end on Alabama's 1934 Rose Bowl team, agreed to leave his coaching position at Texas A&M and come back to Tuscaloosa to serve as head coach of the Crimson Tide. Bryant, who had previously coached at Maryland and Kentucky, had actually agreed to take the job a month before during secret meetings with key Alabama officials. He left Texas A&M with seven years remaining on his contract. When asked why he wanted to leave such a lucrative job to take over a program in trouble, Bryant simply said: "Mama called."

Over his next twenty-five years at Alabama, Bryant dominated Southern college football like no man before or since, posting 232 wins and only 46 losses, thirteen Southeastern Conference championships, 24 straight bowl games, and six national championships.

But the numbers don't reveal the true size of the shadow Bear Bryant cast over the game for an entire generation. To this day, when people talk about Bryant they usually spend more time praising the man than the football coach.

"He was the most impressive man I've ever been close to," said the late John Forney, Alabama's radio broadcaster from 1953 to 1983. "When he walked into a room a hush came over it."

ESPN broadcaster Ron Franklin agrees: "When he walked in a room, it was like his presence got there thirty seconds before he did. There was just something really special about him."

Bryant's philosophy of coaching was simple: He was willing to pay the price to win and demanded that those around him—players, coaches, managers, and university presidents—do the same. He was relentless but never pushed anybody harder than he pushed himself.

"Coach Bryant could get more out of his people than anybody I have ever known," says Danny Ford, who played for Bryant from 1967 to 1969 and then later became the head coach at Clemson and Arkansas. "He expected you to win and you expected to win for him."

Bryant's knack for winning inspired a grudging respect among his fellow coaches. Jake Gaither, the Hall of Fame coach from Florida A&M, paid Bryant the ultimate compliment when he said, "He could take his'n and beat your'n, and take your'n and beat his'n."

One of twelve children, Bryant grew up poor on a farm in Moro Bottom, Arkansas. He earned his nickname at fourteen years old when he wrestled a bear on stage in Fordyce, Arkansas. He grappled with the bear for only a few minutes, but the nickname stuck with him for a lifetime.

On November 28, 1981, Bear Bryant won his 315th game, breaking the major college record of 314 wins set by Amos Alonzo Stagg. Stagg needed fifty-seven years to set the record. Bryant did it in just thirty-seven.

After breaking the record, Bryant coached one more season before announcing his retirement. On December 29, 1982, he coached his last game, a 21–15 win over Illinois in the Liberty Bowl.

Toward the end of his career, Bryant was asked when he would retire: "Retire?" he replied. "Hell, I'd probably croak in a week!" His words were prophetic: on January 26, 1983, just forty-two days after he announced his retirement from coaching, Bear Bryant died at the age of sixty-nine.

SCHOOL	YEARS	RECORD
Maryland	1945	6–2–1
Kentucky	1946–53	60–23–5
Texas A&M	1954–57	25–14–2
Alabama	1958–82	232–46–9
Total	38 years	323–85–17

SEC championships: (14)—'50, '61, '64, '65, '66, '71, '72, '73, '74, '75, '77, '78, '79, '81
National championships: (6) —'61, '64, '65, '73, '78, '79

Georgia Tech legend Bobby Dodd (photo courtesy of the *Atlanta Journal-Constitution*).

Robert Lee "Bobby" Dodd Georgia Tech **1945–66**

General Robert R. Neyland, Tennessee's legendary coach, knew that Bobby Dodd, his All-American quarterback, was going to be a good coach someday. Neyland assumed it would be at Tennessee. But Dodd broke Neyland's heart and altered college football history in 1931 when he rejected offers at Tennessee and Duke to come to Georgia Tech as an assistant coach to Bill Alexander. He never left. Dodd remained at Georgia Tech as an assistant coach (1931–44), head coach (1945–66), athletic director (1950–76), and a consultant to the school's alumni association until his death on June 21, 1988, at the age of seventy-nine.

In twenty-two seasons as a head coach, Dodd won 165 games plus the love and admiration of a generation of players and fans.

"He was one of the smartest, most innovative people I have ever met," says Kim King, who played quarterback on Dodd's last team in 1966. "He was a man truly ahead of his time."

The word most often used to describe Dodd is "unconventional." While he was a protégé of Neyland, his approach to the game was very different from the General's. Neyland believed in using long, hard practices to drill the fundamentals into his players. Dodd believed that practice should be fun and should merely sharpen skills the players already possessed.

"Coach Dodd believed that you should never leave your best effort out on the practice field," says Ray Beck, who played for Dodd from 1949 to 1951 and is now in the College Football Hall of Fame.

Dodd took a particularly unconventional approach to practice when his team went to the Orange Bowl in 1947.

"As soon as we got to Miami, we assembled at the hotel, and he took us to the beach to go swimming," says Red Patton, who played at Georgia Tech from 1947 to 1950. "We beat Kansas and everyone was happy."

Bobby Dodd was also an unconventional coach once the game started. Instead of pacing the sidelines like other coaches, he would sit at one end of the field in a lawn chair and direct the game, as if he were enjoying a day at the beach.

Dodd retired as Georgia Tech's head coach after the Orange Bowl on January 1, 1967, and in 1993 he was inducted into the College Football Hall of Fame as a coach. He is one of only three men in history (along with Amos Alonzo Stagg and Tennessee's Bowden Wyatt) to have been elected to the Hall of Fame as both a player and a coach.

SCHOOL	**YEARS**	**RECORD**
Georgia Tech	1945–66	165–64–8

SEC championships: (2)—'51, '52
National championships: (1)—'52

Mike Donahue Auburn, LSU **1904–27**

Three men are given the lion's share of the credit for bringing college football from the North and making it an institution in the South. They are John Heisman (Auburn, Clemson, Georgia Tech), Dan McGugin (Vanderbilt), and Mike Donahue, who won 99 games at Auburn from 1904 to 1922.

Mike Donahue, Auburn's Hall of Fame coach (photo courtesy of Auburn SID).

Donahue played quarterback for the great Walter Camp at Yale. Tiny in size (5'4") but huge in intellect, Donahue demanded that his players hit hard and think hard as well. According to Wayne Hester's anthology on Auburn football, *Where Tradition Began*, Donahue was one of the most versatile faculty members in the history of the university. He coached not only football but also baseball, track, and soccer and was the school's first basketball coach. In his free time he taught classes in English, math, history, and Latin.

Donahue took a year off from coaching football in 1907 in order to concentrate on his duties as Auburn's athletic director. But he couldn't stay away from the game and returned as head coach for the 1908 season. It was then that he led Auburn to some of its greatest successes on the football field. In a stretch that lasted from 1913 to 1915, Donahue's teams went 23 straight games without a loss and outscored their opponents 600–13.

After the 1922 season, Donahue decided to leave Auburn and become the head coach at LSU, where he was not as successful. He stepped down as head coach after five seasons to become a golf professional at a local country club.

A few years later Donahue got back into coaching at Spring Hill College in Mobile, Alabama, and then returned to LSU in 1937 to serve as the director of intramurals. In 1951 Donahue was inducted into the College Football Hall of Fame. He died in 1958 at the age of eighty-four.

SCHOOL	YEARS	RECORD
Auburn	1904–22	99–35–5
LSU	1923–27	23–19–3
Total	23 seasons	122–54–8

Georgia coach Vince Dooley (1964–88) won 201 games and six SEC titles (photo courtesy of the *Atlanta Journal-Constitution*).

Vince Dooley Georgia 1964–88

November 22, 1963, the day President John F. Kennedy was assassinated in Dallas, is a date that will live in infamy. And it will be doubly remembered in Georgia, thanks to an event that occurred on the same day that would change the course of football history at the University of Georgia.

Just hours before those terrible shots rang out in Texas, Joel Eaves, the basketball coach at Auburn, accepted the position of athletic director at the University of Georgia. On December 4, Eaves made his first major decision: to hire Vince Dooley as the Bulldogs' new head football coach.

Dooley was not a popular choice with the alumni, who wanted a "name" coach to bring Georgia out of its football doldrums. Georgia's fans had suffered through three straight losing seasons under coach Johnny Griffith, who had replaced future Hall of Famer Wally Butts after the 1960 season. Griffith was fired with a 10–16–4 record.

Eaves, who had always been known for his independent streak, went against the alumni and hired Dooley, then a thirty-one-year-old assistant to Auburn coach Shug Jordan. Dooley had played football and basketball at Auburn and had served in the Marines before returning to Auburn to take on his coaching apprenticeship.

"I was convinced he had all the tools it took to be a head coach," Eaves would later say. "And he wouldn't panic."

So, for a salary of $12,500 a year, Dooley became Georgia's new head football coach. Twenty-five years later he retired with 201 victories, six SEC championships, and one national championship. There was no mystery to Dooley—no fancy slogans or secrets to success. He believed in organization. He believed in discipline. And most of all he believed in preparation.

"If you haven't done the preparation on Monday through Friday, there's nothing magical you can do on Saturday to get your team ready to play the game," Dooley often said. "Teams are most confident when they know they are prepared."

Dooley's greatest success came during the four seasons from 1980 to 1983, when his teams won 43 games and lost only 4, earned three SEC championships, and took home a national championship in 1980.

In 1988, after a 9–3 season, Dooley decided to retire as head football coach to become Georgia's full-time athletic director. Under his guidance, Georgia developed one of the most successful college athletic programs in the country. In the 1998–99 academic year, Georgia's teams won four national championships and finished second to Stanford as the nation's best athletic program.

At the time of Dooley's retirement as Georgia's coach, only Alabama's Bear Bryant had won more SEC championships. As of the 2000 season, Dooley was one of fifteen Division I coaches to record more than 200 career victories. In twenty-five years, Dooley had only one losing season (1977). He was inducted into the College Football Hall of Fame in 1994.

SCHOOL	YEARS	RECORD
Georgia	1964–88	201–77–4

SEC championships: (6)—'66, '68, '76, '80, '81, '82
National championships: (1) —'80

John Heisman Auburn, Clemson, Georgia Tech **1895–1919**

Had John Heisman's life gone according to plan, he never would have been a coach and never would have had college football's highest honor named after him. But fate, in the form of an accident, stepped in and changed everything.

Heisman, the son of a German immigrant, first fell in love with football as an undergrad at Brown University. His love for the sport grew at the University of Pennsylvania, where he played while earning his law degree.

John Heisman (photo courtesy of the *Atlanta Journal-Constitution*).

Playing for Penn in the old Madison Square Garden, Heisman's eyes were so damaged by the Garden's galvanic lighting system that doctors prescribed two years of rest for his eyes, which required him to put his law career on hold. In the interim, Heisman decided to try coaching.

His decision changed the face of college football in the South. Heisman coached at eight different colleges, but forged his legend at Auburn (1895–99), Clemson (1900–3), and Georgia Tech (1904–19). He posted winning records at all three schools before returning to Penn in 1919.

A perfectionist who was both rigid and innovative, Heisman could not stand mistakes, especially fumbles. He would often stand holding a football under his arm and say to his players: "Better to have died as a small boy than to fumble this football."

The contradictions in Heisman's personality were legendary. While he played the role of the tough, autocratic football coach on the field, he fancied himself to be an actor and would wander out at night to get ice cream for his pet poodle, Woo. And even though he portrayed himself to be above common human emotion, it was a grudge that led him to set up the most humiliating defeat a team ever devised for an opponent.

Heisman also coached baseball at Georgia Tech, and in the spring of 1916 Tech lost 22–0 to a team of professionals pretending to be players from Cumberland College. That fall, Heisman lured the Cumberland football team to Atlanta with an all-expenses paid trip and $500. Georgia Tech won the game 222–0.

Heisman wanted to finish his coaching career at Georgia Tech, but in a divorce settlement in 1919 he agreed not to live in the same city as his wife, Evelyn. She chose Atlanta and Heisman returned to Pennsylvania.

Heisman retired from coaching in 1926 to become the director of athletics for New York's Downtown Athletic Club (DAC). He died on October 3, 1936, and two months later the DAC awarded its first Heisman Trophy, which today is still awarded to the nation's best college football player.

SCHOOL	YEARS	RECORD
Auburn	1895–99	12–4–2
Clemson	1900–3	19–3–2
Georgia Tech	1904–19	102–29–7
Total	24 seasons	133–36–11

National championships: (1)—'17

Ralph "Shug" Jordan Auburn 1951–75

In 1947 Ralph Jordan's one goal in life was to return to his alma mater as Auburn's head football coach. When Auburn passed him over in favor of Earl Brown, a former All-American at Notre Dame, Jordan did nothing to hide his feelings.

Auburn Hall of Fame coach Ralph "Shug" Jordan (photo courtesy of the *Atlanta Journal-Constitution*).

"If they don't think an Auburn man can do the job, they ought to close the joint down," he said.

Brown won only 3 games in three seasons at Auburn. His last team in 1950 was 0–10. In 1951, the Auburn trustees had the good sense to finally hire Jordan, but the proud coach, who still held a grudge because he had not been chosen at first, had to be goaded into formally applying for the job.

In the rough and tumble world of college football coaches, Jordan was known as a Southern gentleman throughout his twenty-five years as the head coach at Auburn. But no one ever accused Jordan of being soft. Whenever Jordan felt that he or his players were not receiving their proper due, he would rise up with righteous indignation, like a fire-breathing minister admonishing his congregation for their sins.

In November of 1971, Auburn quarterback Pat Sullivan all but locked up the Heisman Trophy with an unforgettable performance against Georgia in which he completed fourteen of twenty-four passes for 248 yards and four touchdowns. After the game, a reporter had the bad judgment to suggest that despite Sullivan's efforts that day, he still might not receive college football's highest award.

"Maybe not," bellowed Jordan, "but if someone else does get it, I'll bet he's Christ reincarnated!"

Jordan, a deeply religious man, then regained his composure. "Now I'll be up all night saying Hail Marys. Let's just say if someone else gets it, he'll have to be—uh—magnificent."

Sullivan did go on to win the Heisman, Auburn's first.

In *When Tradition Began*, a history of Auburn football published by the Birmingham News, author Wayne Hester recalls Jordan's final years leading up to his retirement in 1975. His opponents' recruiters were spreading the word that his health was failing. Some of that talk was coming from Alabama, Auburn's hated rival, where coach Bear Bryant was enjoying one of the most successful decades in the history of college football. Tired of the talk, Jordan, according to Hester, took a not-so-veiled shot at his counterpart across the state: "At least I don't climb up in a four-story tower and holler through a bullhorn like a plantation owner working his slaves," he said.

Shug Jordan may have struck a grandfatherly pose in public, but he would never back down from anybody once he stepped into a competition.

"Coach Jordan was a true gentleman, but he had a mean, cold streak to do what he had to do," says Liston Eddings, who played defensive end for Jordan from 1973 to 1975.

Jordan's teams won 176 games and produced twenty All-Americans. His 1957 team went undefeated and won Auburn's only national championship. In fact, it was a 40–0 beating of Alabama in the finale of the 1957 season that forced the Crimson Tide to hire Bryant, who would torment Auburn (and the rest of the SEC) for the next twenty-five years.

In April of 1975 Jordan decided that his twenty-fifth season at Auburn would be his last. He served on the Auburn University Board of Trustees until his death in July of 1980. In 1982, Jordan was inducted into the College Football Hall of Fame.

His career at Auburn, and his life, can be summed up by what he called "My Seven D's of Success":

1. *Discipline*
2. *Desire to Excel*
3. *Determination*
4. *Dedication*
5. *Dependability*
6. *Desperation*
7. *Damn It Anyway*

SCHOOL	YEARS	RECORD
Auburn	1951–75	176–83–6

SEC championships: (1)—'57
National championships: (1)—'57

Dan McGugin Vanderbilt 1904–34

The most successful period in Vanderbilt's football history was three minutes away from never happening. That's how close Dan McGugin came to taking another job in 1904.

Vanderbilt's Dan McGugin won 197 games in thirty years as coach (photo courtesy of Vanderbilt SID).

Vanderbilt had asked Michigan coach Fielding Yost for help in finding a new football coach. Yost contacted McGugin, who had been one of Yost's brightest players and was a recent graduate of Michigan's law school. McGugin wrote Vanderbilt and expressed his interest in the job but did not receive an immediate reply. In the interim, McGugin received a telegram from Western Reserve University in Cleveland offering him their head coaching position at a salary of $1,000 a year. Western Reserve needed an immediate reply, and so with no response from Vanderbilt, McGugin wired back and accepted Western Reserve's offer.

When McGugin returned to his room on campus, he found a telegram waiting for him from Vanderbilt, offering him a job at a salary of $850 a year. McGugin really wanted to go south and decided that if he could stop the telegram to Western Reserve, he would take Vanderbilt's offer. If he couldn't, he would go to Ohio. So he ran to the telegraph office and stopped the message just three minutes before it was scheduled to be delivered.

Those three minutes turned out to be the most important in Vanderbilt football history. Over the next thirty-one years (except for 1918, when he served in WW I), McGugin and Vanderbilt dominated Southern college football, winning 197 of 271 games.

McGugin possessed a number of traits that made him a good football coach, his strongest being an uncanny ability to inspire his players. Although he was a graduate of Michigan's law school, he would not hesitate to invoke Southern pride as a motivational tool, particularly when his teams faced opposition from the North. He did it when his team played Yale in 1910 and again when Vanderbilt tied Michigan 0–0 in 1922. Michigan's Yost, who had now become McGugin's brother-in-law, was less than impressed.

"That McGugin and his phony accent," Yost said. "Before he came to Vanderbilt he'd never been farther south than Toledo."

McGugin's thirty Vanderbilt teams not only won 72.6 percent of their games but also outscored their opponents by a whopping 6,662 to 1,668, an average margin of victory of 18.4 points. Citing health problems, McGugin ended his coaching career after the 1934 season. He died in 1936 at the age of fifty-six and was inducted into the College Football Hall of Fame in 1951.

SCHOOL	YEARS	RECORD
Vanderbilt	1904–34*	197–55–19

**McGugin took a leave of absence from coaching during the 1918 season to serve in World War I, where he achieved the rank of lieutenant colonel.*

Tennessee coach Robert Neyland in 1947 (photo courtesy of the *Atlanta Journal-Constitution*).

General Robert R. Neyland Tennessee **1926–34, 1936–40, 1946–52**

It was the University of Tennessee's inability to beat state rival Vanderbilt and coach Dan McGugin that encouraged school officials to take a step that would forever change Tennessee's college football history. In 1926, after losing 18 of the 21 games it had played against Vanderbilt since 1892, Tennessee hired thirty-four-year-old Robert R. Neyland as its head coach.

Neyland brought the discipline and strategy he had learned in the military to the football field. And he got great results. Over the next twenty-six years, with two breaks for active military service, Neyland would win 173 games while losing only 31 as the head coach of the Vols.

Neyland won with a simple formula. He firmly believed that great defense, a sound kicking game, and the elimination of mistakes were the keys to victory. He also believed that constant repetition in practice was the only way to make a football team operate like a well-oiled machine on game day. He applied a clearly defined set of principles to the game of football. One of the first principles was "The head coach must remain a little aloof from the players and, to a certain extent, from the coaches." Neyland believed such detachment was necessary to maintain discipline. No one ever doubted that Neyland saw the Tennessee football team as his army and himself as the general in command.

"The general was always in complete control," says John Michaels, who played for Neyland from 1949 to 1952. "He never got excited. He was highly organized and a great disciplinarian."

"The general was not the easiest guy to work with Monday through Friday, but on Saturday he was a fatherly figure," says Herky Payne (1949–51). "On Saturday he was a warm man who gave you a lot of confidence."

But Neyland believed that that confidence came from thorough preparation, not from emotional speeches in the locker room before the game.

"Proper mental attitude on game day stems almost entirely from attitudes built up over a considerable period of time," Neyland once wrote. "Pregame harangues, as a rule, do more harm than good. Inspiration at zero hour is a poor thing to rely on."

Neyland was not, however, above a little psychological gamesmanship. Before Tennessee's 1928 game with Alabama, he approached Alabama coach Wallace Wade and asked Wade if he would mind shortening the second half of the game if the Vols, a decided underdog, fell too far behind. Neyland told Wade that he didn't want his players to get too discouraged in defeat. Wade smiled and said he would shorten the game if necessary.

Tennessee ran the opening kickoff back for a touchdown. In the end, the Vols upset Alabama 15–13.

The week before the big game with Vanderbilt in 1929, Neyland sent ten of his starting players to scout the Commodores, who were playing Georgia Tech in Nashville. But Tennessee had scheduled a game that same day against Carson-Newman. Neyland didn't care. He sent his starters to watch Vanderbilt and the Volunteer scrubs beat Carson-Newman 73–0. The next week Tennessee beat Vanderbilt 13–0.

Neyland won five SEC championships, and at times Tennessee completely dominated the other teams in the South. From 1938 through 1940, the Volunteers won 31 games and lost only 2, a run that included a 22-game winning streak. The Vols lost only once in 1950 and went through the 1951 regular season unbeaten, winning the national championship.

Because of illness, Neyland would make the 1952 season his last as Tennessee's coach. The Vols went to the Cotton Bowl that year, but Neyland was too sick to coach in the game. After his retirement as coach, Neyland became Tennessee's athletic director, a position he held until his death on March 28, 1962. He was elected into the College Football Hall of Fame in 1956.

Appropriately, Tennessee's football stadium, the second-largest on-campus facility in the nation (102,854 capacity), is named after General Robert R. Neyland.

The Ten Basic Principles of General Robert R. Neyland

1. The head coach must remain a little aloof from the players and, to a certain extent, from the coaches.

2. The first qualification of a head coach is to possess a cool head so that he may see things in their true relation to each other and so in their proper perspective. There are things in football of which the head coach alone can comprehend the importance.

3. His first principle must be to calculate what he must do to win and see if he has the necessary means to surmount the obstacles with which the enemy will oppose him. Once the decision is made, see that all do their respective parts to earn the victory.

4. Football is composed of nothing but accidents. The great art is to profit from such accidents. This is the mark of genius.

5. It follows that all plans must be made to minimize our own mistakes and to magnify the effect of the opponents' mistakes.

6. On the nature of the struggle between two equal teams: The difference is never physical but invariably mental.

7. It is important to keep the squad eternally aware of the very nature of football and so not dismayed when things are going wrong.

8. To defeat a weak opponent is not the problem. The problem is to win when he is as good as or better than you.

9. Almost all close games are lost by the losers, not won by the winners.

10. Proper mental stance on game day stems almost entirely from attitudes built up over a considerable period of time. Pregame harangues, as a rule, do more harm than good. Inspiration at zero hour is a poor thing to rely on.

SCHOOL	SEASONS	RECORD
Tennessee	1926–34, 1936–40, 1946–52	173–31–12

SEC championships: (5)—'38, '39, '40, '46, '51
National championships: (3)—'38, '40, '51

Eddie Robinson Grambling **1941–97**

Some people are well into adulthood before they find their calling in life. Eddie Robinson was unique; he discovered his passion in the third grade.

A local high school football coach brought his team to Robinson's elementary school in an effort to sell season tickets. While Robinson's classmates focused on the players in their fancy uniforms, Robinson's eyes were riveted on the coach.

"I liked the way he talked to the team. I liked the way he could make us all laugh," Robinson recalls. "I liked the way they respected him."

Grambling coach Eddie Robinson (photo courtesy of the *Atlanta Journal-Constitution*).

By the time Robinson was in the ninth grade he was organizing and coaching teams in the neighborhoods around his home in Baton Rouge, Louisiana. As a twenty-one-year-old college graduate, Robinson worked at a feed mill for twenty-five cents an hour. Then a relative told him that the Louisiana Negro Normal and Industrial Institute was looking for someone to coach football, basketball, and baseball at a starting salary of $63.75 a month. He would have to take a cut in pay if he got the job.

"But coaching was all I ever wanted to do," he said.

His decision to accept the position launched the most successful and distinguished career in the history of college football. When Eddie Robinson became the head coach at Louisiana Negro Normal, which would later become Grambling, Japan had not yet bombed Pearl Harbor. By the time he retired in 1997, the man they all called "Coach Rob" had won more games (408) than any coach in college football history.

The sheer numbers are staggering:

- He is and will likely forever remain the only coach to ever win 400 college football games.
- He won or shared seventeen Southwestern Athletic Conference (SWAC) championships and nine national black college championships.
- During his fifty-seven-year career, 210 of Robinson's players found their way onto NFL rosters.

But the numbers don't even begin to tell the whole story. Like any coach, Robinson wanted to win, but he cared more about turning out good men who would become good husbands and fathers. Former player Trumaine Jackson once said that if a player used incorrect English on the practice field, Robinson would stop the workout and correct the player on the spot. He would not tolerate profanity from his players, on or off the field. When traveling to and from games, Robinson would insist that his players wear jackets and ties. He required his players to take etiquette classes from Grambling's home economics department so that they would know how to behave in public.

When Grambling did not field a team in 1943 or 1944 due to World War II, Robinson coached for the local high school football team. One day, the father of Robinson's star running back came to practice wanting to take his son home to pick cotton. Robinson responded by taking his whole team to the fields. Once the cotton was picked, the running back was allowed to return to practice. Grambling High School went on to win a state championship that season.

"The football players are the most important people in the world to me," he said. "Without them, there would be no me."

Robinson said that his greatest accomplishment was not winning 408 games, but going for fifty-seven years with "one job and one wife." Robinson married Doris, his high school sweetheart, the same year he came to Grambling.

When Robinson took over at Grambling, the school had 175 students and five buildings. He made the school, and himself, internationally famous. In 1997 Robinson retired from coaching at the age of seventy-eight. The National Football Foundation and College Hall of Fame waived its customary three-year waiting period and immediately inducted him that December.

"No one has ever done or ever will do what Eddie Robinson has done for this game," says Penn State coach Joe Paterno. "Eddie Robinson and Jake Gaither [of Florida A&M] stand alone. Our profession will never, ever be able to repay Eddie Robinson for what he has done for the country and the profession of football."

SCHOOL	YEARS	RECORD
Grambling	1941–97	408–165–15

SWAC championships: (17)—'60, '64, '65, '66, '67, '71, '72, '73, '74, '77, '78, '79, '80, '83, '85, '89
National Black College championships: (9)—'50, '67, '72, '74, '75, '77, '80, '83, '92

Frank Thomas Alabama **1931–46**

After Wallace Wade decided to leave Alabama for Duke in 1930, the search began for a coach to continue the Crimson Tide's winning tradition. Alabama found its coach in Frank Thomas, a short, quiet man who possessed a large and innovative football mind.

Alabama coach Frank Thomas (1931–46) (photo courtesy of the *Atlanta Journal-Constitution*).

Thomas had been a quarterback on Knute Rockne's Notre Dame teams of 1921 and 1922. After graduating from the Notre Dame law school in 1923, he set out to establish a career in coaching. He was an assistant at Georgia when Wade recommended that Alabama hire him for the 1931 season.

Over the next sixteen seasons Thomas would win eighty-one percent of his games (115–24–7), two national championships (1934, 1941), and four SEC championships and make three trips to the Rose Bowl.

A brilliant tactician who had an uncanny ability to make adjustments during the course of a game, Thomas is best remembered for introducing the South to the "Notre Dame box," a shifting, wide-open offense unlike anything his opponents had ever seen.

Harry Gilmer, a former All-American halfback for the 1945 Crimson Tide team, recalls a pregame speech Thomas gave to the team in which he emotionally implored them to play for the honor of those who had worn their Alabama jerseys before them. At the end of his impassioned plea, it dawned on Thomas that the team was wearing brand new, lightweight jerseys—not the heavy, woolen jerseys he had referred to in his speech.

"The last thing he made us do before the game was get off the bus and put on those old, woolen, hot jerseys," says Gilmer, who was the SEC Player of the Year in 1945 and is a member of the College Football Hall of Fame.

Thomas's nervous personality made him do strange things before big games. In *Century of Champions*, Wayne Hester recalls that in 1933, just prior to Thomas's first win over Tennessee, he stuck the lighted end of a cigar in his mouth. Before another game, according to Hester, Thomas was so nervous that he literally urinated in his pants. A player saw what was happening and asked Thomas about it. "Aw, yeah, I'm just nervous," he said.

Thomas's nervousness eventually caught up with him. In 1945 he was diagnosed with high blood pressure and by 1946 he was in such poor health that he had to coach the entire season while riding around in a homemade cart. He retired after that season at the age of forty-eight.

When the College Football Hall of Fame was established in 1951, Thomas was one of the charter members. He died on May 10, 1954.

SCHOOL	YEARS	RECORD
Alabama	1931–46	115–24–7

SEC championships: (4)—'33, '34, '37, '45
National championships: (2)—'34, '41

Mississippi coach John Vaught (photo courtesy of the *Atlanta Journal-Constitution*).

John Vaught Mississippi **1947–73**

In January of 1947 thirty-seven-year-old John Vaught had a difficult decision to make. Mississippi head coach Harold "Red" Drew was leaving after just one season to become the head coach at Alabama, replacing Frank Thomas. Vaught could go with Drew to Alabama, one of college football's most successful programs, or stay in Oxford and take over as head coach. The Rebels had just completed a difficult 2–7 season and the immediate future looked uncertain. Both jobs would pay about $12,000 per year.

While Drew's other assistants were waiting in the car to take Vaught to Tuscaloosa, Vaught decided to remain in Oxford and see if he could make it as a head coach.

His decision turned out to be the most important in the history of Ole Miss football. Vaught was the Rebels' head coach for twenty-five seasons. In that span he won 190 games, six SEC championships, and three national championships. To this day, Vaught's tenure is considered the golden age of football at Ole Miss.

The sixth of eleven children who grew up together on a Texas farm, Vaught possessed a number of qualities that made him a successful head coach. At an early age, he learned the importance of hard work, discipline, and attention to detail from his grandmother. In his book, *Rebel Coach*, Vaught writes that when he lived with his grandmother, she would not tolerate anything that was not done perfectly. If he mowed the lawn improperly, she would make him mow it again and again until it was done to her standards of perfection.

"I didn't realize it at the time, but Grandmother taught me the qualities of good leadership," Vaught wrote. "She taught me that something half done was a failure, and that fits my coaching philosophy."

Vaught was a master of game preparation, a quality he learned from Coach Francis Schmidt when he was a player at Texas Christian from 1929 to 1932. Schmidt was obsessive about everything, but especially about game preparation. During practice one day he forced his team to run a play seventy-two consecutive times until they got it right.

Schmidt was one of the first coaches to study films of opponents and would invite Vaught, a smallish offensive guard, into the physics lab to watch with him. Vaught began using film to prepare for every possible situation he might face in a game, a method he would use throughout his career.

As head coach at Ole Miss, Vaught got off to a strong start. With the help of quarterback Charlie Conerly and end Barney Poole, Ole Miss upset Kentucky and coach Bear Bryant 14–7 in Vaught's first game. The Rebels went on to finish the regular season 8–2 and win the SEC championship.

In 1947 the Sugar Bowl extended an invitation to Ole Miss, but during the previous summer Vaught had agreed to send his team to the new Delta Bowl in Memphis to play Texas Christian. Vaught wanted to help the Delta Bowl get started and liked the idea of playing against his alma mater. Ole Miss fans wanted Vaught to break the contract with the Delta Bowl, but he remembered another lesson his grandmother had taught him: Always keep your word. Ole Miss played TCU in the Delta Bowl, winning 13–9.

Vaught's teams in 1959, 1960, and 1962 were named national champions by various wire services, and his 1959 team was voted the SEC Team of the Decade.

On January 13, 1971, sixty-one-year-old Vaught stepped down from his post as head coach in compliance with his doctor, who had said that Vaught would have to retire or risk a fatal heart attack. But a stunning series of events brought Vaught out of retirement in 1973. After the Rebels started 1–2, which included a 17–13 loss to Memphis State, both head coach Billy Kinard and athletics director Frank "Bruiser" Kinard were abruptly fired. Vaught took over both positions and coached the team for the rest of the season, winning 5 of the remaining 8 games.

After winning his final game, a 38–10 victory over Mississippi State, Vaught retired again—this time for good. He remained at Mississippi as the athletics director until 1977. He was inducted into the College Football Hall of Fame in 1979.

SCHOOL	YEARS	RECORD
Mississippi	1947–71, 73	190–61–12

SEC championships: (6)—'47, '54, '55, '60, '62, '63
National championships: (3)—'59, '60, '62

Wallace Wade Alabama, Duke **1923–50**

If it had not been for the poor timing of a search committee at Kentucky, Alabama could have been deprived of the man who established the great Crimson Tide tradition.

Duke coach Wallace Wade (left) left the school in 1942 to serve in World War II (photo courtesy of the *Atlanta Journal-Constitution*).

In 1923 Wallace Wade, an assistant at Vanderbilt, was up for the head-coaching job at both Kentucky and Alabama. Wade visited Kentucky first, and after the interview the search committee asked him to step outside while they had a discussion. They left him out in the hall for three hours.

Wade, a temperamental man who did not take such slights lightly, stormed into the room and announced that he was going to Alabama. He further vowed that no team of his would ever—ever—lose to Kentucky.

Wade made good during his brilliant career at Alabama, where he was 61–13–3 in eight seasons, and at Duke, where he was 110–36–7 in sixteen seasons. In those twenty-four seasons his teams met Kentucky a total of 11 times and won each time.

Ironically, Wade would be called "The Bear" some thirty-five years before Paul "Bear" Bryant came to Alabama in 1958. But when Wade's players called him "Bear," it was not with affection. Wade was rough and tough and a total disciplinarian.

But he got results. In just three seasons Wade had led Alabama to the Rose Bowl, where the Crimson Tide upset Washington 20–19 in one of the biggest wins ever in the history of Southern football. That season Wade also led Alabama to the first of its twelve national championships. In 1926 Alabama went back to the Rose Bowl, tying Stanford and winning another national championship.

Then Alabama faced three straight difficult seasons (5–4–1, 6–3, 6–3), at least by Alabama standards. Wade could not understand the criticism he was receiving in light of his national championships in 1925 and 1926. Feeling unappreciated, he announced in April of 1930 that he had accepted an offer from Duke and would leave Alabama after the next season. Wade went out with his guns blazing as Alabama earned a 10–0 record and won the Rose Bowl and another national championship.

At Duke, Wade won 110 games in sixteen years. He took the Blue Devils to the Rose Bowl and won six conference championships. In 1942, at the age of fifty-two, Wade left Duke and joined the Army. He fought in World War II in the Battle of Normandy and received the Bronze Star.

After four seasons away from coaching, Wade returned to Duke in 1946 and retired after the 1950 season.

In *Century of Champions*, Wayne Hester tells the story of the day in 1980 when eighty-eight-year-old Wade returned to the Alabama campus for a reunion of his 1930 Rose Bowl team. When he arrived in Tuscaloosa, he was driven directly to Bear Bryant's practice field. Bryant, in the waning years of his career, came down from his famous tower and gathered the Alabama players around him. Then Bryant pointed to Wade and said, "Boys, this man standing here is responsible for the great tradition of Alabama football."

Wallace Wade died on October 6, 1986, at the age of ninety-four. He was inducted into the College Football Hall of Fame in 1955.

SCHOOL	YEARS	RECORD
Alabama	1923–30	61–13–3
Duke	1931–50*	110–36–7
Total	24 seasons	171–49–10

**From 1942 to 1945, Wade did not coach because he was serving in World War II.*

Southern Conference championships: (10)—'24, '25, '26, '30, '33, '35, '36, '38, '39, '41
National championships: (3)—'25, '26, '30

The Best of the Rest

Here are twenty more coaches who have earned a special place in the history of Southern college football.

WILLIAM ALEXANDER took over at Georgia Tech when John Heisman left Atlanta to return to Pennsylvania in 1920. He stayed for twenty-five seasons, winning 134 games and the 1928 national championship and leading his teams to all four major bowls. He also had the vision to hire Bobby Dodd away from Tennessee and General Robert Neyland—for the exorbitant sum of $300 a month. As a student, assistant coach, head coach, and athletics director, Alexander was on the Georgia Tech campus for forty-four years. He was inducted into the College Football Hall of Fame in 1951.

Frank Broyles (photo courtesy of *Atlanta Journal-Constitution*).

FRANK BROYLES played for Bobby Dodd at Georgia Tech. He was an offensive coordinator for the Yellow Jackets when he was named head coach at Missouri in 1957. After one season at Missouri, Broyles was named head coach at Arkansas. In nineteen seasons at Arkansas Broyles won 144 games, six Southwest Conference championships, and the 1964 national championship. Broyles retired as coach after the 1976 season but remained at Arkansas as the athletic director, a post he continues to hold going into the 2000 football season.

WALLACE BUTTS, "The Little Round Man," won four SEC titles and 140 games in his twenty-two seasons at Georgia. He developed twelve All-Americans, including Fran Tarkenton, the Hall of Fame quarterback, and running backs Frank Sinkwich and Charley Trippi. In 1997, Butts was posthumously inducted into the College Football Hall of Fame.

JERRY CLAIBORNE won 179 games in a twenty-eight-year coaching career that included stops at Virginia Tech, Maryland, and Kentucky. Claiborne played for Bear Bryant at Kentucky and began his head-coaching career at Virginia Tech in 1961. He was named coach of the year in three different conferences—Southern (1963), ACC (1973, 1975, 1976), and SEC (1983)—and won three straight ACC titles at Maryland (1974–76). His 1976 team finished 11–1. Claiborne was inducted into the College Football Hall of Fame in 1999.

Georgia coach Wally Butts with Fran Tarkenton (10) and Pat Dye (60) in 1959 (photo courtesy of the *Atlanta Journal-Constitution*).

BILL DOOLEY, brother of Hall of Fame coach Vince Dooley of Georgia, won 161 games in twenty-six seasons at North Carolina, Virginia Tech, and Wake Forest. His greatest success occurred at North Carolina, where he won three ACC championships (1971, 1972, 1977). He retired after coaching his final season at Wake Forest in 1992.

PAT DYE was an All-American guard at Georgia but served his coaching apprenticeship as an assistant to Alabama's Bear Bryant from 1965 to 1973. He coached for six seasons at East Carolina and one at Wyoming before becoming head coach at Auburn in 1981. Dye won 99 games and four SEC championships in twelve seasons at Auburn. He fielded Heisman Trophy winner Bo Jackson in 1985 and as athletic director was responsible for bringing the Auburn-Alabama game to the Auburn campus for the first time in history. Dye retired from coaching after the 1992 season.

JAKE GAITHER coached at Florida A&M for twenty-five years, winning 203 games. His 84.4 winning percentage is sixth among all-time college coaches.

RAY GRAVES won 70 games in ten seasons at Florida (1960–69) and was inducted into the College Football Hall of Fame in 1990.

FRANK HOWARD was Clemson's colorful coach for thirty years. He won 165 games, eight conference championships (Southern and ACC), and a million more hearts during his tenure as the coach of his beloved Tigers. Howard passed away on January 28, 1998,

Harry Mehre (photo courtesy of the *Atlanta Journal-Constitution*).

at the age of eighty-five and was inducted into the College Football Hall of Fame in 1989.

ROY KIDD will enjoy his thirty-sixth season at Eastern Kentucky in the year 2000. His total of 293 career victories is sixth nationally among active coaches at all levels.

HARRY MEHRE was the Notre Dame center who snapped the ball to the fabled Four Horsemen when they were sophomores in 1922. Six years later Mehre became the head coach at Georgia on Knute Rockne's recommendation. After ten years and 58 wins at Georgia, Mehre coached at Ole Miss for eight seasons.

CHARLIE McCLENDON played for Bear Bryant at Kentucky and then went on to coach LSU to the most consistent success in its history—137 wins in eighteen seasons (1962–79).

ALLYN MCKEEN remains the most successful coach in Mississippi State history, having won seventy-six percent of his games (65–19–3) in nine seasons (1939–48). The Tennessee graduate took the Bulldogs to the Orange Bowl after their 10–0–1 season in 1940. He was inducted into the College Football Hall of Fame in 1991.

JOHNNY MAJORS won a national championship (1976) as Pittsburgh's head coach before returning to Tennessee, his alma mater, in 1977. Majors won three SEC championships at Tennessee and left after the 1992 season to finish out his career at Pittsburgh. He won 185 games in twenty-nine seasons as a head coach. Majors was inducted into the College Football Hall of Fame as a player.

Alabama coach Bear Bryant with his friend, LSU's Charlie McClendon (photo courtesy of the *Atlanta Journal-Constitution*).

JOHN MERRITT won 232 games in thirty-one seasons—the fifteenth highest win total of all time—as head coach at Jackson State and Tennessee State. He was inducted into the College Football Hall of Fame in 1994.

JESS NEELY coached at Clemson for only nine seasons (1931–39), but he had a profound effect on the Tigers' program. In 1939, his final season, Clemson went 9–1 and then beat Boston College in the Cotton Bowl, the school's first bowl appearance ever. The Tigers finished twelfth in the final Associated Press poll, their first-ever Top 20 season. Neely left Clemson and spent the next twenty-six years at Rice, where he led the Owls to four Southwest Conference championships. He retired with 207 career wins and was inducted into the College Football Hall of Fame in 1971.

Georgia Tech's Bobby Dodd (right) with Rice coach Jess Neely in 1960 (photo courtesy of the *Atlanta Journal-Constitution*).

JIM TATUM had three ten-win seasons from 1951 to 1955 at Maryland and won a national championship in 1953. He won seventy-two percent of his games, but his career was tragically cut short after fourteen seasons. In the summer of 1959, two years after he returned to his alma mater, North Carolina, Tatum died of Rocky Mountain Spotted Fever.

From left to right, Oklahoma's Bud Wilkinson, Maryland's Jim Tatum, and Kentucky's Bear Bryant in 1952 (photo courtesy of the *Atlanta Journal-Constitution*).

CLARK SHAUGHNESSY won 149 games as the head coach at Tulane, the University of Chicago, and Loyola of New Orleans, but he is best remembered as the most successful coach in Tulane history. He won 59 games in ten seasons with records of 8–1 in 1924 and 9–0 in 1925. He was inducted into the College Football Hall of Fame in 1968.

THAD "PIE" VANN lettered for four years in baseball and football at Ole Miss. In 1937 he came to Southern Mississippi as a line coach and baseball coach and he never left. Vann became the head football coach for the Golden Eagles in 1949 and held the post for twenty years, winning 139 games and capturing the mythical small-college national championship in 1958 and 1962. He was inducted into the College Football Hall of Fame in 1987.

GEORGE WELSH took over at Virginia in 1982 and led the Cavaliers to their most successful period in the school's history. From 1987 to 1999 Virginia posted thirteen consecutive winning seasons. Through the 1999 season Welsh had won 183 games in twenty-six seasons. He is the winningest coach at two schools—Virginia (128 wins) and Navy (55 wins), where he finished third in the Heisman Trophy voting as a player in 1955.

Southern Coaches in the College Football Hall of Fame

NAME	SCHOOL(S)	YEARS COACHED	INDUCTED
Joe Aillet	Louisiana Tech	1940–66	1989
Bill Alexander	Georgia Tech	1920–44	1951
Charlie Bachman	Florida, Michigan State, Kansas State, Northwestern	1919–53	1978
Dana X. Bible	Mississippi College, Texas A&M, Texas, LSU, Nebraska	1913–46	1951
Bernie Bierman	Tulane, Montana, Mississippi State, Minnesota	1919–50	1955
Frank Broyles	Missouri, Arkansas	1957–76	1983
Paul W. Bryant	Maryland, Texas A&M, Kentucky, Alabama	1945–82	1986
Wallace Butts	Georgia	1939–60	1997
Jerry Claiborne	Virginia Tech, Maryland, Kentucky	1961–82	1999
Bobby Dodd	Georgia Tech	1945–66	1959
Mike Donahue	Auburn, LSU	1904–27	1951
Vince Dooley	Georgia	1964–88	1994
Bill Edwards	Wittenberg, Vanderbilt, Western Reserve	1935–68	1986
Ray Graves	Florida	1960–69	1990
Andy Gustafson	Miami (Florida), Virginia Tech	1926–63	1985
Jack Harding	Scranton, Miami (Florida)	1926–47	1980
John Heisman	Auburn, Clemson, Georgia Tech, Oberlin, Akron, Pennsylvania, Washington & Jefferson, Rice	1892–1926	1954
Frank Howard	Clemson	1940–69	1989
Biff Jones	Army, Oklahoma, LSU, Nebraska	1926–41	1954
Ralph "Shug" Jordan	Auburn	1951–75	1982
Charlie McClendon	LSU	1962–79	1986
Dan McGugin	Vanderbilt	1904–34	1951
Allyn McKeen	Memphis State, Mississippi State	1937–48	1991
John Merritt	Jackson State, Tennessee State	1953–83	1994
Scrappy Moore	Chattanooga	1931–67	1980

Bernie Moore	Mercer, LSU	1925–47	1954
Ray Morrison	SMU, Vanderbilt	1915–51	1954
Bill Murray	Duke, Delaware	1940–65	1974
Frank Murray	Marquette, Virginia	1922–49	1974
Jess Neely	Clemson, Rice, Rhodes	1924–66	1971
Robert R. Neyland	Tennessee	1926–52	1956
Eddie Robinson	Grambling	1941–97	1997
Darrell K. Royal	Mississippi State, Washington, Texas	1954–76	1983
Red Sanders	Vanderbilt, UCLA	1949–57	1996
Francis Schmidt	Tulsa, Texas, TCU, Arkansas, Idaho, Ohio State	1919–42	1971
Clark Shaughnessy	Tulane, University of Chicago, Loyola (New Orleans)	1915–65	1968
Buck Shaw	N.C. State, Nevada, California, Santa Clara, Air Force	1924–57	1972
Carl Snavely	North Carolina, Bucknell, Cornell	1927–58	1965
Jim Tatum	Maryland, Oklahoma, North Carolina	1942–58	1984
Frank Thomas	Chattanooga, Alabama	1925–46	1951
Thad "Pie" Vann	Southern Mississippi	1949–68	1987
John H. Vaught	Mississippi	1947–73	1979
Wallace Wade	Alabama, Duke	1923–50	1955
Glenn "Pop" Warner	Georgia, Pittsburgh, Cornell, Carlise	1895–38	1951
Bowden C. Wyatt	Tennessee, Wyoming, Arkansas	1955–62	1972

GREAT TEAMS

Southern Fried Football's All-Time Teams and Dynasties

THE TOP 25

1. Sewanee, 1899 (12–0)

The Tigers from Tennessee's Sewanee went 12–0 in 1899, but that's not why this team is No. 1. In November Sewanee took the ultimate road trip, playing 5 games in six days, all on the road. And not only did the Tigers win them all, but all 5 wins were by shutouts. The Tigers began their trip at Texas (12–0) and then beat Texas A&M (10–0), Tulane (23–0), LSU (34–0), and Ole Miss (12–0) by a combined score of 91–0. Before the trip, Sewanee had beaten Georgia, Georgia Tech, and Tennessee. After the trip the Tigers closed out the season with an 11–10 win over Auburn (the only team to score on the Tigers all season long) and a 5–0 win over North Carolina. As a result, Sewanee confidently declared itself the champion of Southern college football.

The Sewanee team of 1899 won 5 games in six days—all by shutouts, all on the road (photo courtesy of Sewanee SID).

2. Ole Miss, 1959 (10–1)

Ole Miss was so good in 1959 that despite having suffered one loss, the team was named the SEC Team of the Decade by the Associated Press. Coach John Vaught knew this team had a chance to be special, but he didn't know that his 1959 Ole Miss team would close out the season just two yards short of perfection. The Rebels were deep at every position and had two future Hall of Famers in quarterback Jake Gibbs and fullback Charlie Flowers. The team was undefeated and ranked No. 3 in the nation when it traveled to play No. 1 LSU, the defending national champion, on Halloween night. The world will always remember Billy Cannon's eighty-nine-yard punt return that gave LSU a 7–3 lead. What the world doesn't remember is that the Rebels drove all the way down to the LSU 2-yard line inside the final minute. On fourth down Ole Miss was stopped and LSU won the game. The Rebels went on to finish 9–1 and were able to avenge their only loss of the season by beating the Tigers 21–0 in the Sugar Bowl.

3. Duke, 1938 (9–1)

The 1938 Blue Devils, led by future Hall of Fame center Dan Hill and coach Wallace Wade, went through the regular season unbeaten and unscored upon. That success earned the Blue Devils a trip to the Rose Bowl, the first post-season game in school history. Duke led 3–0 after a field goal early in the fourth quarter and was within one minute of perfection when Southern California drove the length of the field with three quick passes and scored a touchdown with only forty seconds left, winning 7–3. Despite the

The 1938 "Iron Dukes" did not allow a point during the regular season (photo courtesy of Duke SID).

George "Bad News" Cafego led the great Tennessee team of 1938 (photo courtesy of Tennessee SID).

disappointing loss, the "Iron Dukes," as the team became known, are remembered as one of the greatest teams in Southern football history.

4. Tennessee, 1938 (11–0)

Many fans believe the 1938 team was Tennessee's best under legendary coach Robert Neyland. The Volunteers gave up ten points in their first 2 wins against Sewanee and Clemson and were not scored on again during the rest of the season. Tennessee was declared the national champion by several wire services after its 10–0 regular season and then went on to snap Oklahoma's 14-game winning streak with a 17–0 win in the Orange Bowl. Future Hall of Famers George "Bad News" Cafego and Bowden Wyatt (who would later become the head coach at Tennessee) were the stars of the team.

5. Alabama, 1934 (10–0)

Coach Frank Thomas, who took over at Alabama after Wallace Wade left in 1931, led the 1934 Crimson Tide team to the Rose Bowl in his fourth season as coach. With the passing combination of Dixie Howell to Don Hutson, the best of that era (or any era, some might say), the Crimson Tide rolled to a 9–0 regular-season record and then beat Stanford 29–13 in the Rose Bowl. The 1934 Alabama team outscored its regular season opponents 316–45, and only one team, Tennessee, came within twenty points of the Tide. After falling behind Stanford 7–0 in the Rose Bowl, Howell and Hutson dazzled the crowd with twenty-two unanswered points in the second quarter. Famed sportswriter Grantland Rice called it "one of the greatest all-around exhibitions football has ever known." Howell and Hutson went on to the College Football Hall of Fame, as did the "other" end on the 1934 team: Paul "Bear" Bryant.

Alabama coach Frank Thomas with starting quarterback Dixie Howell in 1934 (photo courtesy of the *Atlanta Journal-Constitution*).

Maryland coach Jim Tatum with All-Americans Dick Modzelewski (left) and Jack Scarbath in 1951 (photo courtesy of the *Atlanta Journal-Constitution*).

6. Maryland, 1951 (10–0)

Maryland's 1953 team won the national championship, but many Terrapin fans still believe the 1951 team, led by quarterback Jack Scarbath and head coach Jim Tatum, was better. Scarbath and Tatum were just two of many on the 1951 team who would later be inducted into the College Football Hall of Fame. Offensive guard Bob Ward, at the bruising weight of 165 pounds, was a first-team All-American, and Dick "Little Mo" Modzelewski was an All-American defensive lineman. Dick's brother Ed ("Big Mo") made several All-America teams as a running back. The Terps did not play a ranked team during the regular season and beat eight of nine opponents by nineteen points or more. Despite the objections of Southern Conference officials, the No. 3–ranked Terps accepted a bid to play mighty No. 1 Tennessee in the Sugar Bowl. The Volunteers were 10–0 and had already been declared the national champions. But Maryland jumped out to a 21–0 lead against the stunned Volunteers and won the game 28–13. The beating was so thorough that General Robert Neyland, the famed Tennessee coach, simply said after the game: "We were soundly beaten by a superior team."

7. Tennessee, 1951 (10–1)

If the national championship had been decided after the bowl games, Tennessee would have won it all in 1950. The Volunteers lost their second game of the season to Mississippi State (7–0) but then rolled through the rest of their schedule, beating No. 3 Texas 20–14 in the Cotton Bowl while No. 1 Oklahoma and No. 2 Army also lost their respective games. As it turned out, the disappointment of 1950 set the stage for a 10–0 regular season in 1951. The Vols were led by running back Hank Lauricella, the Heisman Trophy runnerup

Georgia Tech's 1952 national championship team had six All-Americans (left to right): Leon Hardeman, George Morris, Buck Martin, Bobby Moorehead, Pete Brown, and Hal Miller (photo courtesy of Georgia Tech SID).

that year, and Doug Atkins, the only Tennessee player in both the college and pro football halls of fame. Tennessee was declared the national champion after the regular season and missed out on a perfect season by losing to Maryland 28–13 in the Sugar Bowl.

8. Alabama, 1992 (13–0)

After a 12–0 regular season that included a 28–21 victory over Florida in the first SEC championship game, few gave No. 2 Alabama a chance against No. 1 Miami in the Sugar Bowl. The Hurricanes were the defending national champions and were led by Heisman Trophy–winning quarterback Gino Torretta. The Crimson Tide had not won a national championship since 1979, but third-year coach Gene Stallings said his team was not an underdog. Stallings was right. Thanks to a brilliant game plan devised by defensive coordinator Bill "Brother" Oliver, Alabama, led by ends Eric Curry and John Copeland, hounded Torretta and defeated Miami 34–13. Seven players on Alabama's defense made one of the various All-SEC teams.

9. Georgia Tech, 1952 (12–0)

Bobby Dodd called the 1952 Yellow Jackets "the best team I ever coached," and for a very good reason. The Yellow Jackets, with future Hall of Fame linebackers George Morris and Larry Morris, gave up double-digit points in only 1 game, a 17–14 win over Florida. In its other 11 games, Georgia Tech allowed only forty-five points. Still, there were some anxious moments along the way. Quarterback Pepper Rodgers had to kick a field goal to beat Florida, and Jakie Rudolph, a 5'7", 155-pound running back, had to tackle Alabama's Bobby Marlowe on fourth down on the 4-yard line to preserve a 7–3 win. Georgia Tech then went on to defeat unbeaten Mississippi 24–7 in the Sugar Bowl. The AP and UPI polls named Michigan State, which had finished 9–0 but had not played in a bowl game, the national champion, but the International News Service awarded the honor to the Yellow Jackets.

10. Georgia, 1942 (11–1)

Arguably the best team in Georgia's football history, the 1942 Bulldogs had what became known as the "Dream Backfield" of Frank Sinkwich, the Heisman Trophy winner that season, and Charley Trippi, who would receive the Maxwell Award as college football's best player in 1946. The Bulldogs rolled through nine straight opponents, including a sound beating of No. 1 Alabama 21–10 in Atlanta. On November 21, No. 1–ranked Georgia traveled to Columbus, Georgia, to play Auburn. Although Georgia was a heavy favorite against Auburn, which had a 3–4–1 record, the Bulldogs lost 27–13 in one of the biggest upsets in the history of both schools. Still, Georgia closed out the regular season with a 34–0 win over No. 2 Georgia Tech and then went on to the Rose Bowl, where it beat UCLA 9–0. Georgia was named the national champion in six polls recognized by the NCAA.

11. Tennessee, 1998 (13–0)

In 1998, the year after the departure of quarterback Peyton Manning, many Volunteer fans worried that the program would sag. Instead, Tennessee went 13–0, won its second straight SEC championship, and then beat Florida State in the Fiesta Bowl for the national championship, the school's first since 1951. But it wasn't easy. Three times the Volunteers had to rally from behind in the fourth quarter to win. In the opener, a 34–33 victory over Syracuse, the Vols had to drive the length of the field to set Jeff Hall up for a field goal as time expired. Hall also kicked a field goal in overtime to beat Florida 20–17. The Vols' offense was led by the big-play combination of quarterback Tee Martin and wide receiver Peerless Price, while the defense was anchored by linebacker Al Wilson.

12. Auburn, 1957 (10–0)

Coach Ralph "Shug" Jordan thought his seventh Auburn team would be able to realize its full potential if only he could find a strong quarterback. Having kicked his No. 1 quarterback off the team for disciplinary reasons, Jordan turned to left-hander Lloyd Nix, who had been a halfback the season before, and the rest was Tiger history. Nix knew his job was not to win the game but to keep from making mistakes so the team

Auburn's 1957 team went 10–0 and won the national championship (photo courtesy of Auburn SID).

wouldn't lose it. He could afford to play conservatively because Auburn's defense, led by Zeke Smith, the 1958 Outland Trophy winner, was tremendous. Before the season ended, Auburn had shut out six opponents and the other four were held to just seven points each. The offense did only what it had to do. The Tigers scored seven points against Tennessee, six against Kentucky, three against Georgia Tech, and six against Georgia—and won all 4 games. Unranked when the season began, Auburn was No. 1 by the final game with Alabama. The Tigers then went out and pounded Alabama 40–0 and were named the consensus national champions. Ironically, it was this beating by Auburn that forced Alabama to go to Texas A&M and hire Paul "Bear" Bryant as its head coach. Despite Auburn's successful season, the team did not play in a bowl game due to NCAA penalties.

13. Florida State, 1993 (11–1)

For six straight seasons leading up to 1993 Florida State had won 10 or more games and had finished in the final top four of the polls. But in spite of all that success, coach Bobby Bowden did not have a national championship to show for it. Critics were beginning to say that Bowden, in his eighteenth season at Florida State, couldn't win the big one. Every year the Seminoles would lose a big game, usually against Miami, that would keep Florida State out of the national championship hunt. It had apparently happened again in 1993 when No. 1 Florida State lost at No. 2 Notre Dame 31–24 on November 6. Even Bowden conceded at the time that losing a big game so late in the season would make it almost impossible to get back into the national championship race. But then fate stepped in.

Florida State quarterback Charlie Ward leads the Seminoles to a win over Nebraska in the 1994 Orange Bowl (photo courtesy of Florida State SID).

The following week, Notre Dame, now ranked No. 1, was stunned by Boston College 41–39 at home, and dropped to No. 4 in the polls. Florida State, which had only dropped to No. 2 after its loss against Notre Dame, jumped back up to No. 1 in the Associated Press poll and stayed there. Florida State then played No. 2 Nebraska in the Orange Bowl for the national championship and won the game 18–16, though it didn't happen without some drama. When Byron Bennett kicked a twenty-seven-yard field goal with 1:16 left to give the Cornhuskers a 16–15 lead, it seemed that Nebraska had won the game. But Florida State quarterback Charlie Ward, that year's Heisman Trophy winner, drove the Seminoles into position for a twenty-two-yard field goal by Scott Bentley with twenty-one seconds left, giving Florida State the lead. Bowden had to hold his breath as Bennett missed a forty-five-yard field goal on the last play of the game.

14. LSU, 1958 (11–0)

After Paul Dietzel had won only 11 games in his first three seasons as LSU's head coach, no one had any reason to think that the Tigers would be anything special in 1958. The Tigers were young, with only three seniors among the top fifty-five players. But Dietzel knew better. He had some weapons, beginning with junior running back Billy Cannon, who would go on to win the Heisman Trophy the next year. Dietzel also had talented depth, so much so that he fielded two separate offenses: the White Team (the first team)

The LSU Chinese Bandits of 1958 (photo courtesy of LSU SID).

and the Gold Team, which was later shorted to "Go Team." Dietzel called his defense the "Chinese Bandits," after an old comic strip that said the "Chinese Bandits" were "the most vicious people in the world."

With these three units LSU marched through the regular season 10–0. LSU was named the national champion, but the team had encountered some rough spots along the way. In a game against Florida, the Tigers needed, and made, a twenty-nine-yard field goal in the final three minutes to win 10–7. In a game against Ole Miss, LSU held the Rebels out of the end zone after the Rebels had reached the LSU one-foot line and went on to win 14–0. In a game against Mississippi State, LSU scored a touchdown in the third quarter to win 7–6. LSU beat Tulane 62–0 to win the national championship, which, in those days, the wire services announced at the end of the regular season. LSU then closed out its most memorable season with a 7–0 win over Clemson in the Sugar Bowl.

15. Ole Miss, 1960 (10–0–1)

With the bulk of their 1959 team returning, including quarterback Jake Gibbs, the Rebels expected to win another SEC championship in 1960 and compete for the national title. And that's exactly what they did, topping off an undefeated season with a 14–6 win over Rice in the Sugar Bowl. The Rebels only encountered two anxious moments along the way: on October 22 in Little Rock, when Allen Green kicked a thirty-nine-yard field goal on the last play of the game to beat Arkansas 10–7; and a week later, when Green kicked a forty-one-yard field goal with six seconds left to tie LSU 6–6. The tie with LSU was the

Quarterback Jake Gibbs led Ole Miss to a win over LSU in the 1960 Sugar Bowl (photo courtesy of Mississippi SID).

only mark on Mississippi's record that season. After they won the Sugar Bowl the Rebels were ranked No. 2, but later that day No. 1 Minnesota was upset by Washington in the Rose Bowl, 17–7, and Ole Miss won the Grantland Rice Trophy, which goes to the national champion as selected by the Football Writers Association of America.

16. Clemson, 1981 (12–0)

Clemson had gone 6–5 in 1980 and as a result was not ranked in any of the preseason polls for 1981. Danny Ford, Clemson's thirty-three-year-old coach, had led his teams to a 14–6 record in his first two seasons, and some fans wondered if he was the right guy for the job. But all those doubts were put to rest when Clemson went through the regular season undefeated and beat Nebraska in the Orange Bowl to win the school's first national championship in any sport. Clemson finished the year as the only undefeated, untied team in the country, with wins over three top ten teams—Georgia (13–3), North Carolina (10–8), and Nebraska (22–5). Clemson won the championship with a defense that forced forty-one turnovers in 12 games, still a school record. The Tigers had five different players earn All-American honors, including linebacker Jeff Davis, the team's spiritual leader. Four players from this Clemson team would go on to become NFL first-round draft choices, and twenty-two would play in the NFL.

17. Florida State, 1999 (12–0)

Coach Bobby Bowden will remember the 1999 season for a lot of reasons. On November 8, the grandfather of twenty-one turned seventy years old. On October 23, he became only the fifth coach in the history of Division I football to win three hundred games, a milestone he reached after defeating Clemson, coached by his son Tommy, 17–14 in the first-ever father-son coaching showdown. But on January 4, 2000, the Florida State team gave its coach the best present of all, a 46–29 win over No. 2 Virginia Tech in the Sugar Bowl. The win gave Bowden his second national championship and his very first undefeated season in thirty-four years as a head coach. The 1999 team was not Bowden's most talented by a long shot, but because the players had to face so much adversity, it was one of his closest teams. The previous January, the Seminoles lost to Tennessee 23–16 in the Fiesta Bowl, losing the national title with it. "That day, this group of guys dedicated themselves to getting back in this position again," Bowden said. Then, star receiver Peter Warrick, the Heisman Trophy favorite, was arrested on charges of theft. Warrick was allowed to return to the team after a 2-game suspension. Led by junior quarterback Chris Weinke, the twenty-seven-year-old former pro baseball player, Florida State rallied from a 29–28 deficit in the second half of the Sugar Bowl to win comfortably over the Hokies. Weinke threw four touchdown passes and Warrick went out in a blaze of glory as he caught two touchdown passes and returned a punt for a third. In 1999, Florida State became the first team since the Associated Press created its preseason poll in 1950 to begin a season at No. 1 and stay there.

18. Florida, 1996 (12–1)

As is often the case, the seeds that blossomed into Florida's first national championship team were sown in disappointment. The season before, the Gators had gone through the regular season 12–0, winning their fourth SEC championship that decade. But in the national championship game against Nebraska in the Fiesta Bowl the Gators were humiliated 62–24. It was then that coach Steve Spurrier decided to make some changes. He brought in Bobby Stoops of Kansas State, which had been No. 1 in defense nationally the year before, to serve as the team's new defensive coordinator. His defense, plus a high-powered offense led by Heisman Trophy winner Danny Wuerffel and future NFL receivers Reidel Anthony, Ike Hilliard, and Jacquez Green, put the Gators into the race for the national title in 1996. Still, Florida needed some good fortune to get in position to win the championship. The Gators were 10–0 and ranked No. 1 when they traveled to No. 2 Florida State on November 30. Wuerffel took a severe pounding from the Florida State defense that day and the Seminoles prevailed 24–21. Florida, which dropped to No. 4 in the polls after the loss, thought it had lost its chance at a national championship. But then fate stepped in. On December 7 Florida beat Alabama 45–30 for the SEC championship. Earlier that day, unranked Texas shocked No. 3 Nebraska 37–27 in the Big 12 championship game. No. 2 Arizona State had committed to play Ohio State in the Rose Bowl, so Sugar Bowl officials took the No. 3 Gators in a rematch with No. 1 Florida State. On January 1, No. 2 Arizona State lost to Ohio State, which meant that the winner of the Sugar Bowl on January 2 would be the national champion. Using a shotgun formation against the strong Florida State pass rush, the Gators dominated the Seminoles 52–20 to win the national title.

19. Miami, 1991 (12–0)

The Hurricanes won four national championships from 1983 to 1991. But a strong case can be made that the 1991 squad was Miami's best during this incredible dynasty. That year the Hurricanes went 12–0 against a schedule that included four teams in the top ten. They capped off this strong performance with a solid 22–0 thumping of No. 11 Nebraska in the Orange Bowl. Miami had begun the season ranked No. 3 and had moved to No. 2 after a 31–3 win over Arkansas in their season opener. The Hurricanes were still No. 2 when they traveled to Florida State and knocked off the No. 1 Seminoles 17–16. Miami moved into the No. 1 spot in the next Associated Press poll and stayed there through its victory in the Orange Bowl.

The 1991 Hurricanes were named the national champions in the Associate Press media poll while Washington, which had beaten Michigan in the Rose Bowl to finish 12–0, was ranked No. 1 in the CNN/USA Today coaches' poll. The stellar Miami team fielded five first-team All-Americans plus junior quarterback Gino Torretta, who would go on to win the Heisman Trophy in 1992. The bulk of this Miami team would return the following season. The Hurricanes would again go 11–0 but would be denied their second straight national title after a loss to Alabama in the Sugar Bowl.

Herschel Walker, Georgia (photo courtesy of the *Atlanta Journal-Constitution*).

20. Georgia, 1980 (12–0)

After Georgia went 6–5 in 1979, few thought the Bulldogs could even compete for the SEC championship in 1980. But a freshman running back named Herschel Walker along with a group of players who had a knack for winning close games enabled the Bulldogs to go 12–0 and win the national title. Georgia had to rally from a 15–2 deficit to beat Tennessee 16–15 in the opener and Lindsay Scott caught a miraculous ninety-three-yard touchdown pass from Buck Belue to beat Florida 26–21. Georgia finished the regular season 11–0 and then beat Notre Dame 17–10 in the Sugar Bowl for the national title.

21. Maryland, 1953 (10–1)

In 1953 Maryland had lost quarterback Jack Scarbath and defensive tackle Dick Modzelewski from the great teams of 1951 and 1952. While coach Jim Tatum thought his team's No. 9 preseason ranking was a little ambitious, he privately told friends that this team had a chance to be very, very good—and he was right. Led by quarterback Bernie Faloney and a defense that posted six shutouts, Maryland capped off a 10–0 regular season with impressive wins over Mississippi (38–0) and Alabama (21–0). During the season, Maryland's defense gave up a total of only 31 points while scoring 298. The 1953 Terps were declared the national champions in the three major polls. Maryland hoped to round out the season with a win over Oklahoma in the Orange Bowl, but in the days leading up to the game in Miami, Faloney reaggravated his knee injury in practice and could not play. Without Faloney the Maryland offense could not move and thus lost to Bud Wilkinson and the Sooners 7–0. Despite this final disappointment, the 1953 team is considered one of the best in Maryland history.

22. Georgia Tech, 1928 (10–0)

When Georgia Tech scheduled Notre Dame for a series of games from 1922 and 1929, fans thought coach Bill Alexander had lost his mind. But Alex, as he was affectionately known, knew exactly what he was doing. "They will beat us nine out of ten, but in losing, we will learn a lot of football," he told the Atlanta Journal. "And when we win, it will be a mighty sweet victory." That sweet victory came in 1928, when the Yellow Jackets beat Knute Rockne and the Fighting Irish 13–0 in Atlanta. Georgia Tech used that game as the springboard to a 10–0 season and a national championship honor from the International News Service. The Yellow Jackets completed the season with an 8–7 win over California in the Rose Bowl, which included one of the most infamous plays in college football history. California's Roy Riegels picked up a Georgia Tech fumble but ran sixty-six yards the wrong way and was finally stopped on his team's one-yard line. Tech then blocked a punt for a safety and a 2–0 lead, which turned out to be the winning points in Georgia Tech's perfect season. Coach Bill Alexander and center Peter Pund would later be elected to the College Football Hall of Fame.

Wrong Way Riegels (photo courtesy of Georgia Tech SID/California SID).

23. Alabama, 1978 (11–1)

If you want to start an argument with a group of Alabama fans, ask them which one of Bear Bryant's teams of the '70s was the best. Alabama won 103 games and three national championships in the '70s, and seven of those ten teams won 11 games or more. But considering their sheer guts and determination, it would be hard to deny the Crimson Tide team of 1978 the honor of being the best Bama team of the '70s. Alabama began that season at No. 1, but when the Tide lost to Southern California 24–14, some thought Alabama's chance for a national championship was ruined. Bryant, however, would not let his team quit and promised that if they kept working hard, Alabama could still win the national title. The Tide then rolled through the rest of its schedule to finish 10–1 and earn a chance to compete for the national championship against Penn State in the Sugar Bowl. Alabama was leading 14–7 late in the game when Penn State drove down to the Alabama goal line. On fourth down, Penn State decided to go for the touchdown. Just prior to the play, Alabama tackle Marty Lyons talked to Penn State quarterback Chuck Fusina on the field.

"How far do you have to go?" Lyons asked.

"About ten inches," Fusina responded.

Lyons smiled. "Then you better pass."

Penn State didn't pass, sending tailback Mike Guman over tackle. Alabama linebacker Barry Krauss met Guman head to head and knocked him back, stopping the drive and saving the game for Alabama. Bryant, who would go on to coach just four more seasons for the Tide, called the goal-line stand "something I will never forget."

24. Miami, 1987 (12–0)

In 1986 Miami fielded one of the best college football teams ever. The No. 1 Hurricanes went through the regular season 11–0 but then lost to No. 2 Penn State 14–10 in the Fiesta Bowl for the national championship. With the departure of quarterback Vinny Testaverde, the Heisman Trophy winner, Miami's ability to get back into the national championship hunt in 1987 was questionable. But the Hurricanes, who started the season ranked No. 10, used a 26–25 win over No. 4 Florida State to propel them to an 11–0 regular season. When Miami arrived at the Orange Bowl to play No. 1 Oklahoma, the Hurricanes were ranked No. 2. With sophomore quarterback Steve Walsh, fullback Melvin Bratton, and wide receiver Michael Irvin leading the way, Miami knocked off Oklahoma 14–10 for the national title. It was Miami's first-ever undefeated season and the first national title for head coach Jimmy Johnson. Defensive back Benny Blades and defensive end Daniel Stubbs were consensus All-Americans that year.

25. Kentucky, 1950 (11–1)

Kentucky coach Bear Bryant with quarterback Babe Parilli (left) and tackle Bob Gain in 1950 (photo courtesy of the *Atlanta Journal-Constitution*).

After having coached one year at Maryland, Paul "Bear" Bryant left the Terps to become the Wildcats' head coach in 1946. His goal was to bring the first SEC football championship to basketball-crazy Kentucky, and it took only five seasons for Bryant to give the school its best football season ever. With future Hall of Famers Babe Parilli (quarterback) and Bob Gain (guard) leading the way, Kentucky went through the regular season 10–1 and won the SEC championship. The only blemish on the team's record was a 7–0 loss to Tennessee in Knoxville in the last game of the regular season. With a 5–1 conference record, Kentucky won the SEC championship over Tennessee, which was 4–1 after a 7–0 loss to Mississippi State. On January 1, Bryant coached the biggest win in the school's history—an upset of No. 1 Oklahoma, which broke the Sooners' 21-game winning streak.

Glory Days: The Top 10 Southern Dynasties

Every school has a favorite period in its college football history. The following periods of success may not all qualify as "dynasties" in the classic sense, but they do generate the fondest memories for the fans of that particular school. Here are the best of those Southern dynasties.

Miami, 1983–94

What makes the Miami dynasty different is that it took place under the leadership of three different coaches. Howard Schnellenberger left after the 1983 national championship. Jimmy Johnson took over, won a national championship in 1987, and then became coach of the Dallas Cowboys after the 1988 season. Dennis Erickson won national titles in 1989 and 1991 and left after the 1994 season. Only twice in the twelve years of their dynasty did the Hurricanes fail to win as many as 10 games. Players during this twelve-year run included two Heisman Trophy winners, an Outland Trophy winner, and a Lombardi Trophy winner.

Overall record: 125–20
National titles: (4)—1983, 1987, 1989, 1991
Coaches: Howard Schnellenberger (1983); Jimmy Johnson (1984–88); Dennis Erickson (1989–94)
Top players: Jay Brophy, Jerome Brown, Vinny Testaverde (1986 Heisman winner), Bennie Blades, Danny Stubbs, Steve Walsh, Greg Mark, Russell Maryland (1990 Outland winner), Kevin Williams, Michael Barrow, Gino Torretta (1992 Heisman winner), Warren Sapp (1994 Lombardi winner), and Michael Irvin

Gino Torretta (photo courtesy of Miami SID).

Florida State, 1987–99

It was somehow fitting that Florida State went 12–0 in 1999 and won the last national title of the 1990s, because in that decade, nobody in college football did it better. The 1999 season marked the thirteenth consecutive year that Florida State had won 10 or more games and had finished in the final top four of the Associated Press poll. Both are NCAA records. Here is a closer look at Florida State's incredible thirteen-year run.

Year	Record	Final AP ranking
1987	11–1	2
1988	11–1	3
1989	10–2	3
1990	10–2	4
1991	11–2	2
1992	11–1	2
1993	12–1	1
1994	10–1–1	4
1995	10–2	4
1996	11–1	3
1997	11–1	3
1998	11–2	3
1999	12–0	1

Overall record: 141–16–1
National titles: (2)—1993, 1999
Coach: Bobby Bowden
Top players: Charlie Ward (1993 Heisman winner), Deion Sanders, LeRoy Butler, Marvin Jones, Terrell Buckley, Derrick Brooks, Corey Sawyer, Clifton Abraham, Clay Shiver, Peter Boulware, Reinard Wilson, Warrick Dunn, Chris Weinke, Peter Warrick, Corey Simon

Alabama, 1961–67 and 1971–81

It's rare when one coach puts together two different dynasties at the same school. But Paul "Bear" Bryant, as the world now knows, was no ordinary coach. Bryant came to Alabama in 1958 and by 1961 he had won the first of his thirteen Southeastern Conference titles and the first of his six national championships. Alabama won three national championships in the sixties and should have had a fourth when its 1966 team went 10–0 and thumped Nebraska (34–7) in the Orange Bowl. That national championship went to Notre Dame. After the Tide struggled in 1968, 1969, and 1970, some fans believed that the game had passed Bryant by. But after installing the wishbone offense for the 1971 season, Bryant began an eleven-year stretch during which Alabama dominated the SEC in a way no school has done before or since. In those eleven years, Alabama won 116 games, nine SEC championships, and three national championships.

Overall record: 1961–67 (68–7–3); 1971–81 (116–15–1)
SEC titles: 13
National titles: (6)—1961, 1964, 1965, 1973, 1978, 1979
Coach: Paul "Bear" Bryant
Top players: 1961–67: Lee Roy Jordan, Billy Neighbors, Paul Crane, Cecil Dowdy, Joe Namath, Ken Stabler, Dennis Homan, Steve Sloan, Ray Perkins. 1971–81: Johnny Musso, John Hannah, Leroy Cook, Ozzie Newsome, Marty Lyons, Barry Krauss, E. J. Junior, Woodrow Lowe, John Mitchell, Don McNeal, Dwight Stephenson

Florida, 1990–1999

When 1966 Heisman Trophy winner Steve Spurrier took over as head coach in 1990, Florida had never won an SEC championship. That quickly changed. Florida finished No. 1 in the SEC in Spurrier's first season in Gainesville but could not claim the SEC title because of NCAA sanctions levied against the previous coaching staff. Over the next six years Florida would win five SEC titles (in 1992 Florida lost the title to Alabama, who would go on to win the national title as well, in the SEC championship game 28–21). In 1996, Florida won its fifth SEC title in six years and then went on to beat Florida State in the Sugar Bowl for the school's first national championship. Florida's record of 102–22–1 in the 1990s was the third best (behind Florida State and Nebraska) among schools in Division I.

Overall record: 102–22–1
SEC championships: (5)—1991, 1993, 1994, 1995, 1996
National championships: (1)—1996
Coach: Steve Spurrier
Top players: Huey Richardson, Shane Matthews, Will White, Brad Culpepper, Errict Rhett, Judd Davis, Kevin Carter, Jack Jackson, Jason Odom, Danny Wuerffel (1996 Heisman winner), Reidel Anthony, Ike Hilliard, Jacquez Green, Donnie Young, Jeff Mitchell

Georgia, 1980–83

It was only four years, but for Georgia fans it was the most glorious four years in school history. Georgia's dynasty began in 1980 when the Bulldogs were trying to rebound from a disappointing 6–5 season in 1979. Coach Vince Dooley believed his team had a chance to be special, but he needed to find one more piece to the puzzle. That piece turned out to be freshman running back Herschel Walker, who became an instant legend, leading the Bulldogs to a 12–0 season and the national championship. In 1981, Georgia went 10–2, losing to Clemson, the eventual national champion, and Pittsburgh, who it played in the Sugar Bowl. In 1982, Georgia went 12–0 and was ranked No. 1 before it lost to No. 2 Penn State in the Sugar Bowl, 27–23. In 1983, the year after Walker left school to play professional football, Georgia almost won its fourth straight SEC title. But a 13–7 loss to Auburn and Bo Jackson gave the championship to the Tigers. By the time Georgia's run was over, the team had won 43 games, three SEC championships, and one national championship.

Overall record: 43–4–1
SEC championships: (3)—1980, 1981, 1982
National championships: (1)—1980
Coach: Vince Dooley
Top players: Herschel Walker (1982 Heisman winner), Buck Belue, Lindsay Scott, Terry Hoage, Rex Robinson, Kevin Butler, Jimmy Payne, Freddie Gilbert, Jeff Sanchez, Tommy Thurson, Guy McIntyre, Eddie Weaver

Auburn, 1983–89

When Pat Dye took over as Auburn's head coach in 1981, the Tigers had not been to a bowl game since 1974 and had lost 8 straight games to Alabama, their bitter rival. Dye's timing could not have been better. In his second year he beat Alabama and Bear Bryant, his former mentor. Bryant retired after the 1982 season and Dye used that opportunity to lead Auburn to its most consistent run in history with 67 wins in seven seasons and four SEC championships. The highlight of this stretch came on December 2, 1989, when Auburn upset No. 2 Alabama 30–20 to share the SEC championship. Dye would go on to coach three more seasons before retiring in 1992.

Overall record: 67–16–1
SEC championships: (4)—1983, 1987, 1988, 1989
National championships: None
Coach: Pat Dye
Top players: Bo Jackson (1985 Heisman winner), Gregg Carr, Donnie Humphrey, Ben Tamburello, Brent Fullwood, Aundray Bruce, Kurt Crain, Stacy Searels, Tracy Rocker (1988 Outland, Lombardi winner), Walter Reeves, Benji Roland, Ed King

Pat Dye led Auburn to four SEC championships (photo courtesy of the *Atlanta Journal-Constitution*).

Tennessee, 1938–40

General Robert R. Neyland won 173 games in twenty-one years as Tennessee's head football coach, but his coaching tenure was interrupted twice by military service. The three-year stretch of 1938–40 represents the most dominating period of Neyland's legendary career. During this stretch Tennessee posted three consecutive undefeated regular seasons, losing only to Southern California (14–0) in the Rose Bowl on January 1, 1940, and to Boston College (19–13) in the Sugar Bowl on January 1, 1941. The Vols' defense was the hallmark of this incredible stretch. Of the 33 games Tennessee played in these three seasons, the Volunteers posted 26 shutouts, setting an NCAA record with 17 straight regular-season shutouts and seventy-one straight quarters without giving up a point. In 1939, Tennessee did not give up a point during the entire regular season and then lost to Southern California 14–0 in the Rose Bowl. Only one other team, Duke in 1938, has done that. Four players from these three teams were later inducted into the College Football Hall of Fame. Various wire services awarded the national championship to Tennessee in 1938 and 1940.

Overall record: 31–2
SEC championships: (3)—1938, 1939, 1940
National championships: (2)—1938, Dunkel, Litkenhous; 1940, Dunkel, Williamson
Coach: Robert R. Neyland
Top players: George "Bad News" Cafego, Ed Molinski, Bob Suffridge, Bowden Wyatt, Abe Shires, Bob Fox, Johnny Butler, Ray Graves, Bob Woodruff

Mississippi, 1954–63

For a ten-year stretch, John Vaught's Ole Miss Rebels were the team to beat, not only in the South but in the nation as well. During that period, Vaught won five of the school's six SEC championships and all three of its national championships. With players like quarterback Jake Gibbs and fullback Charlie Flowers, who both went on to be inducted into the College Football Hall of Fame, Ole Miss won 90 games in ten years. The 1959 team is considered to have been the best, having posted 8 shutouts and lost only to LSU 7–3 after Billy Cannon's famous eighty-nine-yard punt return. The Rebels avenged that loss two months later by beating LSU in the Sugar Bowl 21–0. The Ole Miss squad of 1959 was named the SEC Team of the Decade.

Jake Gibbs, Mississippi's All-American quarterback, led the Rebels to a 10–0–1 season in 1960 (photo courtesy of Mississippi SID).

Ole Miss quarterback Jake Gibbs led the Rebels to the national championship in 1959 and 1960 (photo courtesy of Mississippi SID).

Overall record: 90–13–4
SEC titles: (5)—1954, 1955, 1960, 1962, 1963
National championships: (3)—1959, Dunkel; 1960, Football Writers Association; 1962, Litkenhous
Coach: John H. Vaught
Top players: Rex Reed Bogan, Paige Cothren, Jackie Simpson, Charlie Flowers, Jake Gibbs, Bill Ray Adams, Treva Bolin, Jim Dunaway, Kenny Dill, Jimmy Patton, Billy Brewer

Georgia Tech, 1951–56

After a disappointing 5–6 season in 1950, coach Bobby Dodd decided to make some changes. He hired former Georgia Tech player Frank Broyles, who would later become the head coach at Arkansas, to run the Georgia Tech offense. Ray Graves, who would later become the head coach at Florida, would direct the defense. Broyles and Graves, plus talent that included future Hall of Famers Ray Beck, George Morris, and Larry Morris, created what would be Georgia Tech's most consistent period of success. In six seasons the Yellow Jackets won 58 games, two SEC championships, and one national championship. In 1951, only a 14–14 tie with Duke kept the Yellow Jackets from posting an undefeated season. Georgia Tech finished with a No. 5 ranking after beating Baylor in the Orange Bowl. That win set the table for the 1952 season, when Georgia Tech went 12–0, including a 24–7 win over Mississippi in the Sugar Bowl.

Overall record: 58–7–3
SEC championships: (2)—1951, 1952
National championships: (1)—1952, International News Service
Coach: Robert Lee "Bobby" Dodd
Top players: Ray Beck, Pete Brown, Leon Hardeman, Buck Martin, Bobby Moorhead, Larry Morris, George Morris, Don Stephenson, Lamar Wheat, Hal Miller, Franklin Brooks, Allen Ecker

Grambling, 1960–89

Although the other teams listed here all played Division I football, Grambling's accomplishments under coach Eddie Robinson are simply too great not to include in the list of Southern dynasties. Robinson coached an unprecedented fifty-five seasons at Grambling but was particularly dominating during this thirty-year stretch, winning 247 games, an average of more than 8 wins per season. The Tigers won or shared sixteen Southwestern Athletic Conference championships and seven national black college titles.

Overall record: 247–76–8
SWAC championships: 16
National championships: (7 national black college championships)—1967, 1972, 1974, 1975, 1977, 1980, 1982
Coach: Eddie Robinson
Top players: Buck Buchanan, Ernie Ladd, Charlie Joiner, Alphonse Dotson, Frank Lewis, Richard Harris, James Harris, Gary Johnson, James Hunter, Doug Williams, Dwight Scales, Everson Walls, Sammy White, Willie Brown

Honorable Mentions

(In Chronological Order)

LSU, 1908 **(10–0)**: The Tigers, led by quarterback E. G. "Doc" Fenton, scored 442 points in 450 minutes of play in an era when touchdowns only counted five points.

Alabama, 1925 **(10–0):** The Crimson Tide won its first national championship and beat Washington 20–19 in the Rose Bowl in a game that put Southern College Football on the map.

Tulane, 1925 **(9–0–1):** After an undefeated season that included a tie with Missouri, the Green Wave turned down a chance to go to the Rose Bowl.

Florida, 1928 **(8–1):** The Gators led the nation in scoring, but after they lost to Tennessee in Knoxville they no longer had a chance to go to the Rose Bowl.

Alabama, 1930 **(10–0):** Wallace Wade's last Alabama team won the national championship, which included a 24–0 win over Washington State in the Rose Bowl.

Tulane, 1931 **(11–1):** Tulane finished its regular season undefeated with eight shutouts but lost to Southern California in the Rose Bowl.

Tennessee, 1939 **(10–1):** The Volunteers were unbeaten and unscored upon until they lost to Southern California 14–0 in the Rose Bowl.

Tennessee, 1940 **(10–1):** After another undefeated regular season, the Vols lost to Boston College 19–13 in the Sugar Bowl.

Mississippi State, 1940 **(10–0–1):** The Bulldogs were tied by Auburn 7–7 but beat Georgetown in the Orange Bowl.

Duke, 1941 **(9–1):** The Blue Devils went through the regular season undefeated but lost to Oregon State 20–16 in the Rose Bowl, which was played that year in Durham, N.C.

Georgia, 1946 **(11–0):** After sitting out two seasons to serve in World War II, Charley Trippi returned to Georgia to close out his brilliant career by leading the Bulldogs to a glorious undefeated season, which included a win over North Carolina in the Sugar Bowl.

Alabama, 1945 **(10–0):** The great Harry Gilmer led the Crimson Tide to a perfect season, including a 34–14 win over Southern California in the Rose Bowl.

Clemson, 1948 **(11–0):** Frank Howard's Tigers won the Southern Conference championship and beat Missouri in the Gator Bowl.

Clemson, 1950 **(9–0–1):** A tie with South Carolina (which finished 3–4–2) kept the Tigers from playing for the national championship.

Auburn, 1958 **(9–0–1):** Only a 7–7 tie with Georgia Tech kept the Tigers from a perfect season.

Ole Miss, 1962 **(10–0):** The Rebels gave up only fifty-three points in 10 games on their way to a national championship.

Arkansas, 1964 **(11–0):** The Razorbacks beat Nebraska 10–7 in the Cotton Bowl to win their first national championship.

Arkansas, 1965 **(10–1):** The Razorbacks went 10–0 during the regular season. Their 22-game winning streak was broken by a 14–7 loss to LSU in the Cotton Bowl.

North Carolina linebacker Lawrence Taylor went on to a Hall of Fame career with the New York Giants (photo courtesy of the *Atlanta Journal-Constitution*).

Alabama, 1966 **(11–0):** Alabama should have won its third straight national championship with this team, led by quarterback Ken Stabler. Instead, Notre Dame, which had tied a game against Michigan State, won the national title.

Alabama, 1971 **(11–1):** The Crimson Tide's only loss this year was to national champion Nebraska in the Orange Bowl.

Alabama, 1973 **(11–1):** Despite losing 24–23 to Notre Dame in the Sugar Bowl, the Crimson Tide was still named the UPI national champion.

Arkansas, 1977 **(11–1):** The Razorbacks, under first-year coach Lou Holtz, upset No. 2 Oklahoma 31–6 in the Orange Bowl.

North Carolina, 1980 **(11–1):** The Tar Heels, led by future superstar linebacker Lawrence Taylor, lost only to Oklahoma in the regular season.

Georgia, 1982 **(11–1):** The Bulldogs, with Heisman Trophy winner Herschel Walker, lost the national championship to Penn State in the Sugar Bowl.

Miami, 1986 **(11–1):** Led by Heisman Trophy winner Vinny Testaverde, the Hurricanes lost the national championship to Penn State (14–10) in the Fiesta Bowl.

Florida State, 1987 **(11–1):** The Seminoles' only loss this year was to Miami (26–25) on a failed two-point conversion. Miami won the national championship.

Miami, 1988 **(11–1):** The Hurricanes' only loss this season was to Notre Dame (31–30), the eventual national champion.

Miami, 1989 **(11–1):** Despite a loss to Florida State, the Hurricanes still won the national championship in Dennis Erickson's first year as head coach.

Georgia Tech, 1990 **(11-0-1):** Only a tie to North Carolina kept the UPI national champion from perfection.

Auburn, 1993 **(11-0):** First-year coach Terry Bowden led the Tigers to an unbeaten season, but Auburn did not play in a bowl because of NCAA sanctions.

Florida, 1995 **(12-1):** Thanks to a great Gators offense, Florida went undefeated until they lost to Nebraska 62–24 in the Fiesta Bowl.

Florida State, 1997 **(12-1):** Only a 32–29 loss to Florida in the last game of the season kept the Seminoles from playing for the national title.

GAME DAY

The Towns, the Traditions

Webster defines *tradition* as a set of customs transmitted from one generation to another. Tradition more than anything else is the cornerstone of college football in the South. Each college town has its own special set of traditions that makes it a unique place to visit on game day, such as Tennessee, with its checkerboard end zones and Volunteer Navy; Ole Miss, with the Grove; Auburn, with the Tiger Walk and Toomer's Corner; and Clemson, with the Esso Club.

These traditions are the glue that binds the generations of Southern college football fans to one another and keeps them coming back to their beloved campuses year after year. People in the South take these football traditions very, very seriously. To many fans, the renewal of these traditions each fall provides all the physical and emotional comfort of a warm blanket on a cold winter's night.

"As soon as the last bowl game is over in January, most of the people I know start counting the days until the next season gets here," says Brandon "Booger" Seely, a longtime Georgia fan from Albany. "A lot of us live and die by the kick off in the fall. A lot of friendships are built and maintained for a lifetime thanks to college football."

Game day routines in the South differ at each campus, but they do have several things in common. For example, almost every hotel in a college town in the South requires a two-night minimum stay during football weekends, meaning that fans who want a room have to pay for both Friday and Saturday nights. Many hotels in Southern college football towns make a significant portion of their yearly income during those six or seven football weekends a year, when they are totally booked and, because of the demand, able to charge premium rates.

This policy guarantees that the pregame parties will begin in earnest on the Friday night before the game. These celebrations can get a little rowdy, as Alabama coach Bear Bryant discovered in 1976 when his team played at Georgia. The Crimson Tide had won the SEC championship in 1975 and was favored to do it again in 1976. But Georgia and

Georgia fans, like most fans around the South, can get a bit rowdy at times (photo courtesy of the *Atlanta Journal-Constitution*).

its fans had been preparing for their October 2 game against Alabama since the end of spring practice the previous April. When the Alabama team arrived in Athens on the Friday before the game, Georgia's fans were waiting for them.

Bryant had made the mistake of housing his team in the Athens Holiday Inn, just a few blocks from Georgia's Sanford Stadium. Word of the team's location got out, and at about midnight on Friday, some "enthusiastic" Georgia fans parked their cars outside the hotel, where the Crimson Tide players were trying to get some sleep. Then the fans turned on their headlights and began blaring their horns to wake up the Alabama players. The commotion got so out of hand that Bryant finally ordered his troops to take their mattresses out of their rooms and sleep in the hall. The next day Georgia won the game 21–0. The Bulldogs went on to win the SEC championship.

"That's one of the biggest differences I've seen between football in the South and football anywhere else," says Frank Broyles, the former head coach at Arkansas. "On game day, the South has the most aggressive fans in America. In other parts of the country, fans are there to enjoy the game. But in the South, the fans believe they are there to participate!"

Because the supply of hotel rooms in a Southern college football town can never match the demand, some fans become very possessive of their rooms once they have acquired them. It is not usual to meet fans who have been staying in the same room in the same hotel for more than twenty-five years. Some fans, however, take this possessiveness to the extreme.

"We had a man who had been staying in the same room with us for at least twenty years," says Leroy Dukes, the former manager of the Ramada Inn in Athens. "Unfortunately, one year he died during the off season. Come fall, the man's son showed up saying he was there to claim his daddy's room. He just assumed that the room would be passed down to him after his daddy died."

Another tradition that all Southern college football towns have in common is tailgating. *Tailgating* is the term used to describe the pregame and postgame ritual of eating, drinking, and socializing with one's fellow fans. The name comes from the practice of opening the tailgate of a station wagon or pickup truck and spreading food out on it for everyone to share.

Fans all over the country practice some form of tailgating, but those who follow Southern college football have turned it into nothing less than an art form. Just as the players on the field want to be the best, Southern fans want their tailgating parties to be bigger and better than anyone else's. In the Grove, the most popular tailgating spot at Ole Miss, fans tailgate with style: often you'll see a complete buffet spread out on a white linen tablecloth held in place by a silver candelabra.

At Clemson or South Carolina, you'll often see fans enjoying a Low-Country Boil, a delicious combination of shrimp, potatoes, corn, and sausage cooked to perfection in one huge pot. At Auburn and Alabama, fans start up their barbeque grills well before dawn on game day and by lunch produce some of the best eats on the planet. Fans put a Cajun twist on tailgating at LSU, where the jambalaya and crawfish etouffee flow freely.

But all tailgating parties in the South, regardless of their locale, must have a few basics: fried chicken, potato salad, deviled eggs, pimento cheese sandwiches (no crust on the bread, please!), pecan pie, and plenty of iced tea (sweet, of course) to wash it all down. Some fans choose to serve beverages a little on the harder side of iced tea, and by kick-off these hardy souls already have on their "game faces." Sometimes fans get so involved in the fun of tailgating that they forget about the game.

"Our folks make a mad rush for the gates a few minutes before kickoff," says Bob Bradley, Clemson's sports information director emeritus. "They've just got to have that last bourbon and that last chicken leg."

After the game, Southern fans begin their second round of tailgating to celebrate the victory or drown their sorrows of a defeat. Many fans will stay around town for an hour or more in order to let the traffic thin out. Then it's time to pack up the food and the folding chairs and begin what, in some cases, is a long drive home. Of course the drive is a lot shorter after a win than after a loss.

"Between the Hedges" at Georgia's Sanford Stadium (photo courtesy of Georgia SID).

Here is a look at some of the Southern college football towns where game day is always something magical.

Game Day at Georgia

The Revolutionary War had barely been over two years when the University of Georgia was founded in 1785. The nation's first state university is located in Athens, approximately seventy-five miles north of the state capital in Atlanta, and has a student body of more than thirty thousand.

The Bulldogs' fans love to tailgate at Georgia, which has earned the reputation of being one of the most beautiful campuses on which to enjoy a fall football Saturday. For more than sixty years, fans have been turning out to support their troops at Sanford Stadium, which was named after the late S. V. Sanford, the former president of the university. The stadium was dedicated on October 12, 1929, with a 15–0 upset of Yale, at the time one of college football's national powers. Sanford's original seating capacity of 30,000 was expanded to 86,117 in 1994.

Surrounding the field is a row of English privet hedge. The original hedges were installed in 1929 and then removed to make way for the soccer competitions that were to be held there in the 1996 Olympics. Playing "between the hedges" has never been easy for opposing teams. Since the team's first win at Sanford in 1929, Georgia is 258–95–11 (a 73.08 winning percentage) at home.

The historic Arch is the gateway to the University of Georgia (photo courtesy of Georgia SID).

Here are a few other reasons why game day at Georgia is so special:

The Arch: This gateway to the lovely Georgia campus was installed in 1964. For years, upperclassmen did not allow freshmen to walk beneath the arch, and although the tradition has since ended, some freshmen still keep it alive.

The Chapel Bell: In the 1890s, freshmen were ordered by upperclassmen to ring this bell until midnight after a Georgia victory. Today the bell is still intact and students and fans remain on campus after every home win to take turns ringing it.

Silver Britches: When Vince Dooley became coach in 1964, he changed the school's uniform, which had included silver pants since former coach Wally Butts introduced them in 1939, to include white pants. But in 1980, Dooley decided to go back to the silver pants, or "britches," as he called them. That year Georgia went 12–0 and won the national championship. With the exception of a few games, Georgia has worn the silver britches ever since.

UGA I–VI: The most recognized mascot in all of college football is the English Bulldog UGA (pronounced ugh-ga) that has been Georgia's official mascot since 1956. UGA I was born on December 2, 1955, and made his debut on the Georgia sidelines the following fall. In 1997 UGA V, the most famous of the lineage, appeared on the cover of Sports Illustrated as college football's best mascot. UGA V also appeared in the movie *Midnight in the Garden of Good and Evil*, which was directed by Clint Eastwood. UGA V retired prior to the 1999 season and was replaced by UGA VI.

"Glory, Glory": Sung to the tune of "The Battle Hymn of the Republic," "Glory, Glory" has been the official Georgia fight song since 1915: "Glory, Glory to Old Georgia Glory, Glory to Old Georgia Glory, Glory to Old Georgia G-E-O-R-G-I-A." Often, the last line of the song is replaced with "And to hell with Georgia Tech."

The Redcoat Band: Known for their uniforms, which feature brilliant red coats, the Georgia band plays a big part on game day in Athens. About an hour before kickoff, the band walks through the east entrance of Sanford Stadium to begin the pregame ceremonies. After the game, in one of Georgia's longstanding traditions, the Redcoat Band remains in the stadium for a brief concert, which includes "Tara's Theme" from *Gone with the Wind*. Concluding with the school's fight song, this concert officially marks the end of game day at the University of Georgia.

Game Day at Auburn

Located about fifty miles north of the Alabama state capital of Montgomery, Auburn has long been known as "the loveliest village on the plain," and never is this more true than on a football Saturday.

The town has only thirty-five thousand residents, but more than eighty-five thousand turn out for each home game at Jordan-Hare Stadium, which was named for former coach

Aubie, the Auburn mascot, gets a push (photo courtesy of the *Atlanta Journal-Constitution*).

"War Eagle!" Auburn's eagle, named Tiger, guards the sidelines (photo courtesy of the *Atlanta Journal-Constitution*).

Ralph "Shug" Jordan (1951–75) and Cliff Hare, a member of Auburn's first football team, who went on to become a dean in the School of Chemistry. The stadium was dedicated in 1939 with seventy-five hundred seats and ten years later was named after Hare. The facility was renamed Jordan-Hare Stadium in 1973, two years before Jordan retired as head coach. The final expansion, to 85,214 seats, was completed in 1987.

Auburn got its nickname, "Tigers," from a line in Oliver Goldsmith's poem "The Deserted Valley," which reads "where crouching Tigers await their hapless prey." The town of Auburn got its name from the same poem.

Here are just a few reasons why game day at Auburn is so special:

The Tiger Walk: A couple of hours before each home game, Auburn's players walk up Donahue Drive from Sewell Hall, the school's athletic dormitory, to Jordan-Hare Stadium, several hundred yards away. Fans line either side of the street to form a human corridor. This tradition serves to get both fans and players fired up before the game. The largest Tiger Walk, which began as a tradition in the early 1960s, occurred prior to the Auburn-Alabama game on December 2, 1989, when more than twenty thousand attended.

"War Eagle!": This battle cry of the Auburn faithful was born on February 20, 1892, when Georgia and Auburn met for their first football game, which was held at Atlanta's Piedmont Park. According to a popular legend, a member of the Auburn faculty brought with him an eagle that the man had raised since his days in the Civil War. After Auburn's first touchdown, the eagle broke loose from its handler and soared above the crowd.

Auburn fans celebrate a big victory by "rolling" Toomer's Corner (photo courtesy of Auburn SID).

When the fans saw the familiar figure flying overhead, they shouted "War Eagle!" and a tradition was born. Auburn still has a live golden eagle, which, ironically, is named "Tiger," on the sidelines for each home game. A student dressed in a Tiger costume who goes by the name of "Aubie" shares the sidelines with Tiger. When one Auburn fan greets another on game day, they don't say hello. They shout, "War Eagle!"

Toomer's Corner: This corner, located where the university campus meets the town of Auburn at the intersection of Magnolia Avenue and College Street, is the official gathering place for fans after a home football game. Students, fans, players, and sometimes even coaches will join together at Toomer's Corner to roll the trees with toilet paper in celebration of a big victory.

Game Day at LSU

On a campus rich with tradition, one of the most enduring events at Louisiana State University is a night football game at Tiger Stadium. LSU started playing under the lights in 1931, and over the years a Saturday night game in Baton Rouge has provided one of the most intimidating atmospheres for opponents in all of college football. From 1960 to 1990, LSU won more than seventy-eight percent of its home games played at night.

"You were at a distinct disadvantage when you went into Baton Rouge to play," says Ron Franklin, ESPN's longtime college football voice. "Nine times out of ten they wanted you to take the field first and feel the sense of terror. Because when they came out of the south tunnel, the night erupted. Their players were lifted by it as well."

The tailgating scene at LSU games is unique to all of college football. With New Orleans located about an hour down Interstate 10, the pregame meal consists of Cajun

Mike the tiger (photo courtesy of LSU SID).

foods instead of the usual fried chicken and potato salad found in most places around the South.

In the best Mardi Gras tradition, fans arrive in Baton Rouge as early as Thursday evening for a Saturday night game. To walk across campus on Friday night is to enjoy a smorgasbord of smells that includes crawfish, boiled shrimp, and jambalaya. In 1996, ESPN named LSU's tailgating scene the best in all of college football.

Here are just a few of the other sights and sounds you'll enjoy on a football weekend at Baton Rouge:

Mike the Tiger: Since 1935, a real Bengal tiger has roamed the LSU sidelines as the school's official mascot. Today's tiger, Mike V, lives just north of the stadium in a plush permanent residence that includes a pool and an area encased in glass where fans can watch him. Before home games, Mike is placed in a rolling cage that is parked just outside the opposing team's locker room so that players from the other team are forced to walk past his cage. The sight of him can be a little intimidating. One year, when LSU was playing Alabama, Mike was particularly feisty, and according to legend Bear Bryant had a student feed Mike a steak laced with tranquilizers.

"Tiger Rag": One of the most popular pregame rituals at LSU is the march of the school's Golden Band from Tigerland down North Stadium Drive into Tiger Stadium. Once the band takes the field it remains silent for a few moments before it suddenly pounds out the first few notes of the "Tiger Rag"—"Hold-That-Ti-ger! Hold-That-Ti-ger!"—causing the crowd to erupt. "That sound," noted a veteran sportswriter, "will make the hair stand up on a dead man's chest."

Victory Hill: Two hours before each home game, the Tigers walk down a hill near the Journalism school, down North Stadium Drive, and into Tiger Stadium accompanied by the Golden Band from Tigerland and the Golden Girls. Coach Curley Hallman started this tradition in 1990 and Gerry DiNardo continued it when he took over as head coach in 1995.

White Jerseys: Unlike other schools in the South, LSU likes to wear white jerseys for home games. The tradition, which dated back to the 1950s, ended in 1983 when the NCAA ruled that home teams must wear dark jerseys. When Gerry DiNardo became coach in 1995, he lobbied the NCAA to make an exception for LSU so that he could bring the tradition back to the school. The NCAA then passed a rule that teams could wear white at home if the visiting team agreed, and the only team not to agree with LSU's decision was Vanderbilt, which still held a grudge that DiNardo had left the school to go to LSU. But instead of going with its old purple jerseys, DiNardo introduced gold ones for the game against Vanderbilt, and LSU won 35–0.

Clemson coach Danny Ford pleads with quarterback Rodney Williams in 1987 (photo courtesy of the *Atlanta Journal-Constitution*).

The Earthquake: How loud can it get in Tiger Stadium? On October 8, 1988, after LSU scored the winning touchdown against Auburn, the explosion of sound was so great that it registered on the seismograph at the LSU Geology Department.

Game Day at Clemson

You don't have to wonder if you are on the right road to Clemson, South Carolina. All you have to do is follow the trail of orange tiger paws that begins just a few miles outside of the city limits on Highway 76 and leads you to one of the most unique college towns in the South. Rising up out of the foothills of the Blue Ridge Mountains and near the shores of scenic Lake Hartwell, Clemson is located in the northwestern corner of the state, just two hours north of Atlanta, Georgia.

The population of Clemson is only eleven thousand, but on fall Saturdays more than eighty-one thousand fans pack Memorial Stadium, better known as Death Valley, making it the second largest city in the state, just behind Columbia, the capital.

Going into the 2000 season, Clemson has won or shared thirteen Atlantic Coast Conference titles. But its shining moment in football came in 1981 when the Tigers won their first and only national championship. Every year fans fill Memorial Stadium hoping that the Tigers will make another run for the title.

Here are a few of the sights and sounds you'll experience on a game day at Clemson:

Howard's Rock: Mounted on a pedestal on a grassy hill at the east end of Memorial Stadium, this rock from Death Valley, California, was given to Frank Howard, Clemson's legendary coach from 1940 to 1969. Howard wanted to throw the rock away, but one of his assistants convinced him to keep it. Looking for something to motivate his team, Howard brought out the rock prior to a game with Virginia in 1966. He said his players could touch the rock for good luck, but only under a few conditions.

Touching Howard's Rock before kick-off is a Clemson tradition (photo courtesy of Clemson SID).

"I told all them that was going to give me 110 percent that they could touch my rock and if they weren't going to give me 110 percent, keep your filthy hands off my rock," said Howard, who died in 1996.

While touching the rock before a home game has since become a tradition, not everyone is as impressed with it as Howard was.

"I got a letter from a lady over at Travelers Rest [South Carolina] who said, 'Coach, if you believed more in the Lord than you do that rock, you'd be a much better football coach,'" said Howard.

Running down the Hill: ABC broadcaster Brent Musberger once termed it "the most exciting twenty-five seconds in college football." About ten minutes before kickoff, the

Tigers leave their locker room under the west stands and are bused around Memorial Stadium to the east side of the stadium, where a grassy hill about one hundred feet long leads directly onto the playing field. At a given signal, a cannon is fired, the band plays "Tiger Rag," and the team charges down the hill as the crowd goes wild. The tradition began in 1942, and for all but 15 home games since, the Clemson team has run down the hill. For the record, Clemson is 6–9 when it doesn't run down the hill before a game, 189–65–7 (73 percent) when it does. In 1966, touching Howard's Rock at the top of the hill officially became a part of the pregame ceremonies.

The Esso Club: Not all the partying at a Clemson game goes on in the parking lot surrounding the stadium. At Clemson, fans gather before and after the game at the Esso Club, a converted gas station that has become the area's most popular watering hole and a Southern institution. "The Esso Club [is] a place where professors used to go to get a cold beer when nobody else in town had one," says Bob Bradley, the former sports information director at Clemson.

The Graveyard: Clemson has beaten a lot of ranked teams at home. But at its practice fields, which are located just across the street from Memorial Stadium, the team has constructed a "graveyard" to celebrate those victories it has earned over ranked teams on the road. Since 1948, Clemson has posted 15 road victories over ranked teams.

Tiger Mascot Pushups: Since 1954, a Clemson student dressed in a Tiger suit has served as the school's mascot. After every Clemson score, the mascot does pushups to match the current number of Tiger points. If Clemson scores and goes ahead 7–0, the mascot does seven pushups. If the team scores again and goes up to 14–0, the mascot does fourteen pushups. The record number of pushups for one game was 465, performed by Ricky Capps during an 82–24 win over Wake Forest in 1981.

Game Day at South Carolina

Football fans say that a special place in heaven is reserved for all fans of South Carolina football—for they have certainly been through hell on earth.

In the history of college football, no group of fans has suffered so much and yet been so supportive of their school's program. Going into the 2000 season, the 109th in the school's history, South Carolina has experienced only six years of winning 8 games or more. In more than a century of football South Carolina has won 10 games in a season only once (1984).

Still, every year Gamecock fans flock to Williams-Brice Stadium in Columbia, the capital of the Palmetto State. During the 1999 season, the first for new coach Lou

South Carolina players run through the smoke during the "2001" pregame ceremony (photo courtesy of South Carolina SID).

Holtz, South Carolina fans set a record by purchasing fifty-three thousand season tickets. That was after a 1–10 season in 1998. In 1999 the Gamecocks went 0–11, but the fans kept coming.

South Carolina has won only 1 bowl game in its history (the 1994 Carquest Bowl over West Virginia) but still is ranked among the top fifteen of the nation in attendance each year.

"We have the greatest fans in the world," says Holtz, the former coach at Notre Dame. "We raise more money per win than any school in America."

The tailgating scene at the State Fairgrounds, which is located directly across the street from the stadium, is as good as any you will find in the South. But I will offer a few words of advice: Get there early. Only two roads lead into the stadium area, and more than eighty thousand fans must use them.

Here are just a few of the things you need to know about game day and its traditions at South Carolina:

2001: When Joe Morrison took over as head coach at South Carolina in 1983, he wanted to find something that would bring excitement into Williams-Brice Stadium at the beginning of each game. Thus he instituted this tradition. In the moments prior to when the South Carolina team takes the field, the public address system begins to blare out the opening notes to the theme song from *2001—A Space Odyssey*. As the music plays, the crowd's enthusiasm builds. When the music hits the highest note, the Gamecocks rush onto the field through a tunnel of smoke and the crowd goes wild.

The Chicken Curse: Legend has it that former governor and U.S. Senator "Pitchfork" Ben Tillman, who founded Clemson University, South Carolina's arch rival in the state, is responsible for this curse. A farmer, Tillman felt that the bluebloods who attended South Carolina looked down their collective noses at him and his people. Over the years, Tillman's curse has been used to explain why the Gamecocks have experienced so many disappointments in its athletic ventures. Among the disappointing events attributed to the curse are South Carolina's 38–21 loss to heavy underdog Navy in 1984, which may have cost them a shot at the national title; Joe Morrison's death in 1989 by a heart attack; and a loss at home to Division I-AA Citadel in 1990.

The Cockaboose: South Carolina fans take a backseat to no one when it comes to creativity in tailgating. In 1990 a couple from Columbia decided to put to good use a set of abandoned train tracks that run along one side of Williams-Brice Stadium. They installed twenty-two rail cars, decorated to the hilt and outfitted with all the amenities, such as running water, air conditioning, and cable TV, and rented them out to the "serious" tailgaters among Gamecock fans.

Game Day at Florida

Until 1990, the University of Florida had always had a good but not great college football tradition. This lack of enthusiasm was perhaps in part a result of the fact that the Gators, while having had their share of great players and great teams, had never won a championship of any kind in football. In fact, Florida had earned the reputation of being a school that, despite its talent, would always come up short in the big game.

But all that changed when Steve Spurrier, a former Florida player and the 1966 Heisman Trophy winner, returned to Gainesville to serve as head coach. Before Spurrier took over in 1990, Florida had never won an SEC championship; in his first seven seasons as the head coach of the Gators, Spurrier won five. Then, in 1996, with Heisman Trophy quarterback Danny Wuerffel at the controls, Florida won its first national championship. But what Spurrier did at Florida in the '90s went beyond mere wins and losses. He changed the attitude of Florida's entire fan base and made game day in Gainesville, Florida, very, very special.

Florida players celebrate their win over Alabama in the 1994 SEC championship game (photo courtesy of the Associated Press).

First off, Spurrier came up with an appropriate nickname for Ben Hill Griffin Stadium. He labeled it "The Swamp" because, he said, "that's where Gators live. We feel comfortable there, but we hope our opponents feel tentative. A swamp is hot and sticky and can be dangerous." Over the next ten years, Spurrier's Swamp would become one of the toughest venues for opponents in all of college football. Going into the 2000 season, Spurrier's teams are 57–4 in the Swamp.

With the warm weather and a campus surrounded by palm trees, Florida offers a pregame and postgame tailgating scene that is unlike just about any other in the South.

Here are but a few of the things that make game day at Florida a unique experience:

"We Are the Boys from Old Florida": At the end of the third quarter at each Florida home game, Gator fans stand arm-in-arm, swaying back and forth while singing this tune, which dates back to World War II.

> *"We are the boys from old Florida.*
> *F-L-O-R-I-D-A.*
> *Where the girls are the fairest*
> *The boys are the squarest*
> *Of any old state down our way.*
> *We are all strong for old Florida*
> *Down where the old Gators play.*
> *In all kinds of weather*
> *We'll all stick together*
> *For F-L-O-R-I-D-A.*

Florida's Mr. Two Bits, George Edmondson (photo courtesy of Florida SID).

Mr. Two Bits: George Edmondson, a retired insurance salesman from Tampa who attended every Florida game dressed in saddle oxford shoes, a yellow oxford-cloth shirt, and a blue and orange tie, earned this nickname because before every game he would run to the middle of the field, holding a crumpled sign that said "Two Bits," and lead the most recognized cheer in college football. Edmondson retired as Mr. Two Bits after the 1998 season but still comes back for "special" Florida games such as those against Tennessee and Florida State.

"He-e-e-e-e-e-r-e Come the Gators!": In 1964 Jim Finch, the Gators' public address announcer, began this tradition of stretching out the word "Here" for approximately twenty to twenty-five seconds as the Florida players take the field. The Ben Hill Stadium crowd grows louder and louder, and after Finch's long "Here," he finishes with a quick "Come the Gators!" By then the Florida crowd is going crazy.

North End Zone: The north end zone of Ben Hill Griffin Stadium was rebuilt in 1991 in order to raise the stadium's capacity to eighty-three thousand. This reconstruction also made the Florida stadium one of the loudest in all of college football. The Victory Bell, which was once located on the battleship USS Florida, was installed in the north end zone in the '30s, when the ship was decommissioned. Fans and students ring the bell after each home win.

Game Day at Georgia Tech

To attend a game day at the Georgia Institute of Technology, known as one of the leading technological universities in the world since its founding in 1888, is to partake in a totally different kind of college football experience.

Whereas most campuses in the South are located in smaller towns and have stadiums surrounded by wide-open spaces, the Georgia Tech campus spreads across more than three hundred acres of prime real estate in the heart of downtown Atlanta. In most college towns around the South, only pine trees tower above the rim of the stadium. At Tech's historic Grant Field/Bobby Dodd Stadium, fans instead see overhead the skyscrapers that mark the empire city of the South.

The Georgia Tech stadium was originally built in 1913, making it the oldest on-campus stadium in Division I football. Georgia Tech students built the original west stands, which seated five thousand fans at the time. The stadium was originally named Hugh Inman Grant Field, after the deceased son of John W. Grant, a member of the Georgia Tech Board of Trustees and a well-known Atlanta merchant who donated $15,000 toward the stadium's construction costs. In the almost ninety years of its existence, the stadium has undergone several renovations. In 1988 Georgia Tech added the name of former coach Bobby Dodd to the stadium's name.

Parking is limited on the narrow streets around Grant Field/Bobby Dodd Stadium, so game day traffic can be quite a nightmare. Some fans take MARTA, Atlanta's commuter rail system, which runs into the city from the suburbs. Other fans choose to drive to the campus several hours before the game so they can take part in the street fair held on Bobby Dodd Way, the street that runs behind the north entrance to the stadium.

Fraternity houses and residence halls line Fowler Street and Techwood Drive, the two streets located on either side of Grant Field/Bobby Dodd Stadium. After a big Georgia Tech victory those houses keep the party going and music blaring well into the wee hours of the morning.

On the night of November 3, 1990, the Georgia Tech students living in those houses experienced their finest moment. Earlier that day, several hundred miles away in Charlottesville, Virginia, Georgia Tech had upset No. 1 Virginia 41–38 in one of the greatest games ever played in the South. Immediately after the game, Georgia Tech students stormed into the empty Bobby Dodd Stadium, tore down the goalposts and, while holding them aloft, staged a victory parade down the streets of Atlanta. One goalpost was tossed into a bonfire that was set at the corner of Techwood Drive and Bobby Dodd Way.

In *Focused on the Top*, Jack Wilkinson's book on Georgia Tech's 1990 national championship season, Tech president Patrick Crecine discussed the antics of his fire-wielding students on that fateful night. "Maybe someone learned something about thermodynamics," Crecine said. "Heat rises."

Georgia Tech's famed "Ramblin' Wreck" (photo courtesy of Georgia Tech SID).

Welcome to game day at Georgia Tech. Here are a few other things you should look out for:

Ramblin' Wreck (the car): This restored 1930 Model A Ford Sports Coupe has been leading the Georgia Tech team onto the field at home games since September 30, 1961. Ted J. Johnson, a former Delta pilot, had restored the car as a gift to his son and later donated it to the school. The car was restored again in 1982 under the supervision of Tech alumnus Pete George, a manager of the Ford assembly plant near Atlanta.

"Ramblin' Wreck" (the song): With the possible exception of the Notre Dame fight song, this is the most recognized tune in college football. It is so well known that, according to Georgia Tech records, Richard Nixon and Nikita Khrushchev sang it together during their historic face-to-face meeting in Moscow in 1959.

If you're going to visit Georgia Tech on game day, learn the lyrics. It's a big part of game day on the Flats, as the school is also known:

"I'm a Ramblin' Wreck from Georgia Tech.
And a hell of an engineer.
A helluva, helluva, helluva, helluva, hell of an engineer
Like all the jolly good fellows
I drink my whiskey clear
I'm a Ramblin' Wreck from Georgia Tech
And a hell of an engineer."

Rat Caps: Since 1915 all members of the freshman class at Georgia Tech have worn these gold-colored caps. The term "rat" was originally used for first-year military students but was later expanded to include all freshmen. The freshmen decorate their rat caps with winning football scores written right side up and losing scores written upside down. If Tech experiences a tie, the score is written sideways.

George P. Burdell: He won't be there in body, but he will be there in spirit. In 1927 Georgia Tech student Ed Smith decided to play a prank and enroll a fictitious classmate, George P. Burdell, in some classes. He took the ruse to the point of actually turning in papers for Burdell. Other students joined in the fun over the years and kept Burdell enrolled until he eventually got a bachelor's degree from Georgia Tech. In 1969, when registration became computerized, students feared that Burdell's attendance string would end. But Burdell beat the system and registered for all three thousand classes at Georgia Tech.

The Varsity: Located on North Avenue, just two blocks from the stadium, the Varsity is one of the South's most famous drive-in restaurants and serves as a gathering place for fans before and after the game. The Varsity is famous for its onion rings and its counter service people who will always greet you with "Whaddaya have?"

Over the years, a Varsity lingo has developed between Varsity employees and customers:

Varsity employee: "Whaddaya have?" Customer: "I want two dogs walkin' through the garden, a ring, a fry, and a PC." Translation: "I want two chili dogs to go, with slaw, some onion rings, some french fries, and a container of chocolate milk."

Game Day at Tennessee

Located in East Tennessee near the base of the Smoky Mountains, Knoxville is a relatively small city (pop. 167,000). But on those fall Saturdays when Tennessee plays at home, the seat of Blount County swells with an additional 107,000 fans who turn out to watch their beloved Volunteers battle the week's opponent.

Technically, the capacity of Neyland Stadium/Shields-Watkins Field is 102,854. Among on-campus facilities, that's second only to Michigan Stadium (107,501) in Ann Arbor. But since 1996, when the stadium was last expanded, Tennessee has averaged more than 106,000 fans per game.

The stadium is named after legendary coach Bob Neyland, the man most responsible for establishing the school's football tradition, and Colonel W. S. Shields, the president of Knoxville's City National Bank, who provided the initial capital to build the original facility. Shields added the name of his wife, Alice Watkins, when the field was completed in 1921.

Tennessee's Volunteer Navy docks near Neyland Stadium before every game (photo courtesy of Tennessee SID).

Tennessee became known as the "Volunteer State" in the nineteenth century because of the willingness of its men to fight in the War of 1812 and the Mexican War. So it was only fitting that the teams of the state's largest university, which was founded in 1794, would take on that name.

Tennesseans are proud of their heritage and proud of a football tradition that dates back to 1891. Like most Southerners, Volunteer fans live for football season. When the Pride of the Southland Band marches onto the field and the players dressed in orange and white run through the block "T," Volunteer fans know, as radio announcer John Ward always said right before kickoff: "It's football time in Tennessee!"

Here are just a few of the game day traditions at Tennessee:

Volunteer Navy: By 1962 radio broadcaster George Mooney had grown weary of Knoxville's traffic on game days. So he got creative, taking his small boat down the Tennessee River and docking it just across Neyland Avenue in the shadow of Neyland Stadium. The idea caught on and the "Volunteer Navy" was born. Today, more than two hundred boats make their way down the river on game day. For big games, some fans

Tennessee's checkerboard end zones (photo courtesy of Tennessee SID).

dock several days in advance, because in Big Orange Country, as the vast majority of Tennessee is known, it's never too early to put on your game face.

Checkerboard End Zones: The checkerboard design on the end zones at Neyland Stadium was introduced in the mid-sixties when Doug Dickey, now Tennessee's athletic director, became head coach. The orange and white checkerboard end zones, which are unique to Tennessee, went on a hiatus for a while when the stadium switched from natural grass to artificial turf in 1968. In 1989, Tennessee brought back the checkerboard end zones, which remain in place to this day.

Block T: One of the most recognizable symbols in college football, the Block T was added to the Tennessee football helmet by coach Doug Dickey in 1964. Prior to each game, the Pride of the Southland Band forms a Block T with the bottom of the letter facing the Tennessee tunnel. The Volunteers then run through the "T" onto the field.

Smokey: The bluetick coonhound, a native dog to the state, became Tennessee's official mascot in 1953. Over the years Tennessee has had eight Smokeys, and each has been among the most beloved figures in the state. Smokey leads the team onto the field before every home game.

Tennessee's mascot Smokey, the blue-tick hound (photo courtesy of Tennessee SID).

"Rocky Top": Tennessee has several official fight songs, but "Rocky Top," an old country-bluegrass tune, has become the school's unofficial fight song. Some advice: If you don't like this song, do not go to a Tennessee home game. No band plays its fight song more during the course of a game than Tennessee plays "Rocky Top":

"Wish that I was on ol' Rocky Top,
down on the Tennessee Hills.
Ain't no smoggy smoke on Rocky Top,
ain't no telephone bills.
Once I had a girl on Rocky Top,
half bear, other half cat.
Wild as mink and sweet as soda pop,
I still dream about that.

(CHORUS)
Rocky Top, you'll always be
home sweet home to me,
Good ol' Rocky Top,
Rocky Top, Tennessee
Rocky Top, Tennessee."

(Music and lyrics by Boudleaux Bryant and Felice Bryant)

Game Day at Ole Miss

Few places in the South have more charm than Oxford, Mississippi, home of the University of Mississippi, which is affectionately known as Ole Miss.

Located about an hour south of Memphis, Tennessee, Oxford combines small-town warmth with an intellectual, literary, and artistic community that is second to none. Many writers, such as William Faulkner, Willie Morris, and John Grisham, have called Oxford home and have drawn inspiration from its tree-lined streets and eclectic community of people.

The University of Mississippi was founded in 1844 under a unique set of circumstances. When Oxford was founded in 1840, the city's officials hoped that it would someday be the site of the State University of Mississippi. Looking for every edge, the founders named the city Oxford, after the famous university city in England. The strategy paid off. By a vote of 58–57, the state legislature placed the university in Oxford.

The name "Ole Miss" has been synonymous with the university for more than one hundred years. It first surfaced as the winning entry in a contest to name the school yearbook. The name eventually became so popular that it was linked with the school itself.

Over the course of its 150-year history, Ole Miss has seen both success and turmoil. In 1962 riots broke out on campus and the National Guard was called to restore order when James Meredith became the first black student to attend the university. But out of that adversity, Ole Miss has emerged as a school strongly committed to the best possible education for all.

One reason why the people of the state have pulled together is their love of football and of those special fall Saturdays in Oxford. But the thing that sets Ole Miss apart, more than the Grove or any of its other great traditions, is the love its alumni and the people of the state have for the institution. It has been said that Ole Miss is not just a location on a map, but a place in the heart. The late Frank E. Everett Jr., an Ole Miss grad, wrote this tribute to his alma mater many years ago:

"There is valid distinction between the University and Ole Miss even though the separate threads are closely interwoven. . . . The University is buildings, trees, and people. Ole Miss is mood, emotion, and personality. One is physical and the other is spiritual. One is tangible and the other intangible. . . . The University is respected, but Ole Miss is loved. The University gives a diploma and regretfully terminates tenure, but one never graduates from Ole Miss."

Here are just a few of the things that make game day at Ole Miss special:

The Grove: This ten-acre park on campus is the center of the pregame tailgating scene in Oxford. On game day, fans begin arriving to the Grove at 7 A.M., regardless of the kickoff time. In just a few hours, the entire space is filled with tents, tables, chairs, and anything else that is necessary for a pregame tailgate party. About two hours before each game, the Ole Miss team leaves Kinard Hall and walks across campus to Vaught-Hemingway Stadium. Fans form a human corridor in the Grove for the players to walk through. This "Rebel Walk" is one of the most stirring sights in all of college football.

The Lyceum: Built in 1848, the year the university held its first classes, the Lyceum was the state of Mississippi's first public building of higher education. Named after the tract of earth where Aristotle taught in ancient Greece, this building serves as the historic focal point of the Ole Miss campus and contains the offices of the chancellor and other key administrators. Built in the Greek-revival style with six columns, the Lyceum is a popular meeting place for fans on game day at Ole Miss.

Vaught-Hemingway Stadium: Even though Oxford is the home of Faulkner, the town's football stadium was originally named for a Hemingway. Judge William Hemingway (1869–1937) was a professor of law at Ole Miss and the longtime chairman

Before each home game, the Ole Miss players take their "Rebel Walk" through the Grove (photo courtesy of Mississippi SID).

of the University's Committee on Athletics. On October 16, 1982, the name of John Vaught, the most successful coach in Ole Miss history (1947–73), was added to the stadium's name. Ole Miss students built the first seats of the stadium in 1915. Today, with a seating capacity at just over fifty thousand, Vaught-Hemingway Stadium is considered one of the coziest venues for college football in the South.

Number 38: For the Ole Miss football team, this number is worn each season by the winner of the Chucky Mullins Courage Award. The award is given every spring at Ole Miss by the Phi Beta Sigma fraternity in honor of Mullins, a football player who suffered a paralyzing injury in a game with Vanderbilt in 1990 and died from complications the following May. The winner has the honor of wearing Mullins's number the following season.

"Hotty Totty Cheer": This cheer is the favorite among Ole Miss fans:

"Hotty, Totty, gosh a mighty
Who the hell are we?
Flim fam, bim bam
Ole Miss, by damn!"

Game Day at Florida State

While most Southern college football powers trace their roots back to the nineteenth century, Florida State got a relatively late start in the sport. But it didn't take long for the Seminoles and their fans to catch up and make game day in Tallahassee one of the most colorful and exciting in the South.

Located in the state capital of Tallahassee, the school was originally founded in the nineteenth century as a seminary. Later it became the Florida State College for Women (FSCW). In 1947 the state legislature voted to make the school coeducational and to change the name to Florida State. With these changes came the understanding that football would also be coming to the campus.

Game day in Tallahassee has a different feel than most game days in other college towns across the South. Tallahassee, located in the Florida panhandle just twenty miles north of the Gulf of Mexico, is certainly characterized by constant heat, which the Seminoles have used to their advantage over the years. Many schools outside of the South simply will not come to Tallahassee because their teams literally melt in the hot and humid weather September brings.

The last non-Southern team to try and tame the Tallahassee heat was Southern California. The game was close for a half, but in the final thirty minutes fans could see that the Trojans were wilting. Florida State won easily, 30–10.

Florida State's Chief Osceola takes his pregame ride around Doak Campbel Stadium on Renegade (photo courtesy of Florida State SID).

"Now I remember why we don't like to come down here," said USC coach Paul Hackett after the game.

Accordingly, Florida State fans do not curse the heat but embrace it as an ally. At most Southern stadiums, it is considered inappropriate for men to take off their shirts during the game. At Florida State, it is expected. Game day with the Seminoles is like a giant beach party.

While Tallahassee has the Florida heat, its landscape includes the hills of Georgia and Alabama, its two neighboring states to the north. Many roads leading to the city run beneath canopies of moss-draped oaks, giving an old Southern feel to one of the youngest institutions on the college football scene.

Florida State has been playing football for only forty-four years, but its fans have already become legendary. Fans in their campers begin to arrive at the lots surrounding Doak Campbell Stadium on Thursday night and the party does not stop until they begin to head home on Sunday morning.

One more thing to keep in mind while you're visiting Florida State: The school uses the nickname "Seminoles" and various other Native American references with the complete blessing and participation of Florida's Seminole tribe. Both parties see Florida State's use of the symbols as a tribute.

Here are just a few other things to look for on your game-day trip to Tallahassee:

Chief Osceola and Renegade: The Seminoles have one of the most famous pregame traditions in all of college football. Just minutes before the kickoff, all eyes turn to the stadium's north end zone, where Chief Osceola, an FSU student carefully chosen and trained for this moment, leads the Florida State team onto the field while riding Renegade, his majestic Appaloosa. After the coin toss, Chief Osceola rides Renegade back to midfield while holding a flaming spear above his head. As the crowd goes wild, Renegade rocks back on his hind legs and Chief Osceola plants the spear into the turf. The game is on. The tradition began on September 16, 1978, in a game against Oklahoma State. Over the years FSU has had nine different riders and three different horses to appear as Chief Osceola and Renegade.

War Chant: Shortly after the kickoff, the Florida State fans will begin their famous "War Chant" accompanied by the FSU Band, the Marching Chiefs. While fans sing the war chant, they make a tomahawk chop motion in the air to the rhythm of the music.

Sod Cemetery: When Florida State wins a big game on the road, someone digs up a piece of sod from the opposing team's field and brings it back to Tallahassee. The sod is buried in a "sod cemetery" located near the Florida State practice field. A small monument marks each win. The tradition began in 1962 with an 18–0 win at Georgia, and the most recent "Sod Games" played by the Seminoles were a 30–23 win at Florida on November 20, 1999, and a 46–29 win over Virginia Tech in the Sugar Bowl on January 4, 2000, which gave Florida State the national championship. Over the years the criteria has changed to include bowl games and significant wins regardless of which team was favored.

Doak Campbell Stadium: When it was first built in 1950, Doak Campbell Stadium had a meager seating capacity of fifteen thousand. Today it is a state-of-the-art facility that seats more than eighty thousand. Named after Doak S. Campbell, the first FSU president, the stadium underwent its most recent renovation—in which the entire structure was encased in brick—in 1996. Now the noise of those eighty thousand fans cannot escape. Florida State plays night games whenever possible, and on those nights Doak Campbell Stadium is among the loudest in all of college football. Florida State will enter the 2000 season with a 46-game unbeaten streak at the stadium.

Burt Reynolds: In 1954, Buddy Reynolds was a highly regarded freshman running back for Florida State. The native of West Palm Beach appeared headed for a strong football career until an auto accident left him with a bad knee. His football dreams over, Buddy Reynolds decided to try acting. Burt Reynolds may have become a star, but he never forgot Florida State. He is a regular on the Florida State sidelines during football season and has made significant contributions to the school's drama and film departments. Robert Urich, another famous actor, was an offensive lineman at Florida State in 1964 and 1965.

Game Day at Alabama

Getting to the University of Alabama on a game day is really pretty simple. You exit off I-65 at McFarland Boulevard and turn onto University Avenue. Then bear left on Paul W. Bryant Drive. After about a mile you'll pass the Paul W. Bryant Museum on your right. Across the way you'll see Paul W. Bryant Hall. Finally you'll pass the Paul W. Bryant Conference Center and the Bryant-Denny Hospitality House before reaching your final destination: Bryant-Denny Stadium.

Obviously, Paul "Bear" Bryant, the Crimson Tide coach from 1958 to 1982 who won more games (323) than any coach in Division I history, was pretty important at Alabama. The influence of this one man dominates the state of Alabama in general and the city of Tuscaloosa in particular. Bryant died in 1983, only 28 days after he coached his last game, but his spirit still hangs over everything and everybody at the University of Alabama.

While the people who love Alabama still cling dearly to Bryant's memory, some major changes have been made in how Crimson Tide fans celebrate on game day.

During Bryant's career Alabama played at least three of its key games each year at Legion Field in nearby Birmingham. The stadium was bigger and Bryant believed that a strong presence in Birmingham, the center of financial and corporate power in the state, could only help his program. But in 1999 school officials decided to move those big games back to Bryant-Denny Stadium. The stadium was named for the former coach and former university president George H. Denny, whose leadership enabled the original facility to be built in 1929. That structure held twelve thousand people. The most recent expansion was completed in 1998, increasing the capacity to 83,818. Moving Alabama's big games, including the season-ending rivalry game with Auburn, was a huge break with tradition, something that isn't taken lightly in Tuscaloosa.

Tradition at Alabama isn't just a word, it's a way of life. Read on to learn about just a few of the things that make a football Saturday at Alabama special.

Dreamland: Located on the outskirts of Tuscaloosa, this modest but historic restaurant has a simple menu: barbeque ribs, white bread, and cold drinks. Don't even ask for coleslaw! Everyone, from royalty to common folk, who attends an Alabama football game must sooner or later make the pilgrimage to Dreamland.

The Paul W. Bryant Museum: A game day at Alabama is not complete, particularly for first-time visitors, without a visit to this museum, which not only traces the career of the former coach but also provides a history of Alabama football that dates back to 1892.

The Paul W. Bryant Museum traces the career of the famous coach and the history of Alabama football (photo courtesy of the University of Alabama).

The Quad: The Quad is the central on-campus gathering place for pregame and postgame activities. At the edge of the Quad is Denny Chimes, a tower built in 1929 as a tribute to the university's president. Denny Chimes also serves as the standard meeting place for friends and family who arrive from different parts of the state.

The Million Dollar Band: Alabama's marching band travels in relative comfort now, but back in the 1920s the only way it could get to the school's road games was by asking for contributions from the local merchants in Tuscaloosa. They were so good at fundraising that W. C. Pickens, Alabama's football manager, nicknamed the group the "Million Dollar Band." The name stuck.

When the Million Dollar Band arrives at Bryant-Denny Stadium and plays the first five notes of the school fight song, "Yea, Alabama," it is a sign for Crimson Tide fans everywhere that game day in Tuscaloosa has officially begun:

"Yea, Alabama! Drown 'em Tide.
Every Bama man's behind you, hit your stride.
Go teach the Bulldogs to behave,
Send those Yellow Jackets to a watery grave
And if a man starts to weaken, that's his shame
For Bama's pluck and grit have writ her name in Crimson flame,
Fight on! Fight on! Fight on, men!
Remember the Rose Bowl we'll win then.
Go! Roll to victory! Hit your stride!
You're Dixie's football pride, Crimson Tide!

The Best of the Rest

Jacksonville, Florida, site of the annual Georgia-Florida game: When both teams are competitive, there is nothing quite like the Georgia-Florida game, which is better known as the "The World's Largest Outdoor Cocktail Party."

North Carolina (Chapel Hill, N.C.): Although the school is more famous for its basketball, few places are more beautiful than a fall Saturday at Kenan Stadium, which sits majestically among the Carolina pines.

Mississippi State (Starkville, MS): If you go to Mississippi State to watch a football game, be prepared to hear a whole lot of ringing. Even though hand-held cowbells, which have been a fixture at Bulldog games since the 1940s, were banned from conference games by the SEC in 1974, fans still ring them proudly at nonconference games and bowl games. And some brave fans still occasionally defy the SEC ban in order to keep the unique tradition alive.

Kentucky (Lexington, KY): In September and October, Kentucky schedules its home football games at night so that fans can enjoy thoroughbred racing at the nearby Keeneland racetrack in the afternoon and then enjoy the football game that evening. The school started the practice in 1949, and it remains one of the greatest traditions in the South.

Virginia (Charlottesville, VA): Just to be able to stroll through the grounds of Mr. Jefferson's University is worth the trip to Charlottesville. The football Cavaliers have earned some success over the years, but this place has lost none of its small-town charm. The Virginia pep band is sometimes irreverent and always entertaining.

Virginia Tech (Blacksburg, VA): You "can't get there from here," but if you do find your way to Blacksburg, you'll soon learn that nothing is wilder than a bunch of Hokies on a fall Saturday night.

Duke (Durham, N.C.): Back in the days of Wallace Wade, for whom Duke's stadium is named, Duke was a national powerhouse and played in both the 1939 and 1942 Rose Bowls. Duke's football glory days are gone, but the memories still linger on at this gorgeous campus.

Southern Mississippi (Hattiesburg, MS): The Hub City of the state has more than held its own against big brothers Mississippi and Mississippi State.

East Carolina (Greenville, N.C.): Greenville is the one college town in the state where the fans love football more than basketball.

Honorable Mention

Maryland (College Park, MD): Bear Bryant spent one year (1945) at Maryland as the coach of the Terps, who experienced some glory days under Jim Tatum in the '50s.

Louisville (Louisville, KY): The Cardinals have always wanted to be a major player in Southern college football. With their new stadium, they may have a chance.

Memphis (Memphis, TN): The Tigers take a backseat to Tennessee in their home state, but if you like ribs and watching the ducks march in the Peabody Hotel lobby, this is your town.

Miami (Miami, FL): Although the days of being a national powerhouse may be over for the Hurricanes, there is no place like the Orange Bowl when it's rocking.

Vanderbilt (Nashville, TN): While Vanderbilt is still considered the SEC's doormat, its home games are unique. After all, in what other college football town can you find stars from the Grand Ole Opry in the stands?

Tulane (New Orleans, LA): Tulane was once a member of the SEC and a football power, and although both are no longer the case, New Orleans still loves its football, and fans still love to come watch a game in New Orleans.

N.C. State (Raleigh, N.C.): In North Carolina's state capital, fans love their hometown football, even though the conversation sometimes turns quickly to basketball.

Wake Forest (Winston-Salem, N.C.): Although there have been few moments of football glory in this conservative, old-money town, Groves Stadium is a small but beautiful place to watch a football game.

GREAT RIVALRIES

The passion of a Southern college football fan is fierce and indestructible, so it only stands to reason that when the passions of one group of fans encounters those of another, sparks fly. What is born of this collision of passions is a rivalry, the cornerstone of college football in the South.

Each college football rivalry has its own history, its own record of greatness and controversy, of triumph and disappointment, and with each new season another chapter of that history is written. Every year schools get the opportunity to avenge a defeat or extend their domination over the others. In the South, college football rivalries turn friend against friend, brother against brother, and husband against wife—at least for a week. What's at stake that would put such a strain on these otherwise strong relationships?

Simple. It's called bragging rights. More than anything, you want your team to win the big game so that the jerk in your office (or in your family) won't be able to hold it over you for an entire year. Hell, no. *You* want to hold it over your rival for an entire year.

Isn't all this a little childish? Perhaps. But in the South, folks would rather have bragging rights in college football than oil rights in the Middle East.

With these kinds of passions at work, it's no surprise that the great rivalries in the sport have given fans some of the best games and most unforgettable moments in college football history. Here are a few of the greatest Southern college football rivalries.

Alabama vs. Auburn: It Lasts 365 Days a Year

Alabama Leads 36–26–1

To call what exists between state foes Alabama and Auburn a rivalry would be like calling St. Patrick's Cathedral a nice little church. People even argue over what to call it. To Alabama fans it is the Alabama-Auburn rivalry. To Auburn fans it is the Auburn-Alabama rivalry. Regardless of its name, it is really a cultural battle between two groups of people. Football is simply the vehicle that has been used to wage the conflict. When it comes to a single event that affects the entire fabric of a state, not only on game day but all year round, nothing beats the annual Alabama-Auburn game.

"People talk about the Alabama-Auburn game on New Year's Day," says former Alabama coach Gene Stallings. "They talk about it on Christmas Day. They talk about it on the Fourth of July. It's the only game I've ever heard of where people talk about it 365 days a year. And if you don't live here, you couldn't possibly understand."

The two teams played twelve times from 1893 to 1907. But, as is befitting a rivalry, they did not play in 1908 because of contract disagreements and charges and countercharges that the two teams were using illegal players. The feelings were so bitter that the two schools did not play again until 1948 and then only at the insistence of the Alabama state legislature.

A lot of bad feelings can build up over forty years, and the two schools have been making up for it ever since. Every coach who has been thrust into the heat of this rivalry quickly learns that his success will be measured by one thing and one thing only: how he fared in the last game of the season.

When Auburn lost 2 of its first 3 games to Alabama after the series was resumed in 1948, the school fired coach Earl Brown and hired an Auburn man, Shug Jordan, who would stay for twenty-five years.

Auburn coach Pat Dye (1981–92) played a major role in bringing the Alabama game to Auburn for the first time in 1989 (photo courtesy of the *Atlanta Journal-Constitution*).

In 1957, Auburn beat Alabama 40–0 for its fourth straight win over the Crimson Tide. Then Auburn rubbed salt into Alabama's wounds by winning the national championship that year. Alabama officials decided that they had had enough. A delegation from the school went to Texas A&M and hired Paul "Bear" Bryant as its new head coach. Bryant would be the dominant figure in Southern college football for the next twenty-five years, beating Auburn nineteen times.

When Bryant and Alabama won 10 out of 11 games played from 1971 to 1981, Auburn's fans wondered if they would ever win again. Jordan retired after the 1975 season having lost four of his last five games against Alabama. His successor, Doug Barfield, went 0–5 against Alabama before he was fired after the 1980 season. Looking for someone to get Auburn back on top in the rivalry, the school hired Pat Dye, a former assistant to Bryant. Dye beat Bryant in his second season and won 6 of the 8 meetings with Alabama from 1982 to 1989.

Auburn returned two blocked punts for touchdowns to upset Alabama in 1972 (photo courtesy of Auburn SID).

If there is one overall truth about the football rivalry between Alabama and Auburn it is this: If you live in the state of Alabama, you can't be in the middle of the road when it comes to this game.

"If you're from Alabama you're either for the University of Alabama or you're for Auburn," says Jim Fyffe, who has been Auburn's radio broadcaster since 1981. "You can't be both. And once you move here, you're asked to declare."

Here are but a few of the great moments that these two teams have contributed to the history of Southern college football:

1948: On December 4 the two teams met for the first time in forty-one years. Sophomore Ed Salem threw three touchdown passes to lead Alabama to a 55–0 victory.

1967: Kenny Stabler ran forty-seven yards on a muddy field for a touchdown, giving Alabama a controversial 7–3 win. It was controversial because Auburn coach Shug Jordan said after the game that Alabama blocker Dennis Dixon had tackled Auburn defender Gusty Yearout on the winning play.

1971: Alabama held Auburn's Pat Sullivan, the Heisman Trophy winner that season, to the lowest yardage total of his career and won 31–7.

1972: One of the most incredible finishes in college football history took place between Auburn and Alabama in this year's game. Trailing 16–3 with only nine minutes

Auburn's James Joseph (10) scores against Alabama in 1989 (photo courtesy of the *Atlanta Journal-Constitution*).

left, Auburn blocked two punts, and David Langer returned both for touchdowns. Auburn won the game 17–16 over second-ranked Alabama. Among many Auburn fans, it still ranks as the greatest win in school history. Today the game is remembered simply as "Punt, Bama, Punt!"

1982: Auburn beat Alabama 23–22, snapping the Crimson Tide's 9-game winning streak. No one knew that it would be Bear Bryant's last regular-season game.

1985: Alabama's Van Tiffin kicked a fifty-two-yard field goal as time ran out, leading the Crimson Tide to a 25–23 win.

1989: For sheer drama, no game will live up to the 1989 game, when Alabama finally came to play at Auburn. Since 1948, the game had been played at Birmingham's Legion Field, which Auburn people felt was a home stadium for the Crimson Tide. Bryant and his successor, Ray Perkins, vowed that Alabama would never play at Auburn. But in 1989 it happened.

"It was a conquest of sorts for Auburn because it had been playing the game in Legion Field," says Fyffe. "It was the most electric moment I've ever seen."

Alabama was undefeated and ranked No. 2. A win over twice-beaten Auburn would put them in the Sugar Bowl with a shot at the national championship. But Auburn won the game 30–20 in one of the most emotional afternoons in college football history.

That's when Alabama coach Bill Curry learned the true depth of the school's rivalry with Auburn. Despite his 10–1 regular season, Curry had lost his 1 game to the wrong opponent. He had won 26 games and had taken Alabama to bowls in all three of his seasons as coach. But he was 0–3 against Auburn. The next season Curry was the head coach at Kentucky.

Auburn vs. Georgia: Brother Against Brother

Auburn Leads 49–46–8

On the day in February of 1892 when Auburn and Georgia played the South's first big football game, it is likely that most of the fans present in Atlanta's Piedmont Park had no idea that the two teams would still be playing each other at the dawn of the twenty-first century. Little did they know then that when both schools have fielded teams, they have met every year since 1894, making theirs the longest continuous football rivalry in the South.

In 1897 Georgia disbanded its team for the rest of the season after a player was killed in the third game. Neither school fielded a team in 1917 or 1918 because of World War I. In 1943 Auburn did not field a team because of World War II. The two teams have played every season without interruption since 1944.

From 1917 until 1958 Auburn and Georgia played all but 1 game in Columbus, Georgia, near the Alabama state line. After that, the game went to the respective campuses.

Going into the 2000 season, Auburn "officially" holds a 49–46–8 record in the series. Auburn's records give the Tigers an extra win because of the disputed game of 1899. Reports indicate that Auburn held an 11–6 lead late in that game when play was suspended. Some stories say that play was suspended because of darkness. Others claim that it was because of an unruly crowd. In any event, the game went into the books as a 0–0 tie. Auburn later appealed, but the ruling was allowed to stand.

Despite the long-standing rivalry, the relationship between the two schools has always been good.

"It's hard to explain to others, but when Auburn and Georgia play it's like a game between you and your best friend," says former Georgia coach Vince Dooley, an Auburn grad and former player for the Tigers from 1951 to 1953.

Fran Tarkenton's touchdown pass to Bill Herron in the final seconds beat Auburn 14–13 in 1959 (photo courtesy of the *Atlanta Journal-Constitution*).

Over the years a number of players and coaches have crossed the Alabama-Georgia state line to work at the other school. Pat Dye, who won 99 games as Auburn's coach from 1981 to 1992, had been an All-American guard at Georgia in 1960. As Auburn's head coach, he recruited heavily in Georgia.

"When Auburn and Georgia play, it's like two brothers going at it in the backyard," says Dye. "I love my brother, but I want to whip him."

This unique relationship has brought about some of the more memorable games in Southern football history.

1942: Georgia was undefeated and ranked No. 1 with the dream backfield of Frank Sinkwich, the Heisman Trophy winner that season, and the great Charley Trippi. But the Bulldogs, looking ahead to a big showdown with No. 2 Georgia Tech, lost 27–13 to Auburn. It remains the biggest upset in the series.

1959: Georgia had lost 6 straight to Auburn and was in danger of losing again, trailing 13–7 with less than a minute to go. With the ball at the Auburn 13-yard line, Georgia quarterback Fran Tarkenton kneeled in the huddle and drew up a play in the grass.

Running that play, Tarkenton hit Bill Herron for the touchdown. Georgia won 14–13 and captured its last SEC championship for coach Wally Butts.

1971: In one of the most hyped games ever between the two schools, Auburn's Pat Sullivan threw for 248 yards and four touchdowns as No. 5 Auburn knocked off No. 6 Georgia 35–20 in Athens. Twelve days later, thanks to his performance against Georgia, Sullivan won the Heisman Trophy.

1985: Bo Jackson had a sixty-seven-yard touchdown run against the Bulldogs in Athens and led Auburn to a 24–10 victory in this game. Jackson finished the game with 121 yards and his performance gave him the edge he needed to win the Heisman Trophy.

1986: Every rivalry needs some comic relief, and in 1986 it came to Auburn and Georgia. Using second-string quarterback Wayne Johnson, the Bulldogs upset the Tigers 20–16 at Auburn. The Georgia fans were so excited that they stormed the field and began tearing up pieces of the turf. Auburn officials turned the water hoses on the Georgia fans, hoping to get control of the situation. The 1986 game has since been known as "The Battle Between the Hoses." Ironically, the Auburn official who decided to turn the hoses on the Georgia fans was Kermit Perry, a Georgia grad who had run track for the Bulldogs.

1994: Auburn had won 20 straight games under second-year coach Terry Bowden and were favored to make it 21 when 4–4–1 Georgia came to Jordan-Hare Stadium. Behind senior quarterback Eric Zeier, the Bulldogs rallied from a 23–9 deficit to tie the game 23–23.

1996: The one hundredth game played between Georgia and Auburn was one of the most exciting ever. Led by quarterback Dameyune Craig, Auburn dominated the first three quarters of the game, leading 28–14 going into the fourth quarter. But Georgia rallied and tied the score on the last play of regulation time with Mike Bobo's thirty-yard touchdown pass to Corey Allen. Georgia eventually prevailed in four overtimes, winning 56–49.

Alabama vs. Tennessee: The Third Saturday in October

Alabama Leads 42–33–7

It was October 20, 1928, and for the first time in fourteen years, Alabama and Tennessee were going to meet on the football field. Alabama, in its fourth year under coach Wallace Wade, had been to the Rose Bowl in 1925 and 1926, winning the national championship both years. Tennessee had won 16 games and lost only 1 in its first two years under coach Robert R. Neyland, but the Vols had not yet faced a team as good as Alabama.

Prior to the game in Tuscaloosa, Neyland engaged in some psychological gamesmanship. He humbly walked up to Wade and asked if Wade would mind shortening the fourth quarter if Alabama was dominating the game, as most expected it would. Neyland told Wade that he wanted to save his players from too much embarrassment. Wade said yes, he would allow Tennessee to save face.

Tennessee's Gene McEver ran the opening kickoff ninety-eight yards for a touchdown, and the Volunteers went on to win the game 15–13. That game put Tennessee on the college football map. The rivalry, which would become one of the richest in the South, was on.

Since that day in 1928, with a few exceptions, Tennessee and Alabama have met each year on the third Saturday in October. Theirs is a rivalry so legendary that author Al Browning of Birmingham penned a book with that title.

Over the years, both schools have considered this game to be the true measuring stick of their respective teams. More often than not, during the twentieth century the winner of this game had the inside track to the SEC championship.

Here are but a few of the highlights in this legendary rivalry:

1932: Played in Birmingham, this game featured what many believe was the greatest punting duel of all time. Alabama's Johnny "Hurry" Cain averaged forty-eight yards on nineteen kicks, while Tennessee All-American Beattie Feathers averaged forty-three yards on twenty-one kicks. Tennessee won the game 7–3 and went on to a 9–0–1 record and the Southern Conference championship.

1939: On October 21 in Knoxville, Tennessee beat Alabama 21–0 behind Johnny Butler's fifty-six-yard touchdown run. The run, in which the sophomore running back went sideline to sideline, is still considered the greatest single play in the school's history. Tennessee went on to finish the regular season undefeated and unscored upon.

1965: Bear Bryant's defending national champions had already been upset by Georgia 18–17 in the season opener and were tied with Tennessee 7–7 in Birmingham in the final minutes of this game. The Crimson Tide drove inside the Tennessee 5-yard line and was setting up for the winning field goal when quarterback Ken Stabler lost track of the downs and threw the ball out of bounds to stop the clock—on fourth down. The game ended in a tie, but Alabama still won the national championship. After the game, an angry Bryant kicked in the locker room door.

1966: This time it was Tennessee's turn to have its heart broken. Trailing 11–10, the Vols drove deep into Alabama territory inside the final minute. Tennessee's Gary Wright missed a twenty-yard field goal with sixteen seconds left in the game and the Crimson Tide held on. Both Wright and the Tennessee bench erupted, saying the field goal was good, but the ruling stood. Alabama went 11–0 that season, but Notre Dame was declared the national champion.

1971–81: With Alabama enjoying its greatest period of dominance ever, the Crimson Tide beat Tennessee in 11 straight games. Only once, in 1976 (20–13), did Alabama win by less than double digits.

1982: Bryant won 16 of his 25 meetings against Tennessee, but not the last. On October 16 in Knoxville, Tennessee knocked off 5–0 Alabama 35–28 to snap the Crimson Tide's 11-game winning streak. The Tennessee players carried coach Johnny Majors to the middle of the field to meet Bryant. No one knew it at the time, but it would be Bryant's last game against Tennessee.

1986–94: During these years Alabama reeled off a string of nine years without a loss. Alabama defeated Tennessee eight times and the teams tied 17–17 in 1993 in Birmingham when the Crimson Tide scored a late touchdown and a two-point conversion. After that Alabama streak ended, Tennessee won the last 5 games of the nineties.

Clemson vs. South Carolina: Still Going Strong After Big Thursday

Clemson Leads 58–35–4

Officials from the University of South Carolina and Clemson College met in 1896 and decided to hold an annual football game between the two schools. But they wanted to do something different to make the game an event for the entire state to enjoy, so they agreed that rather than play the game on a Saturday, it would be held on the Thursday during the annual State Fair in Columbia, South Carolina.

On November 12, South Carolina won the first game 12–7, and the tradition of Big Thursday was born. Except for a one-year break in 1901 and a seven-year hiatus from 1903 to 1909 due to strained relations between the two schools, South Carolina and Clemson played on Thursday every year until 1959. It was quite a celebration, as students from both schools were excused from class in order to attend the game.

While the two teams played a number of great games, Big Thursday is best remembered for the events of 1946, when counterfeiters printed thousands of bogus tickets. The crowd finally stormed the gates and surrounded the field, standing as many as six deep.

Clemson coach Frank Howard kisses Big Thursday good-bye in 1959 (photo courtesy of Clemson SID).

The Big Thursday tradition ended after the 1959 game because Clemson's fans had grown tired of playing in Columbia every year. Clemson had just expanded its stadium by eighteen thousand seats and could now make more money playing at home.

But it didn't matter if the Clemson–South Carolina game was played on Big Thursday in Columbia or on a Saturday on the teams' respective campuses; it was and still remains a big-time football rivalry. Here are a few of the highlights:

1902: Because of a train accident, only one official was available for the game. Not a single penalty was called and South Carolina won 12–6. The night after the game a riot broke out between the fans of the two schools. As a result, the teams did not play again until 1909.

1939: On October 19, future Hall of Famer Banks McFadden rushed for seventy-six yards and threw for eighty-five more, leading the Tigers to a 27–0 win. Clemson would go on to finish 9–1 and play in the Cotton Bowl, the first bowl in the school's history. The Tigers finished with a No. 12 ranking, the team's first ranking in a final poll.

1947: Both teams scored three touchdowns, but Clemson's Mavis "Bull" Cagle missed two extra points and South Carolina won 21–19 in what is still considered one of the better games in the series.

1948: While his team trailed 7–6 with 4:15 remaining, Clemson's Phil Prince blocked a South Carolina punt and Oscar Thompson picked up the ball on the 11-yard line, running it in for a touchdown to give the Tigers a 13–7 win.

1961: A group of South Carolina students pretending to be Clemson players came onto the field and warmed up prior to this year's game. When Clemson's fans eventually discovered that the team on the field was not the real Clemson team but members of the Sigma Nu fraternity from South Carolina, some Clemson students went onto the field and fought with the imposters. State police were called in to restore order.

1962: Clemson's Rodney Rogers kicked a twenty-four-yard field goal with 1:31 left to lift the Tigers to a 20–17 victory. The win was secured when South Carolina quarterback Dan Reeves was sacked on the last play of the game.

Jerry Butler's touchdown catch in the final moments helped Clemson beat South Carolina in 1977 (photo courtesy of Clemson SID).

1965: Clemson scored a touchdown with forty seconds left in the game to get within one point of South Carolina, 17–16. But instead of kicking the extra point to tie, Clemson faked the kick and tried a pass for two points. South Carolina linebacker Bobby Gunnels batted the ball away and South Carolina held on for the one-point win.

1977: Clemson was ranked No. 15 and had been invited to the Gator Bowl when the team arrived in Columbia to play the Gamecocks. The Tigers led the game 24–0 only to have South Carolina rally from behind to take a 27–24 lead. Clemson drove the length of the field and with forty-nine seconds left Steve Fuller hit Jerry Butler with a twenty-yard touchdown pass to win the game 31–27.

1984: Prior to this game, South Carolina's undefeated season and shot at the Orange Bowl was ruined after a loss to Navy. The Gamecocks were still in a funk when they played the Tigers the following week and trailed Clemson 21–3 in the first half. But South Carolina rallied with a touchdown, a safety, and a field goal to come within six, 21–15. Quarterback Mike Hold then drove the Gamecocks eighty-four yards down the field for a touchdown to tie the game with fifty-four seconds left. South Carolina missed the extra point, but Clemson was penalized for having twelve men on the field. This time the extra point was good, giving South Carolina a 22–21 win.

Florida vs. Florida State: The Sunshine Showdown

Florida Leads 26–16–2

In 1947 the Florida state legislature proclaimed that the Florida State College for Women, located in Tallahassee, would become coeducational. That fall Florida State fielded its first football team and went 0–5. The most notable omission on the first Florida State schedule was the University of Florida.

Florida quarterback Danny Wuerffel dives into the end zone during a 31–31 tie at Florida State in 1994 (photo courtesy of Florida SID).

Florida wanted no part of the upstart school in Tallahassee. Athletics director Bob Woodruff was quoted as saying that as long as he was at Florida the school would not play Florida State. The rationale was simple from Florida's perspective: the Gators had nothing to win by playing Florida State. Florida was the bigger school and had a stronger football tradition. The Gators were supposed to win. By playing Florida State, Florida would only enhance the visibility of a rival program and make recruiting against them in the state that much tougher.

Florida State in turn started flexing some of its political muscle. In 1955 a bill reached the floor of the legislature demanding that the schools play each other in all sports. But Florida had enough pull to get the bill voted down 19–15.

Not too long after that, however, Governor Leroy Collins brought the two school's athletics directors together and ordered them to schedule a game against each other as soon as possible. Florida finally relented and the first Florida–Florida State game was played on November 22, 1958.

On the very first play of that first game, Florida State's Bobby Renn took a handoff and rambled seventy-eight yards. Florida State later scored to take a 7–0 lead and ignite the passion of the FSU fans. Although Florida came back to win 21–7, a rivalry, whose heat has only grown hotter over the years, was born.

Here are some of the highlights:

1964: After playing the first 6 games in Gainesville (all won by Florida), Florida State finally got the Gators to come to Tallahassee. Florida coach Ray Graves, in an attempt to mentally prepare his players to play at Florida State and keep the 6-game winning streak alive, put the words "Never, FSU, Never" on his team's practice jerseys. When Florida showed up for the game, the Gator players had the words "Go for Seven" printed on the fronts of their jerseys. But none of this gamesmanship worked for Florida, as the Seminoles won 16–7 on the way to a 9–1–1 season.

1966: After losing at Florida 30–17 in 1965, Florida State again had a chance to win in Tallahassee. Trailing 22–19 with twenty-six seconds remaining, Florida State's Lane Fenner made a diving catch of a fifty-five-yard pass near the boundary line of the end zone. The official on the play ruled Fenner out of bounds, touching off a huge argument. Florida prevailed by three points, but to this day, Florida State fans still insist that Fenner's catch should have been a touchdown.

1971: Florida State, in its first year under coach Larry Jones, came to Gainesville with a 5–0 record. Florida was rebuilding under second-year coach Doug Dickey and was 0–5, but Florida still won 17–15.

1994: The Seminoles and the Gators have twice played dramatic regular season games only to get a rematch in the Sugar Bowl. In 1994, Florida dominated the rivalry game for almost three quarters, holding on to a 31–3 lead. But then Florida State rallied against a dazed Gator defense and the game ended in a 31–31 tie. Florida went on to beat Alabama in the SEC championship game and was then invited to play Florida State in the Sugar Bowl. This time the Seminoles won, 23–17.

1996: Florida was undefeated and ranked No. 1 when the Gators traveled to Tallahassee to play No. 2 Florida State. The Seminoles pounded Florida quarterback Danny Wuerffel, who would be the season's Heisman Trophy winner, and won the game 24–21. That capped off an 11–0 season for Florida State and put the Seminoles into the Sugar Bowl, where they would play for the national championship. Florida State expected to play Nebraska for the title, but Nebraska lost to Texas in the Big 12 championship game. After Florida beat Alabama in the SEC championship game, the Gators moved to No. 3 in the rankings and got a rematch with Florida State in New Orleans. This time coach Steve Spurrier put Wuerffel in the shotgun formation to slow down the Florida State rush. The Gators dominated 52–20 to win the national championship.

1997: Florida State was undefeated and ranked No. 1 when it arrived at Florida's Swamp. The Seminoles knew that a win would take them to the Orange Bowl to play Nebraska for at least a share of a national championship. A field goal put Florida State in the lead, 29–25, with 2:38 left in the game. With only one more defensive stop Florida State would have had a perfect season. But on Florida's first play from scrimmage, quarterback Doug Johnson fooled the FSU secondary and hit Jacquez Green for a sixty-three-yard completion. Two plays later Florida's Fred Taylor scored from one yard out and the Gators won 32–29. Florida State coach Bobby Bowden would later call it one of the most difficult defeats of his career.

Alabama vs. Georgia Tech: A Great Rivalry Turns Ugly

Alabama Leads 28–21–3

Alabama coach Paul "Bear" Bryant and Bobby Dodd, his counterpart at Georgia Tech, claimed to be friends. But the rivalry between their two schools took an ugly turn during the teams' November 18, 1961, game in Birmingham. In the fourth quarter, Georgia Tech's Chick Graning was running down the field under a Georgia Tech punt when Alabama's Darwin Holt, who was blocking on the play, flipped an elbow which caught Graning in the face. Graning suffered a broken nose and a broken jaw and lost five teeth on the play. No penalty was assessed.

After the 10–0 win by Alabama, a war of words broke out in the newspapers in Atlanta and Birmingham. The Atlanta newspapers were highly critical of Bryant, accusing him of

Alabama's Bear Bryant (left) with Georgia Tech's Bobby Dodd in happier times (photo courtesy of the *Atlanta Journal-Constitution*).

teaching dirty play. Bryant said that the elbow thrown by Holt was unintentional. He further responded by showing the game film to newspaper writers in Alabama, pointing out all the elbows that Georgia Tech had thrown.

The episode put a temporary strain on the relationship between Bryant and Dodd, who put an end to the series with Alabama after the 1964 game. The two teams would not play again until 1979, thirteen years after Dodd retired.

From 1979 to 1984 Georgia Tech and Alabama played every year but have not played since. Still, in its day, the Georgia Tech–Alabama rivalry was one of the best in the South.

Here are some of the highlights:

1952: Georgia Tech was 8–0 and ranked No. 2 when 7–1 Alabama came to Grant Field. The Yellow Jackets were clinging to a 7–3 lead late in the game as Alabama was driving for a potential winning touchdown. On fourth down at the Georgia Tech 4-yard line, Jakie Rudolph, a tiny 5'7", 155-pound defensive back, stopped Alabama running back Bobby Marlowe short of the goal line. Georgia Tech won the game and went on to finish 12–0 and win the national championship.

1960: The bad feelings that surfaced in the 1961 game began the year before in Atlanta with one of the greatest comebacks in Alabama history. Georgia Tech led 15–0 at half time and 15–6 at the beginning of the fourth quarter. Pat Trammell, Alabama's starting quarterback, had been taken out of the game as a result of injuries. Reserve quarterback Bob Skelton led Alabama to a touchdown with 8:44 left to make the score 15–13. Then, in the final minutes, he drove the Crimson Tide down the field, where Richard O'Dell kicked the winning field goal from twenty-one yards out on the last play of the game. It was the first field goal that O'Dell had ever kicked.

1962: When Alabama returned to Atlanta after the Graning-Holt incident the year before in Birmingham, the Georgia Tech students were waiting for Bryant and the Crimson Tide. Bryant, concerned about being hit by a stray liquor bottle, donned a helmet during pregame warm-ups. Alabama was the defending national champion and ranked No. 1, but the Yellow Jackets upset the Crimson Tide 7–6. It was the only game Alabama lost all season, and it very likely cost the Crimson Tide another national championship.

1981: Alabama was 1–0 and ranked No. 4 when it met Georgia Tech in Birmingham. The game was the season opener for the Yellow Jackets, who had been 1–9–1 the year before. Trailing 21–17 late in the fourth quarter, Georgia Tech drove eighty yards for a touchdown with 3:57 left to beat the Crimson Tide 24–21 before a stunned crowd of 78,865 at Legion Field. Alabama's fifty-yard field-goal attempt on the final play of the game fell short.

LSU vs. Ole Miss: Cannon's Eighty-Nine-Yard Run Will Live Forever

LSU Leads 48–36–4

It was Halloween night, 1959, and the fog that hung over LSU's Tiger Stadium only added to the eeriness of what would become a most unforgettable evening. LSU, the defending national champion, was undefeated (6–0) and ranked No. 1 for the second straight year, after an 11–0 season in 1958. Ole Miss was 6–0 and ranked No. 3. The winner would have the inside track to the SEC championship and still be in the hunt for the national championship.

With ten minutes remaining, Ole Miss was clinging to a 3–0 lead. The Rebels had so much confidence in their defense that they began punting on third down. Jake Gibbs, the Ole Miss quarterback and punter, never intended to kick the ball to LSU's Billy Cannon. The ground was mushy and Gibbs figured that the ball would simply slide around when it hit the ground. Instead, the kicked ball took a big hop in front of Cannon, who decided to field it on the run.

By most accounts, eight different LSU defenders touched Cannon, but none could bring him down. With each broken tackle, the roar of the LSU crowd grew louder. Gibbs was the last Ole Miss defender to have a chance to tackle the LSU stallion.

"I got a hand on him," Gibbs recalls, "but he just shook me off like a puppy."

Cannon eventually lumbered eighty-nine yards for a touchdown and a place in history. His run still stands as one of the most famous plays in the history of Southern college football and the defining moment of one of the South's greatest rivalries.

While LSU won that famous game, the Rebels always point out that in their rematch with the Tigers in the Sugar Bowl they beat them 21–0. That Ole Miss team, despite the loss, was later named the SEC Team of the Decade.

Billy Cannon's run in the LSU–Ole Miss game of 1959 (photo courtesy of LSU SID).

In the forties, fifties, and sixties, no rivalry in the South was more competitive than Ole Miss vs. LSU. The most intense period of the rivalry was from 1959 to 1961, when Ole Miss could have posted three undefeated regular seasons if not for two losses and a tie to LSU. LSU had unbeaten seasons spoiled by Ole Miss in 1962 and 1969.

Here are but a few of the great moments of this rivalry:

1947: Perhaps the two greatest college quarterbacks of the era, Y. A. Tittle of LSU and Charlie Conerly of Ole Miss, put together a memorable shootout in Baton Rouge on November 1. Conerly scored all three Ole Miss touchdowns and the Rebels won 20–18.

1960: Ole Miss was for the second year in a row unbeaten and in pursuit of the national championship when LSU came to Oxford with a 1–4 record. After a tough 10–7 win over Arkansas the week before, the Rebels were flat and trailed 6–3. Starting from his own 21-yard line, a hobbled Jake Gibbs drove the Rebels into field goal position.

Ole Miss quarterback Archie Manning (1968–70) threw for 345 yards against LSU in 1969 (photo courtesy of Mississippi SID).

Allen Green made the forty-one-yard field goal for the tie with six seconds left in the game. Ole Miss went on to finish 10–0–1 that season and was declared the national champion by several wire services.

1961: Ole Miss was 6–0 and ranked No. 2 when it arrived at Baton Rouge to play No. 6 LSU. The Rebels led 7–3 at halftime, but in the third quarter, quarterback Jerry Stovall raced fifty-seven yards to set up a touchdown that gave LSU a 10–7 lead. That score stood and the Tigers went on to win the SEC championship.

1964: Coach Charlie McClendon's third LSU team was undefeated and ranked No. 9 when it hosted 3–2–1 Ole Miss. The Rebels crossed LSU territory only twice, but that was enough to allow them a 10–3 lead late in the game. LSU was given a chance to win when Ole Miss punt returner Doug Cunningham fumbled near midfield and the Tigers recovered. LSU scored on a nineteen-yard pass from Billy Ezell to Billy Masters with 3:30 left in the game. When LSU's Doug Moreau caught a tipped pass for a two-point conversion, the Tigers won 11–10.

1969: LSU was 6–0 and seemed to be headed for an SEC championship when it faced 3–3 Ole Miss in Jackson, Mississippi. But the Tigers did not have an answer for junior quarterback Archie Manning of Ole Miss, who threw for 345 yards. The Rebels knocked off the Tigers 26–23 in LSU's only loss all season.

1972: LSU was 6–0 and had its eyes set on another SEC championship. The Tigers trailed 16–10 in the final minutes until quarterback Bert Jones put together one of the most memorable performances of his career. Jones drove his team the length of the field, and on a play that began with ten seconds left, Ole Miss was called for pass interference. That gave LSU a first down at the Mississippi 10-yard line with four seconds remaining. Here the controversy began, according to Marty Mule's outstanding book on LSU football, *Eye of the Tiger*.

Ole Miss fans still insist that the next play, an incomplete pass over the middle, took more than four seconds, and that the game should have been over. But after Jones's pass hit the ground, one second remained on the Tiger Stadium clock.

Given one last chance, Jones hit Brad Davis out of the backfield. Davis juggled the ball and dove into the end zone for a touchdown to tie the game. Rusty Jackson added the extra point and the Tigers won 17–16.

To this day, Ole Miss fans believe they fell victim to bad time keeping. They say that what Jones did—run two plays in four seconds—was impossible.

Just a few days after this historic game, a sign went up on the Louisiana-Mississippi border: "Entering Louisiana—Set your clocks back four seconds."

1979: Ole Miss jumps out to a 17–0 lead in Jackson only to have LSU storm back to win 28–24.

1986: LSU won the SEC championship in 1986 but still lost to Ole Miss 21–19 in Baton Rouge.

Ole Miss vs. Mississippi State: The Egg Bowl

Ole Miss Leads 54–36–6

Most could understand why the fans of Ole Miss wanted to celebrate after watching their team win at Mississippi A&M (now Mississippi State) in 1926. In the 23 previous meetings with their hated state rival, the Rebels had won only 5 times. In his book *Mississippi Mayhem*, author William George Barner III described the scene that would further fuel the rivalry and eventually lead to the creation of the Egg Bowl.

When Ole Miss fans went for the goalposts after the 7–6 win, Mississippi State fans came out of the stands with cane-bottom chairs, according to Barner. Fights broke out all over the stadium until almost all of the chairs were splintered.

Ole Miss coach Billy Brewer holds the Golden Egg trophy after a win over Mississippi State (photo courtesy of Mississippi SID).

The war of words that broke out between the two schools continued long after the postgame scene in Starkville. Officials on both sides feared that more violence would erupt the following year. In an effort to cool the animosity between the two schools, members of Sigma Iota, an Ole Miss honor society, proposed awarding a trophy to the winning team. "The Golden Egg," a regulation-sized, gold-plated football mounted on a pedestal, was designated as the trophy. The two schools shared the $250 cost.

The first Battle of the Golden Egg, or Egg Bowl, as it became known, took place on Thanksgiving Day in 1927. The game was actually the twenty-fifth meeting of the two schools and Ole Miss won 20–12. But this time, instead of a brawl, a formal ceremony was staged during which the president of Mississippi State presented the trophy to the chancellor of Ole Miss. The chancellor, in turn, handed the trophy to the Ole Miss team captain.

Over the years, the Battle for the Golden Egg has always been the highlight of the season for both schools, regardless of their respective records. Even in years when both schools were losing, an entire season could be salvaged for one of them by winning the Golden Egg.

Since 1927, the game has been played every year except 1943, when football at Mississippi colleges and universities was put on hold because of World War II. From 1927 to 1972, the game alternated between the campuses in Starkville and Oxford. In 1973, the game was moved to Jackson, where it remained through 1990. In 1991, the games went back to the respective campuses.

Ole Miss leads the series, 54–36–6. Here are but a few of the most memorable moments in this heated rivalry:

1928: In the second meeting for the Golden Egg, Claude "Tadpole" Smith earned his place in Ole Miss football history. He ran forty yards for a touchdown and then kicked the winning extra point, taking the Rebels to a 20–19 win on Thanksgiving Day.

1941: Mississippi State won 6–0 in Oxford to claim its first and only SEC championship.

1951: Arnold "Showboat" Boykin scored seven touchdowns as Ole Miss routed Mississippi State 49–7. Boykin's performance remains one of the greatest ever in the Rebels' history.

1962: Sophomore quarterback Jimmy Weatherly missed a handoff to David Jennings late in the game but then put the ball on his hip and ran forty-three yards for a touchdown to give Ole Miss a 13–6 victory. The Memphis Commercial Appeal would call Weatherly "The Goof That Laid the Golden Egg."

1983: In the final seconds of the game, a gust of wind caused a potential winning field goal for Mississippi State to fall short, and Ole Miss held on to a 24–23 victory.

1992: Trailing 17–10, Mississippi State ran eleven plays inside the Ole Miss 10-yard line with less than three minutes left and still could not score. Michael Lowry's interception in the end zone stopped a last-second Bulldog drive, preserving the seven-point victory.

1997: Mississippi quarterback Stewart Patridge hit Andre Rone for a ten-yard touchdown pass with twenty-five seconds left in the game. Patridge then hit Cory Peterson open for a two-point conversion to give the Rebels a 15–14 victory. The win sent Mississippi to the inaugural Motor City Bowl, its first post-season game since 1992.

1999: The 1999 Mississippi State team earned a reputation for winning close games, and never was this truer than in the season finale against Ole Miss. The Bulldogs were down 20–6 midway through the third quarter but battled back to tie the Rebels 20–20 with twenty-seven seconds left in the game. It appeared that the game would head into overtime, but a pass from Mississippi's Romaro Miller was intercepted and returned to the 26-yard line with eight seconds left. Mississippi State's Scott Westerfield kicked a forty-four-yard field goal with four seconds left, and the Bulldogs won 23–20.

Georgia vs. Florida: The World's Largest Outdoor Cocktail Party

Georgia Leads 45–31–2

In 1933 officials from the universities of Georgia and Florida decided to move their annual game from the schools' respective campuses to Jacksonville, Florida. They thought the move would bring a more festive atmosphere to the event and give both groups of fans a mini vacation in the fall. Little did they know that they were about to create one of the biggest events in all of college football.

Except for a two-year break during World War II and another two-year break (1994–95) during the renovation of the old Gator Bowl Stadium, Georgia and Florida have fought their border war every year along the banks of the St. John's River.

The tickets are divided evenly between the two schools so that there is no home-field advantage. Fans arrive at Jacksonville several days before the game to play golf, shop,

Georgia's Bulldog drags the Florida Gator (photo courtesy of the *Atlanta Journal-Constitution*/Calvin Cruce).

and do a whole lot of partying. Over the years, the game has become such a social event that it was finally dubbed "The World's Largest Outdoor Cocktail Party."

Parties aside, the Georgia-Florida game is best known for having contributed some truly classic moments to the history of Southern college football.

1964: Georgia won 14–7 when placekicker Bobby Etter picked up a bad snap and ran twenty-two yards for a touchdown.

1965: Florida quarterback Steve Spurrier threw a thirty-two-yard touchdown pass with forty-one seconds left, giving the Gators a 14–10 win.

1966: Spurrier was in the middle of his Heisman Trophy–winning season, but more than anything he wanted to lead Florida to its first SEC title. A win over Georgia would do it. Florida led 10–3 at halftime, but in the second half the Bulldogs pounded Spurrier and won the game 27–10.

1973, 1974: Both of these games came down to a two-point conversion. In 1973 Florida made it and won 11–10. In 1974 the Bulldogs stopped the Gators and won 17–16.

1975: Florida needed a win over Georgia to nail down its first SEC championship in the school's history. The Gators seemed to be in good shape, leading 7–3 with 3:42 remaining. Then Georgia tight end Richard Appleby took the ball on an end-around, and instead of running the ball as he had done earlier in the game, Appleby stopped, planted his foot, and threw an eighty-yard touchdown pass to Gene Washington, giving the Bulldogs a 10–7 victory.

1976: Florida again needed to defeat Georgia to win the SEC championship, and at halftime the Gators appeared to be in control, leading 27–13. With his team still leading 27–20, Florida coach Doug Dickey decided to go for a first down on fourth and 1 at his own 29-yard line. Georgia stopped the play and went on to score three straight touchdowns for a 41–27 victory. The Bulldogs went on to win the SEC championship and Dickey's "Fourth and Dumb" stuck with him for the rest of his days at Florida, which weren't many. In 1978 he was replaced by Charley Pell.

1980: The most famous moment in the rich Georgia-Florida rivalry, at least from the Georgia perspective, took place in 1980. The Bulldogs, led by great freshman Herschel Walker, were 9–0, ranked No. 2, and in the hunt for the national championship. Earlier in the day top-ranked Notre Dame had been tied 3–3 by Georgia Tech, so a win would move the Bulldogs to No. 1 in the next polls.

But with 1:03 remaining, Georgia trailed 21–20 and was stuck on its own 7-yard line. The Bulldogs' chance at a national championship seemed to be over. Then, on third and 11, quarterback Buck Belue hit receiver Lindsay Scott with a pass near the 25-yard line. A Florida defender slipped down and Scott raced the length of the field for the touchdown. Georgia won 26–21 and went on to beat Notre Dame in the Sugar Bowl for the national championship.

1984: Florida quarterback Kerwin Bell hit Ricky Nattiel with a ninety-six-yard touchdown pass to clinch a 27–0 victory and snap Georgia's 7-game winning streak. Florida fans were so excited that they tore down a goalpost and did a victory lap around the Gator Bowl.

As Florida's coach, Steve Spurrier won 9 of his first 10 games against Georgia (photo courtesy of the *Atlanta Journal-Constitution*).

1985: Florida was undefeated and ranked No. 1 when it arrived at Jacksonville to play a 6–1–1 Georgia team that had been tied by Vanderbilt. Tim Worley sparked the Georgia effort with an eighty-nine-yard touchdown run and the Bulldogs upset the Gators 24–3.

1990–present: Vince Dooley retired as Georgia's head coach after the 1988 season with a 17–7–1 record against Florida. Then former Heisman Trophy winner Steve Spurrier was named Florida's head coach in 1990. Spurrier had never forgotten that Georgia had knocked him out of a chance for an SEC championship in 1966 and took great joy in beating the Bulldogs. Under Spurrier, Florida won 9 of its 10 games against Georgia from 1990 to 1999.

Georgia vs. Georgia Tech: A Peach of a Rivalry

Georgia Leads 52–35–5

Is it possible for a player to have his jersey retired based on his performance in 1 game? Yes, if the game is big enough. And for the University of Georgia, few games have been bigger than its 1957 meeting with Georgia Tech.

The Bulldogs had had very little to cheer about that season. Going into the game with Georgia Tech they were 2–7 and headed for their third straight losing record under coach Wally Butts. To make matters worse, Georgia was mired in an unbelievable 8-game losing streak to Bobby Dodd and Georgia Tech, the longest in the history of the series for either team.

After a 10–1 season in 1956, Georgia Tech (4–3–2) was also struggling when Georgia arrived at Grant Field on November 30. The winner of the game would have a chance to salvage its season and get the alumni off its back.

In his book about the rivalry, *Clean Old-Fashioned Hate*, author Bill Cromartie makes it clear that if a game ever belonged to one player, the 1957 Georgia–Georgia Tech game belonged to Bulldog running back Theron Sapp. Sapp, a junior fullback from Macon, scored the game's only touchdown from one yard out late in the third quarter. From his linebacker position, he recovered two fumbles—one of which set up the winning touchdown drive.

The victory touched off a wild celebration among the Georgia fans who had come to Grant Field. From that day on, Sapp became known as "The Drought Breaker" for having ended Georgia's losing streak to Georgia Tech.

Sapp went on to enjoy a solid career at Georgia and was named All-SEC in 1958. In 1959 Sapp became only the third player in Georgia history to have his jersey retired—his touchdown against Tech was that big. Since Georgia and Georgia Tech played their first game in 1893 (won by Georgia Tech 28–6 in what Cromartie describes as a brawl-filled afternoon), this game has stirred passions like few others have.

The two teams stopped playing each other for six years (1919–25) over a disagreement that involved baseball and World War I. Cromartie writes that Georgia was in the

Georgia's Theron Sapp scores to end Georgia Tech's 8-game winning streak in 1957 (photo courtesy of the *Atlanta Journal-Constitution*).

middle of sweeping a 4-game baseball series with Georgia Tech when some of Georgia's students flew a banner pointing out that in 1917–18 Georgia had not fielded a football team because of World War I while Georgia Tech, under coach John Heisman, had continued playing. Georgia Tech students and officials took offense and threatened to break off athletic relations with Georgia if Georgia did not apologize. Georgia indicated that no apology would be forthcoming, and thus the schools did not play each other in any sport until 1925, when the two sides made peace.

When Georgia Tech left the SEC after the 1963 season, the Georgia–Georgia Tech game ceased to be a conference game. Still, the rivalry has not lost any of its passion.

"Georgia has other rivals, like Florida and Auburn, but Georgia Tech is the greatest of all because it's our state rival," says former Georgia coach Vince Dooley, who was 19–6 in 25 meetings with Georgia Tech. "If you lose that one, there are a lot of people on both sides who will not let you forget it."

Dooley arrived at Georgia in 1964 just as Dodd was winding down his legendary career at Georgia Tech. Dodd would retire after the 1966 season with a 12–10 record against the Bulldogs.

Here are but a few of the most memorable moments in this great Southern rivalry:

1927: Georgia, 9–0 and ranked No. 1, was a heavy favorite against Georgia Tech at Grant Field. The Bulldogs knew that a win would earn them an invitation to the Rose Bowl on New Year's Day. But Georgia Tech intercepted four passes, winning 12–0 and dashing Georgia's hopes of a trip to Pasadena.

1942: The week before its scheduled date, the Georgia–Georgia Tech game of 1942 was shaping up to be one of the biggest in the history of Southern football. Georgia, with running back and Heisman Trophy winner Frankie Sinkwich, was undefeated and ranked No. 1 when it met Auburn on November 21. At the Auburn-Georgia game fans were already talking about the next week's game with Georgia Tech, since No. 2 Tech was also undefeated, and an invitation to the Rose Bowl would go to the winner of the game. Georgia stumbled against 4–4–1 Auburn and lost 27–13 but still had to bring in eight thousand extra seats for all its fans at the next week's game with Tech. The Rose Bowl stuck with its promise that the winner of the game would go to Pasadena. It wasn't even close as Sinkwich and Charley Trippi led Georgia to a 34–0 win. Georgia (9–1) went to the Rose Bowl where it beat UCLA. Georgia Tech (9–1) went to the Cotton Bowl where it lost to Texas.

1966: The 1966 game rekindled memories of the 1942 game. No. 5 Georgia Tech arrived at Georgia's Sanford Stadium with a 9–0 record. The Yellow Jackets would be heading to the Orange Bowl later that season. Georgia (8–1) had won the SEC championship two weeks before by beating Auburn. The Bulldogs' only defeat was a 7–6 loss at Miami. Tech coach Bobby Dodd had the glamour backfield combo of quarterback Kim King and running back Lenny Snow, while Georgia featured a hard-hitting defense led by All-American tackle George Patton. Georgia's Kent Lawrence returned a punt seventy-one yards for a touchdown and the Bulldog defense simply smothered King and Snow on the way to a 23–14 victory in the two team's one hundredth meeting. Georgia went on to the Cotton Bowl, where it beat SMU, while Tech lost to Florida and Steve Spurrier in the Orange Bowl. Not long after that, Dodd retired after twenty-two seasons as head coach at Georgia Tech.

1971: On a cold Thanksgiving night at Grant Field, these two old rivals played one of their most exciting games ever. Georgia was 9–1 after losing to Pat Sullivan and Auburn twelve days before. The Bulldogs were still feeling the effects of that loss as they fell behind 17–7 in the second quarter. But just before halftime Georgia quarterback Andy Johnson hit Jimmy Shirer for a twenty-three-yard touchdown to give the Bulldogs new life. Still, Georgia Tech was leading 24–21 when Georgia took possession on its own 35-yard line with 1:29 left in the game. Then, with fifty-seven seconds left, Georgia faced a fourth and 10 at the Georgia Tech 43. With the game in the balance, Johnson hit tight end Mike Green for eighteen yards and a first down. The Bulldogs eventually scored when running back Jimmy Poulous leaped over the top of the Georgia Tech defense from one yard out with fourteen seconds left to give Georgia a 28–24 victory.

1978: Georgia fell behind 20–0 but battled back to take a 21–20 lead with Scott Woerner's seventy-two-yard punt return for a touchdown in the third quarter. But then Georgia Tech answered with a stunning 101-yard return for a touchdown on the ensuing kickoff. A two-point conversion gave the Yellow Jackets a 28–21 lead. Georgia got one last chance to score when it took possession at its own 16-yard line with just under six minutes left. Georgia freshman quarterback Buck Belue converted a fourth-down play to keep the drive alive. Then, on a fourth-down play at the Georgia Tech 43, Belue found Amp Arnold behind the Yellow Jacket secondary and lofted a touchdown pass with 2:25 left in the game. Georgia went for the two-point conversion and the win. Belue passed over the middle incomplete for Mark Hodge, but Georgia Tech was called for pass interference. Given another chance, Belue pitched to Arnold for the two points and a 29–28 victory.

1984: Georgia Tech gave coach Bill Curry his first win over Georgia, 35–18 in Athens. The game snapped Georgia's 6-game winning streak. Back in Atlanta, the Tech students were so excited that they broke into Grant Field and tore down the goalposts, parading the pieces up and down North Avenue.

1985: Tech's Gary Lee returned a kickoff ninety-five yards for a touchdown, which proved to be the winning points Georgia Tech needed to beat No. 20 Georgia 20–16. Georgia still had a chance to win, but quarterback James Jackson fumbled at midfield in the closing minutes.

Just to prove that the rivalry still had steam, Georgia and Georgia Tech closed out the 1990s with three of the most exciting games in the history of the series:

1997: When Charles Wiley scored on a three-yard touchdown run to give the Yellow Jackets a 24–21 lead with forty-eight seconds left in the game, it seemed that Georgia Tech would win this home game. But Georgia took over on its own 35-yard line after the ensuing kickoff went out of bounds. Then two quick passes to Champ Bailey and another to running back Robert Edwards put Georgia deep in Georgia Tech territory. A controversial pass-interference call negated a Georgia Tech interception and gave Georgia a first down at the 8-yard line. Quarterback Mike Bobo hit Corey Allen for the touchdown with eight seconds left and Georgia won 27–24. It was Georgia's seventh straight win.

1998: Georgia appeared to be headed for its eighth straight win over Georgia Tech, leading 19–7 going into the fourth quarter. Georgia Tech, however, would not be denied, driving seventy-four yards for a touchdown early in the final quarter. After a two-point conversion, the Yellow Jackets trailed 19–15. Brad Chambers's forty-nine-yard field goal brought the Yellow Jackets to within one, 19–18, with 5:01 left. Georgia Tech then drove fifty-two yards in the final four minutes and Chambers kicked a thirty-five-yard field goal with two seconds left to give the Yellow Jackets a 21–19 victory.

1999: This game will probably go down in history as the wildest game in the series. Georgia Tech quarterback Joe Hamilton, who would finish second to Wisconsin's Ron Dayne for the Heisman trophy that year, was unstoppable. Twice he posted Georgia Tech to seventeen-point leads in the game and twice Georgia, led by sophomore quarterback Quincy Carter, fought back to tie the game. The game was tied at 48–48 when Georgia started its final drive. Within the final seconds, Georgia had a first down near the Georgia Tech goal line. Coach Jim Donnan instructed his team to take one shot at the end zone and then kick the field goal. But when running back Jasper Sanks was struggling for the touchdown, the ball popped loose and was recovered by Georgia Tech. Television replays later showed that Sanks was down and that the play shouldn't have been ruled a fumble.

But the call stood and the game went into overtime. After Georgia failed to score on its possession in overtime, Georgia Tech lined up for a field-goal attempt on third down. The Bulldogs blocked the kick and Georgia fans thought the drive was over. But Georgia Tech recovered the ball and was given another chance to kick. This time Luke Manget's thirty-eight-yard field goal attempt was good and the Yellow Jackets won 51–48.

THE VOICES

Before television brought dozens of games into the home and before modern transportation made getting to the games much easier, the most important link between college football and its fans was the radio play-by-play announcer.

These men did much more than just explain what was happening on the field. They were the ultimate cheerleaders and, sometimes, the most unforgiving critics. They made no pretense of objectivity, literally living, dying, laughing, and crying along with every first down and last-minute play.

With their voices, they were able to transport fans from every tiny hamlet in the state to that glorious stadium far, far away. Thanks to the announcer's powers of description, the listeners could not only hear the band but could also see it in their mind's eye. And the really good announcers could take their listeners through a full range of emotions on any given Saturday afternoon.

Today, even though most games are shown on television, the emotional bond between Southern college football fans and their radio announcer is still very strong. In stadiums around the South, fans can be seen holding radios up to their ears, listening to their announcer while watching the game on the field. They can see what happens on the field, but they need him to tell them what it all means. His excitement is their excitement. His joy is their joy.

Without these men, the special emotional bond between Southern college football and its fans would never have been completely cemented. These are their stories.

Otis Boggs Florida, **1939–82**

Boggs was not the kind of guy you could pick out of a crowd. A rotund, slightly balding, ordinary-looking man, Boggs did not give the impression that he was capable of extraordinary things. But contrary to his appearance, Boggs, the valedictorian of his high school senior class and a former chemistry major at the University of Florida, could have done anything with his life. But he was bitten by the broadcasting bug.

What happened after Boggs graduated from Florida is a wonderful chapter in Florida football history. In 1939 he became a member of the Florida broadcast team right out of

Florida's Otis Boggs
(photo courtesy of Florida SID).

college. He took over as the Gators' play-by-play man in 1940 and stayed at the job for forty-two seasons and 401 games.

Few radio voices have bonded with a group of fans the way Boggs bonded with the Gator faithful. Tom McEwen, the longtime sports editor of the *Tampa Tribune*, told a story that best illustrated the relationship between Boggs and the Florida fans. When Florida State took a 17–16 lead in the 1965 Sunshine Showdown against Florida, an FSU fan stood up in his seat, turned around, and shouted at the press box: "How you like that, Otis Boggs?" He sat down to applause and laughter.

The point of the story is that the fan would not have known Otis Boggs if Boggs had walked up and asked him to dance. But in his excitement, the fan wanted to lash out at the best-known symbol of Florida football. For forty-two seasons, that symbol was Otis Boggs.

Boggs retired as the voice of the Gators in 1982.

Al Ciraldo Georgia Tech, **1954–97**

A time when "toe meets leather": this signature phrase of the late Al Ciraldo, who served as the voice of the Yellow Jackets for almost a half a century, describes the forty-three unforgettable seasons that comprised Ciraldo's tenure at Tech. Georgia Tech football has always evoked memories of John Heisman, Bobby Dodd, and the Ramblin' Wreck that leads the Georgia Tech team out onto Grant Field. But it was Ciraldo who painted the picture for all those Georgia Tech fans who could not be in Atlanta on game day to see it for themselves.

Georgia Tech's Al Ciraldo
(photo courtesy of the *Atlanta Journal-Constitution*).

Ciraldo, a 1948 graduate of the University of Florida, came to Atlanta in 1949 to broadcast basketball games for the University of Georgia, Georgia Tech's biggest rival. But in 1954 he joined the staff at WGST radio, the flagship station of Georgia Tech athletics. His first football broadcast for Georgia Tech was on September 8, 1954, in a game against

Tulane. Over the next thirty-eight seasons, Ciraldo would do the play-by-play for 416 football and 1,030 basketball games for Georgia Tech.

In 1992 Ciraldo stepped down as Tech's play-by-play announcer but remained involved in the pregame and postgame shows. He officially retired in 1997 after a radio career that had spanned a total of sixty-two years.

Ciraldo passed away on November 7, 1997, at the age of seventy-six.

Jack Cristil Mississippi State, **1953–Present**

In 1953 Jack Cristil was a twenty-seven-year-old Army veteran working at a radio station in Clarksdale, Mississippi, when he sent a tape of his work to Mississippi State athletic director Dudy Noble. Cristil was one of three men up for the job of play-by-play man for Bulldog football. Cristil got the interview and the job. Then he got his marching orders from Noble.

Jack Cristil began broadcasting for Mississippi State in 1953 (photo courtesy of Mississippi State SID).

"You tell them what the score is, who has the ball, and how much time's left, and cut out all that other bulls**t," said Noble, a man known for his ability to plainly speak his mind.

Cristil, now seventy-four, is still taking that advice to heart in the fall of 2000 as he enters his forty-eighth season of broadcasting Mississippi State football games. Going into the start of the 2000 season, Cristil has called 502 Mississippi State games and has endeared himself to several generations of faithful Bulldog football fans.

Cristil knew at an early age that he wanted to be a broadcaster. As a young boy he would make up games in his head and broadcast them out loud. After he got out of the service in 1946, he hitchhiked four hundred miles from Chicago to Minneapolis to take broadcasting courses at the University of Minnesota. He began his radio career in 1948 calling minor league baseball games in Jackson, Tennessee. Then, after several years of traveling through the South to call baseball games, he got the job at Mississippi State.

Cristil was the first nonathlete to be named to the Mississippi Sports Hall of Fame when he was inducted in 1992.

Woody Durham (photo courtesy of North Carolina SID).

Woody Durham North Carolina, **1971–Present**

Woody Durham's love of sports began when he was a 165-pound pulling guard for Albermarle High School, the 1957 Western North Carolina champions.

"I was a terror," he recalled.

Durham loved the excitement that came with being in the arena of athletic competition but knew that he would not be able to play football at the college level. So he went searching for something that would allow him to keep that feeling of excitement. He found what he was looking for in broadcasting, and he began his career a week before his sixteenth birthday. Durham had entered a local oratory contest, and one of the judges was the manager of the town's radio station, WZKY. Soon after the contest Durham got his first job in broadcasting.

College sports in general and college football in particular is lucky that Woody Durham was able to follow his passion. The fall of 2000 will mark Durham's thirtieth season of calling games on the North Carolina Tar Heel Sports Network.

After graduating from North Carolina in 1963, Durham worked briefly at a television station in Florence, South Carolina, before joining a television station in Greensboro, North Carolina, as its lead sportscaster. In 1971, when play-by-play man Bill Currie left North Carolina, Durham was tapped by Tar Heel athletics director Homer Rice.

While Durham is known nationally and internationally as the voice of North Carolina's ultrasuccessful basketball program, his work in football has always been among the best in his profession. A stickler for preparation and detail, Durham has always been able to balance his love for his school and his commitment to making every broadcast the very best it can be.

In thirty years, Durham, who turned fifty-nine in August of 2000, has become one of the state's treasures and one of the most respected people in sports broadcast journalism. He has been named North Carolina Broadcaster of the Year ten times, most recently in 1996.

Durham's son, Wes, followed in his Dad's footsteps and works as the voice of the Georgia Tech Yellow Jackets.

John Ferguson LSU, **1946–87**

Marty Mule, the outstanding sportswriter for the *New Orleans Times-Picayune*, captured the essence of John Ferguson in his book on LSU football, *Eye of the Tiger*. The year was 1942 and Ferguson had just graduated from Louisiana Tech. He stood in the office of a manager of a radio station in El Dorado, Arkansas, and asked for a job.

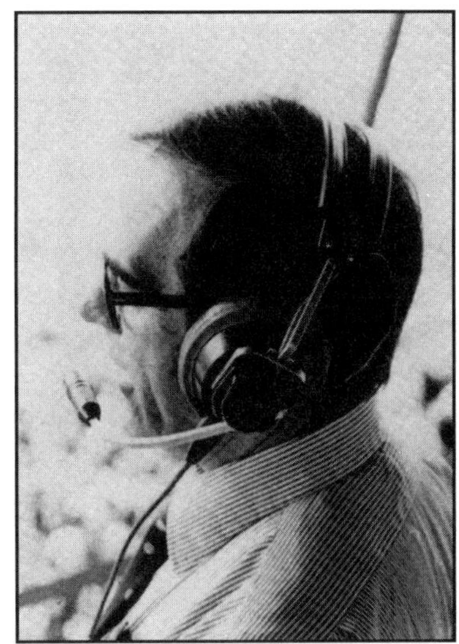

John Ferguson (photo courtesy of LSU SID).

"What makes you think you can do this?" bellowed the manager.

"I'm better than anyone you have," said Ferguson.

That's how Ferguson got his first job in radio, which required him to work seventy hours a week for the princely sum of $17.50. Ferguson broke into the business calling baseball in the Cotton States League. World War II interrupted Ferguson's career, but after completing 144 missions as an Army Air Corps transport pilot, he returned to his native Louisiana and began working on a master's degree at LSU. In 1946 WJBO radio in Baton Rouge won the right to broadcast LSU football games and asked Ferguson if he was available. Ferguson took the job, and on that day a forty-two-year-long relationship with the school and its fans began.

Over the next four decades, Ferguson's rich baritone voice brought LSU fans every heart-pounding moment of Tiger football—that is, every moment but one. Perhaps the most famous play in LSU football history was Billy Cannon's eighty-nine-yard punt return for a touchdown against Ole Miss in 1959. As fate would have it, that year Ferguson took a break from LSU football when he earned the assignment of calling the Southwest Conference game of the week. He returned to the LSU radio booth for good in 1961.

In 1984 Ferguson reluctantly left the radio booth to handle *TigerVision*, the school's cable TV broadcasts. He retired in 1987.

John Forney Alabama, **1953–97**

Few broadcasters have timed their arrival at a major Southern school better than John Forney, who graduated from the University of Alabama in 1948 and by 1953 had landed a job as a member of the Crimson Tide broadcast team. Alabama won an SEC championship that season, but coach Harold "Red" Drew left a year later and Alabama went into a three-year tailspin.

John Forney, the voice of Alabama Football during the Bear Bryant era (photo courtesy of the University of Alabama).

Then, in 1958 Alabama hired former player Paul "Bear" Bryant to serve as its head football coach. Over the next twenty-five years under Bryant, Alabama would win thirteen SEC championships and six national championships. And Forney was there to call every one of them as the voice of the Crimson Tide.

Forney started out in broadcasting at an early age. When all the college-aged talent in Tuscaloosa was heading off to war in 1943, the manager of the local radio station needed someone who wouldn't get drafted soon. He called Tuscaloosa High School and found fifteen-year-old Forney, whom he hired to be a play-by-play announcer.

Forney was not only an accomplished play-by-play announcer but also a shrewd businessman. From 1948 to 1952 he learned the advertising business in New York, and when he returned to Birmingham he established his own agency, in which he was a partner for thirty years.

Forney first retired in 1982, the same year as Bryant. But in 1988 he was asked to rejoin the broadcast team to help out with pregame and postgame shows. He remained with the Alabama radio network until his death on July 31, 1997.

"John will always be the voice of the Crimson Tide," says Eli Gold, who has been Alabama's play-by-play man since 1989. "I may be the current custodian of the title, but he is the man that people always have and always will associate with that title."

Bob Fulton South Carolina, **1952–94**

If people have any doubt about the bond between Southern college football fans and their radio voice, consider the story of South Carolina's Bob Fulton. Fulton had been calling the Gamecocks' games for fourteen years when he received an offer to move over to Georgia Tech, whose team was at that time coached by the legendary Bobby Dodd. So Fulton kept his home in Columbia, South Carolina, and commuted to Atlanta to serve as the voice of Georgia Tech for the 1965–66 seasons.

South Carolina broadcaster Bob Fulton (photo courtesy of South Carolina SID).

The outcry from South Carolina fans was so great that in 1967 Paul Dietzel, in his second year as the Gamecocks' football coach and athletics director, brought Fulton back and made him a full-time employee of the athletics department. No matter who owned the radio rights to broadcast South Carolina football, the contract would stipulate that the voice would be Fulton's. Fulton remained in that position until his retirement after the 1994 season.

Given the school's relative lack of success, South Carolina fans have to be among the most loyal fans in all of college football. Since 1892, the Gamecocks have posted only four seasons with 8 wins or more. That fact makes Fulton's career as the voice of South Carolina football even more remarkable.

"Our fans had a special bond with our football team," says Tom Price, the school's former sports information director and the author of several books on Gamecock athletics. "Bob had a lot to do with that."

When Fulton retired after the 1994 season, his tenure was ranked as the fourth longest with one school in NCAA Division I history.

A native of Ridley Park, Pennsylvania, Fulton had called University of Arkansas football games for nine years before he came to South Carolina. He still resides in Columbia.

Bob Harris Duke, **1975–Present**

Like a number of broadcasters, Harris fell into the profession because it was a way to stay close to the games he loved.

Duke broadcaster Bob Harris. (photo courtesy of Duke SID).

In Matt Fulks's book *The Sportscaster's Dozen*, Harris concedes that he did not have a lot of athletic ability: "My high school baseball coach finally told me after I had graduated that a scout was watching one of my games, and on my card beside "speed" he had written: "Deceptive—slower than he looks."

Harris was too small (5'9", 119 pounds) to play football or basketball, so he went to N.C. State on an academic scholarship that had been provided by his father's company. Harris's father worked for the same textile-manufacturing firm in Albemarle, North Carolina for fifty-five years.

After he graduated from college, Harris went to work for the Goodyear Tire Company, starting out as a salesman and moving up to store manager. He bounced around to five different stores and finally decided that all the moving wasn't good for his wife, Phyllis, and their two young children. He left Goodyear, moved back to Albemarle, and went into the insurance business.

Still, a part of Harris wanted to give broadcasting a try. As a young boy, Harris would sit with his father while he listened to the great radio voices of the day, like Red Barber and Bill Stern. It was something he knew he could do.

In the fall of 1967, when a local radio station needed someone to do tape-delayed broadcasts of high school games, Harris volunteered and quickly discovered his passion. In February of 1968, Harris quit his insurance job and decided to pursue a career in broadcasting. For eight years he toiled in relative obscurity, broadcasting high school sports in Albermarle. Then, on Labor Day in 1975, he took a job at WDNC radio in Durham as a salesman. Out of that position came an opportunity to serve as a guest commentator on Duke football broadcasts. He then moved into basketball. When play-by-play man Add Penfield experienced health problems, Harris finished out the rest of the season in his spot. And he has been there ever since.

It turned out to be the perfect marriage of man and school. While Harris is best known nationally for his work with Mike Krzyzewski's ultrasuccessful Duke basketball program, he has always taken pride in his work in football. He has been named North Carolina Sportscaster of the Year twice and has received numerous awards for his work and contributions to broadcasting. Harris was the sports director at WDNC radio in Durham for twenty-four years before he left to join the Duke Radio Network in a full-time capacity. Today he is the vice president of radio operations for Moore Productions.

Harris and his wife are involved in local charities and have endowed an athletic scholarship at Duke.

Cawood Ledford Kentucky, **1953–91**

Like North Carolina's Woody Durham and Duke's Bob Harris, Ledford forged his reputation as a broadcaster by being the voice of a college basketball dynasty. But Ledford, like Durham and Harris, was one of radio's consummate professionals and never gave Kentucky football any less than his very best.

When Ledford arrived at Kentucky in 1953, Adolph Rupp was in his twenty-third year of what would be a forty-two-year-long career as the school's head basketball coach. Bear Bryant was in his eighth and final season as the school's head football coach. Kentucky football struggled more often than not in his thirty-nine seasons behind the microphone, but Ledford's sharp and clear-headed calls were always among the very best in college football.

Kentucky legend Cawood Ledford (photo courtesy of Kentucky SID).

Ledford possessed many strengths as a broadcaster but is best remembered for his exquisite use of language, which kept his listeners informed and at ease. At the same time, Ledford was anything but a house-man for the Wildcats. If Kentucky was playing poorly or giving less than its best effort, he would not hesitate to report it.

Ledford was named the Kentucky Sportscaster of the Year twenty times in his thirty-nine-year career. He is the only man to have had his jersey retired at Rupp Arena and not be a coach or player. Ledford retired after the 1991 football and 1992 basketball seasons at the age of sixty-five, when he was still very much on top of his game.

"I just didn't want to stay too long," Ledford said at the time.

Cawood Ledford didn't stay too long. In fact, he left much too early.

Larry Munson has been the voice of the Georgia Bulldogs since 1966 (photo courtesy of Georgia SID).

Larry Munson Georgia, **1966–Present**

By the time Larry Munson was hired in 1966 to be Georgia's play-by-play man, he had already earned a reputation as one of the nation's best broadcasters. He had called Vanderbilt football and basketball games for sixteen years and had even done a stint with the Atlanta Braves professional baseball team. But as the radio voice of the Georgia Bulldogs, Munson is immortal. The 2000 season will mark his thirty-fifth of calling the action for yet another generation of adoring fans.

A native of Minneapolis, Minnesota, Munson had to earn the affection of Southern fans. For his first seven years with the Bulldogs, Georgia fans weren't too high on Munson, who replaced the very popular Ed Thilenius. First of all, he was from the North. Second of all, he seemed stiff and unemotional. But all that changed in 1973 when Georgia rallied from a 31–21 deficit to beat Tennessee 35–31. At the end of the game Munson screamed: "My God, we've just beaten Tennessee in Knoxville!" The phrase ruffled some feathers among the more strident church-going crowd, but it endeared him to the rest of the Bulldog Nation.

Munson solidified his legend during the era of Herschel Walker (1980-82), when the Bulldogs won three straight SEC championships and one national championship. As he counted down the final seconds of Georgia's 19–14 win over Auburn in 1982, Munson screamed, "Look at the sugar falling out of the sky! Look at the sugar falling out of the sky!" That was his way of proclaiming that Georgia had won the SEC championship and was headed to the Sugar Bowl.

In 1994 Munson was inducted into the Georgia Association of Broadcasters Hall of Fame and in 1997 he was honored by the Georgia State legislature for his contributions to the university and the state of Georgia.

Clemson broadcaster Jim Phillips (photo courtesy of Clemson SID).

Jim Phillips Clemson, **1968–Present**

One of the more enduring qualities of Southern college football and all the fun and good feelings that go with it is that once the game gets its hooks into you, no matter where you are from, you just can't leave it.

Such is the case with Jim Phillips, a native of Youngstown, Ohio, who had never set foot in the state of South Carolina when he applied in 1968 for the job to broadcast Clemson football and basketball games. But Phillips liked Clemson and they certainly liked him, and in the fall of 2000 he will begin his thirty-third season as the voice of the Clemson Tigers.

In the thirty-two seasons he has worked for the school, Phillips has called 371 Clemson football games, including the historic 12–0 run to the national championship in 1981. He was unable to call Clemson's Orange Bowl win over Nebraska, a win that clinched the national title for the Tigers, because NBC had exclusive TV and radio rights to the game. In thirty-two years Phillips missed only one game that he could have called—the 1988 Citrus Bowl. Phillips returned home to Ohio on that day because his mother had passed away.

Phillips has earned respect from legions of fans as well as his fellow broadcasters because of the credibility he brings to his broadcast. He is enthusiastic about Clemson but always believes in giving the opponents their due. "You should always tell it like it is because you lose credibility if you don't," Phillips said in 1992. "Everyone I have admired in this business over the years has used that approach."

Phillips has been elected South Carolina Sportscaster of the Year no less than five times, and in 1992 Clemson bestowed its highest athletic honor upon Phillips by naming him to the school's Athletic Hall of Fame. Phillips has also received the Marvin "Skeeter" Francis Award, which goes to one person who has given outstanding service and dedication to the ACC.

John Ward Tennessee, **1968–98**

At the end of the 1998 season Ward ended his thirty-first and final year of calling Tennessee football with a broadcaster's dream: a perfect 13–0 season and a national championship. Ward thought that his retirement from broadcasting would take place without a lot of fanfare. He was wrong.

John Ward, Tennessee's longtime radio voice (photo courtesy of Tennessee SID).

"If you're not from Tennessee, you won't understand this," says Jeff Hall, the placekicker on that national championship team. "But John Ward is more important to Tennessee football than any player or coach we've ever had. From the time I was a little boy, he was Tennessee football. He was the man we trusted."

Ward didn't start out to become a broadcasting legend. While getting his law degree from Tennessee, he picked up extra cash by calling the play-by-play for high school football games. He later went to work for an advertising agency and then was given the opportunity to become the voice of the Vols. Because the bulk of his income came from his successful advertising business, he would always call his radio work a hobby. But it was a hobby he performed with passion, passion that was shared by two generations of Tennessee fans.

"You cannot measure what John Ward did for Tennessee football," said coach Phillip Fulmer after Ward had called his last game.

Ward is best known for a series of phrases, or "Ward-isms," that would become his trademark. Here are but a few:

"It's football time in Tennessee!" "The 10, 5, 4, 3, 2, 1. Give him six. Touchdown Tennessee!" "The kick is up. Ladies and gentlemen, that kick is gooood!"

Other Important Voices of Southern College Football

Wally Ausley, Gary Dornburg, N.C. State: Ausley and Dornburg is perhaps the best known broadcasting duo the South has ever known. Ausley became N.C. State's play-by-play man in 1961 and stayed for thirty-six years. In 1974, after the death of Bill Jackson, Ausley's color man, Dornburg joined the Wolfpack broadcasting team. He remained after Ausley retired in 1990. In 1998 Dornburg died of cancer at the age of fifty-one.

Reb Barber, Florida: Barber earned his fame as a baseball play-by-play announcer for the Cincinnati Reds, Brooklyn Dodgers, and New York Yankees from 1934 to 1966. But from 1930 to 1933, the University of Florida graduate was the voice of the Gators.

Gene Deckerhoff, Florida State: Deckerhoff, an eight-time Florida Sportscaster of the Year, has been with the Seminoles for twenty-one seasons, which includes all but three of the seasons in the Bobby Bowden era (1976–present). In April of 2000, Deckerhoff was inducted in the Florida Sports Hall of Fame.

Paul Eells, Vanderbilt, Arkansas: The voice of Vanderbilt from 1967 to 1978, Eells, a native of Iowa, is now the voice of the Razorbacks.

Jim Fyffe, Auburn: Fyffe is a University of Kentucky graduate, but the 2000 season will mark his twentieth as the voice of the Tigers. His signature call of "Touchdown Auburn!" has made him one of the best-known voices in the South.

Johnny Holliday, Maryland: The 2000 season will be Holliday's twenty-second as the voice of the Terrapins. Holliday is one of the nation's most versatile broadcasters and has won numerous awards for his volunteer work. He was named America's No. 1 disc jockey in 1965.

Lindsey Nelson, Tennessee: Nelson was the voice of the Volunteers for only three years (1948–50), but his impact on Tennessee football is still felt. He and General Robert Neyland, Tennessee's legendary coach, formed the Volunteer Radio Network in 1949. Nelson left Knoxville and went on to have a successful career on the national stage as the radio voice of the New York Mets.

EPILOGUE

Why the Game Will Last

You've now met the players and coaches who were the building blocks of Southern college football as you know it today. You've visited the towns and enjoyed the unique traditions that have made the game so special for generation after generation of fans. You've relived the games and remembered those moments that will continue to be discussed and argued about long after we are all gone.

But no story about Southern college football would be complete without an examination of the one thing that above all else keeps the college football fan coming back to campus year after year. It is the thing that

Father and son: Archie Manning (above) of Ole Miss, Peyton Manning (left) of Tennessee (photos courtesy of the *Atlanta Journal-Constitution*).

sends fans running to the newsstands in June, when the first preseason magazines appear, to find out where their team is rated. It is the thing that drives a father to take his children on a tour of his old campus and share some precious memories. It is the thing that encourages friends, who are busy and scattered across several states, to find a way to coordinate their schedules so that they can meet on one of those brilliant fall Saturdays. It is love.

While other sports inspire excitement, enthusiasm, anger, and happiness, in the South, college football is the only sport that generates an emotional attachment that comes from the very core of who we are. Southerners enjoy many other sports, but college football is the one we will always love, and this love can take on many forms.

The love of family. Many Southerners use college football games to bring together their far-flung families several times each year. Unlike the potentially stressful reunions at Thanksgiving and Christmas, college football games give family members a chance to actually relax and enjoy each other.

"When you go to a game in the South, you're likely to see four generations together," says Frank Broyles, the athletics director at Arkansas. "It's part of our heritage, and that heritage is passed along from generation to generation. It means something very important to our people."

Georgia's Porter Payne (left) and his son Billy in 1948 (photo courtesy of Georgia SID).

The love of school. No matter how successful we may become, our college campus will always tug at our heartstrings. It is where we grew up, where we suffered our first major triumphs and disappointments, where we fell in love (at least once). Football gives us the chance to come back and, for a little while, be young again—to remember those days when all of life's possibilities were still ahead of us.

Georgia's Billy Payne (right), the future chief of the 1996 Atlanta Olympics, with dad Porter Payne in 1968 (photo courtesy of Georgia SID).

Friends, you just don't get these kinds of feelings watching the NFL.

Because Southerners love college football, a game is much more than just mere entertainment or a way to pass the time on Saturdays in the fall. In the South, we have a sincere, long-term emotional investment in college football, and each year it pays huge dividends.

If you still think that this is just a game, when there is so much evidence to the contrary, consider this: for Southerners, the passing college football seasons are not just a series of games played. Oh, no. They are the markers that serve to connect the important events of our lives.

"In Alabama, people won't say, 'My child was born in 1972,'" says Roy Kramer, the commissioner of the SEC. "They'll say, 'My child was born the year Auburn blocked two punts and beat Alabama.' That's how ingrained the sport is in our culture."

In the South, the arrival of college football season each September is the return of a long-lost friend. Regardless of how bad things may be in our lives, we know that each

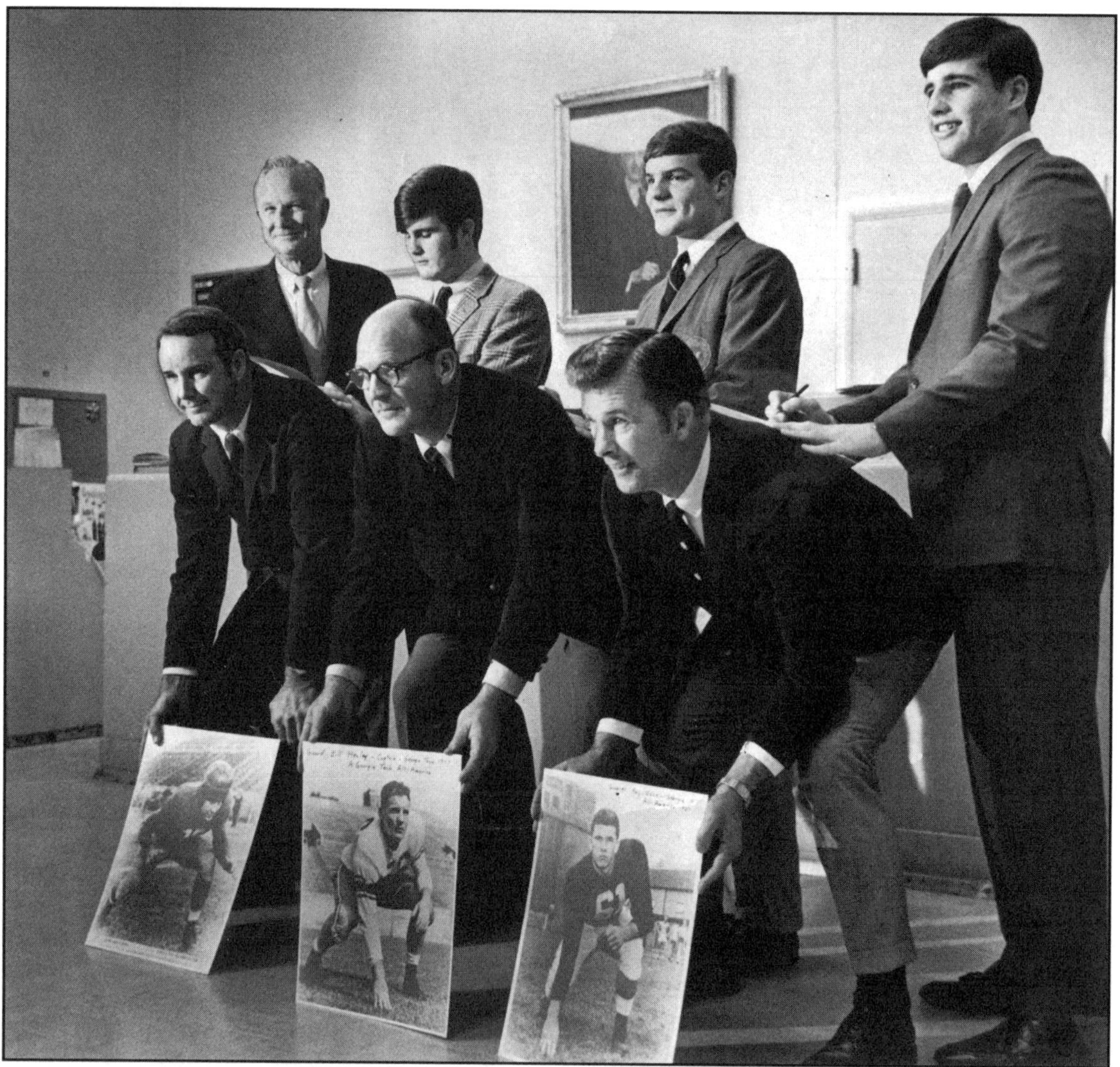

The sons of Georgia Tech All-Americans (left to right) Harvey Hardey (Harvey, Jr.), Bill Healey (Rob) and Ray Beck (Tommy) all signing with former coach Bobby Dodd in 1968 (photo courtesy of the *Atlanta Journal-Constitution*).

fall the leaves will turn, the temperatures will finally drop, and college football will be back. There's a lot of comfort in that thought. And there's some additional comfort in this: when things are going badly in our lives, we can, thanks to college football, think back to a special Saturday afternoon, and it makes us feel better.

One of Tennessee's biggest wins under the leadership of coach Johnny Majors (1977–92) was a 35–7 upset of highly rated Miami in the Sugar Bowl on January 1,

Former Ole Miss great Charlie Conerly in 1987 (photo courtesy of the *Atlanta Journal-Constitution*/Rich Addicks).

1986. Miami was in the middle of a great dynasty, which saw the Hurricanes win four national championships from 1983 to 1991. Oddsmakers didn't give Tennessee a chance in the game. That's why the victory was so sweet and still remains such a pleasant memory today.

Several years after that game, Majors was on the road for a speaking engagement. After his speech, a man walked up to him.

"He told me that whenever he is feeling down and out, he just watches the videotape of that game," Majors says. "And it made him feel better. That's how much that one game meant to the Tennessee people."

No other sport creates that kind of emotional bond with its fans.

So the celebration of college football in the South is ultimately a celebration of love—love of family, love of school, love of beautiful fall afternoons with friends. It is the very best of life in the South today, just as it was one hundred years ago. Bill Curry said it best at the beginning of this book. In the South, college football is not just a game. It's who we are.

And we are all better for it.

In the South, college football fans get an early start. Ashley Green with her dad, Howard, at a Georgia game in 1985 (photo courtesy of the *Atlanta Journal-Constitution*/Joey Ivansco).

WORKS CITED

Adventure Quest, Inc. *The Heisman: Sixty Years of Tradition and Excellence.* Bronxville, NY: Adventure Quest, Inc., 1995.

Attner, Paul. *The Terrapins: Maryland Football.* Huntsville, AL: The Strode Publishers, 1975.

Bradley, Bob. *Death Valley Days: The Glory of Clemson Football.* Marietta, GA: Longstreet Press, 1991.

Bradley, Bob, Sam Blackman, and Chuck Kriese. *Clemson, Where the Tigers Play: The History of Clemson University Athletics.* Champaign, IL: Sports Publishing, Inc., 1999.

Browning, Al. *Bowl, Bama, Bowl, 1926–88: A Crimson Tide Tradition.* Sterrett, AL: Five Points South Productions, 1998.

Clarkson, Julian. *Let No Man Put Asunder: Story of a Football Rivalry.* Ft. Myers, FL: Hillsboro Printing and Lithographing Co., 1968.

Cromartie, Bill. *Clean Old-Fashioned Hate.* Atlanta, GA: Gridiron Publishers, 1984.

Dunnavant, Keith. *Coach: The Life of Paul "Bear" Bryant.* New York: Simon and Schuster, 1996.

Dye, Pat, with John Logue. *In the Arena.* Montgomery, AL: Black Belt Press, 1992.

Forney, John, and Steve Townsend. *Talk of the Tide: An Oral History of Alabama Football.* Birmingham, AL: Crane Hill Publishers, 1993.

Fulks, Matt. *The Sportscaster's Dozen: Off the Air with Southeastern Legends.* Chicago, IL: Masters Press, 1998.

Fulmer, Phillip, with Jeff Hagood. *A Perfect Season.* Nashville, TN: Rutledge Hill Press, 1999.

Givens, Wendell, with Arthur Ben and Elizabeth N. Chitty. *Ninety-Nine Iron.* Birmingham, AL: Seacoast Publishing, 1992.

Hester, Wayne. *Century of Champions: The Centennial History of Alabama Football.* Birmingham, AL: Seacoast Publishing/Birmingham News, 1991.

Hester, Wayne. *Where Tradition Began: The Centennial History of Auburn Football.* Birmingham, AL: Seacoast Publishing/Birmingham News, 1991.

Mule, Marty. *Eye of the Tiger.* Marietta, GA: Longstreet Press, 1993.

Mule, Marty. *Rolling Green: A Century of Tulane Football.* New Orleans, LA: Tulane University Athletic Department, 1993.

Price, Tom. *A Century of Gamecocks: Memorable Football Moments.* Columbia, SC: Summerhouse Press, 1995.

Price, Tom. *The '84 Gamecocks: Fire Ants and Black Magic.* Columbia, SC: University of South Carolina Press, 1985.

Scherer, George. *Auburn-Georgia Football: A Hundred Years of Rivalry.* Jefferson, NC: McFarland and Company, Inc., Publishers, 1992.

Smith, Derek. *Glory Yards: Georgia vs. Florida.* Nashville, TN: Rutledge Hill Press, 1993.

Smith, Loran. *Between the Hedges: 100 Years of Georgia Football.* Marietta, GA: Longstreet Press, 1992.

Smith, Loran, with Lewis Grizzard. *Glory, Glory.* Atlanta, GA: Peachtree Publishers, 1981.

Spurrier, Steve, with Norm Carlson. *Gators: The Inside Story of Florida's First SEC Title.* Orlando, FL: Tribune Publishing, 1992.

Thilenius, Ed, and Jim Koger. *No Ifs, No Ands, And a Lot of Butts: 21 Years of Georgia Football.* Atlanta, GA: Foote and Davis, Inc., 1960.

Wells, Larry. *A Century of Heroes: One Hundred Years of Ole Miss Football.* Marietta, GA: Longstreet Press and Oxford, MS: The University of Mississippi Athletic Department, 1993.

Wenzell, Frank and Rita Cantrell Wenzell. *The Fanatics Guide to SEC Football.* Pensacola, FL: LightSide Productions, Inc., 1993.

Whitten, Don. *The Dog Comes Home: Ole Miss Football in 1983.* Oxford, MS: Yoknapatawpha Press, 1984.

Wilkinson, Jack. *Focused on the Top: Georgia Tech's Championship Story.* Marietta, GA: Longstreet Press, 1991.

Woody, Larry. *A Dixie Farewell: The Life and Death of Chucky Mullins.* Nashville, TN: Eggman Publishing, 1993.

Vaught, John H. *Rebel Coach.* Memphis, TN: Memphis State University Press, 1971.

ABOUT THE AUTHOR

Tony Barnhart (photo courtesy of ESPN).

Tony Barnhart, the 1999 Georgia Sportswriter of the Year, has been covering college football for twenty-five years.

A native of Union Point, Georgia, Barnhart began his newspaper career at the *Union Daily Times* (South Carolina) in 1976 and then spent seven years at the *Greensboro News & Record* (North Carolina) before joining the *Atlanta Journal-Constitution* in 1984.

In addition to his newspaper work, the 2000 season will mark Barnhart's fourth as the national reporter for ESPNs award-winning *College Game Day* show with Chris Fowler, Lee Corso, and Kirk Herbstreit.

In 1996 Barnhart was the screenwriter for "The Southern Game," a documentary on Southern college football produced by Georgia Public Television. The documentary was one of three finalists for a Southern regional Emmy Award.

During his career, Barnhart has been honored by the North Carolina Press Association, the Associated Press Sports Editors, the Georgia Press Association, and the Georgia Sports Writers Association.

He is a past president of the Football Writers Association of America and the Atlantic Coast Sports Writers Association. He currently serves as the Georgia regional voting director for the Heisman Trophy.

A 1976 graduate of the Henry W. Grady School of Journalism at the University of Georgia, Barnhart lives in Atlanta, Georgia.